PORTLAND'S AUDACIOUS CHAMPION

Portland's Audacious Champion

*How Bill Naito Overcame Anti-Japanese Hate
and Became a Fierce Civic Leader*

ERICA NAITO-CAMPBELL

Oregon State University Press   Corvallis

Library of Congress Cataloging-in-Publication Data

Names: Naito-Campbell, Erica, author.
Title: Portland's audacious champion : how Bill Naito overcame anti-Japanese hate
    and became an intrepid civic leader / Erica Naito-Campbell.
Other titles: How Bill Naito overcame anti-Japanese hate and became an intrepid
    civic leader
Description: Corvallis : Oregon State University Press, 2024. | Includes bibliographi-
    cal references and index.
Identifiers: LCCN 2023057119 | ISBN 9781962645096 (trade paperback) | ISBN
    9781962645102 (ebook)
Subjects: LCSH: Naito, William Sumio, 1925-1996. | Japanese Americans—
    Oregon—Portland—Biography. | Civic leaders—Oregon—Portland—Biography.
    | Portland (Or.)—Biography. | Portland (Or.)—History—20th century. | Portland
    (Or.)—Race relations—History—20th century.
Classification: LCC F884.P853 N46 2024 | DDC 979.5/49043092 [B]—dc23/
    eng/20231220
LC record available at https://lccn.loc.gov/2023057119

∞This paper meets the requirements of ANSI/NISO Z39.48-1992
(Permanence of Paper).

Oregon State University
OSU Press

Oregon State University Press
121 The Valley Library
Corvallis OR 97331-4501
541-737-3166 • fax 541-737-3170
www.osupress.oregonstate.edu

*Oregon State University Press in Corvallis, Oregon, is located within
the traditional homelands of the Mary's River or Ampinefu Band of
Kalapuya. Following the Willamette Valley Treaty of 1855, Kalapuya people
were forcibly removed to reservations in Western Oregon. Today, living
descendants of these people are a part of the Confederated Tribes of Grand
Ronde Community of Oregon (grandronde.org) and the Confederated
Tribes of the Siletz Indians (ctsi.nsn.us).*

For my Grandma Donna and Grandpa Don
and my Grandma Micki and Grandpa Bill

CONTENTS

Appreciations

To those who shared their "Bill stories,"
to my incredible editors and publisher,
to my inspiring friends and family,
To the resilient Japanese American community,
to my brilliant partner and beautiful sons,
to my perfect-in-all-ways dogs and cats

PREFACE

I grew up a stone's throw from my grandma and grandpa Naito. It was rare for me to go a couple days without running that short distance up the hill to their house to play with their pets, to share my schoolwork, or simply to enjoy their company. I can't remember a time that I was turned away, and so I was spoiled by their ever-present attention and affection. If I wasn't with them at their home or beach house outside of Lincoln City, Oregon, I was with one of them at their work—my grandma Micki at the Galleria mall downtown or my grandpa Bill at the Norcrest headquarters in the White Stag building in Old Town.

Despite having spent so much time with them and being the eldest grandchild, I knew very little about their childhoods. That my grandmother grew up in poverty in a rural community did not mesh with the urban, sophisticated Grandma Micki that I knew. And I did not know that my grandfather had not been able to speak English when he entered first grade or that he had served in the army in World War II. It wasn't until I was about ten years old that I realized that he spoke Japanese fluently. His face was unavoidably Japanese, but I never saw it. I just saw my grandpa.

The older I grew, the more I realized how important he was to the wider community and how much weight the name "Naito" carried. One time, while my grandma was speeding around Portland with me, a police officer pulled her over. When he saw her driver's license, he handed it back to her, saying, "Excuse me, Mrs. Naito. Have a nice day." I'm sure my adolescent eyes were as big as saucers. It is complicated being in the family of a man who was larger than life, successful, and wealthy, but I was lucky to have the quiet intimacy of the relationship between a grandparent and a grandchild more than anything.

This book is an exploration of my grandfather Bill Naito's life and his impact on the city that had once expelled him and his parents and his brothers. To a certain extent, Portland was a member of our Naito family, too: the wayward but well-meaning relative whose constant need for help took time away from the rest of us. Portland was close to achieving true livability in the 1970s and 1980s, when many other like-minded leaders were guided by similar ideals. But Bill could not leave it to chance, and he spent as much time as possible working on Portland when he wasn't working on his family business. That didn't leave much time for anything else, and so it wasn't easy competing with such a noisy, challenging member of the family. But Bill would not have been Bill without the city. And the city would not be Portland without Bill.

CHAPTER 1

When Bill Naito became a household name in the 1970s, his father Hide (Hee-day) was in his late eighties. Hide was still going to work, sitting at his desk in the main office, and going to the nearby Import Plaza retail store to look over the products and store layout, all the while being shadowed by a Norcrest employee assigned to look after him. Even though he had not directed the business for years, work remained his life. It was how Hide—an Issei, a first-generation Japanese immigrant—had created the business that firstborn son Sam Naito and his brother Bill would build into a real estate empire. For most of his adult life, Hide had worked six to seven days a week, saving enough money to get married, buy a business and a house, and support his wife and three sons. He bore the personality of his adopted hometown of Portland, Oregon, which historian Carl Abbott describes as having a "certain middle westernness" with its "moderate scale," "slow tempo," New England sensibilities, and puritanical work ethic. Hide was conservative by nature; he never borrowed money and never loaned it, and he was not one to make waves. He and Portland were an ideal match.

In early twentieth-century America, many believed it was not possible to be both gifted and Japanese. "Japs" were violent, apelike buffoons, naturally inclined to deceit and savagery. But Hide and other Issei were undaunted by such racist stereotypes and had come to the United States with high hopes. Hide was soft-spoken and introverted, had few close friends, and stayed at an emotional distance from his children—to some extent, the antithesis of the man Bill would come to be. Leaving Japan as a young teenager, he built a life in the United States almost entirely alone, working tirelessly to build a prosperous business that would justify his marriage to Fukiye (Foo-kee-yeh) Naito (no relation), an Issei from his village. Bill admired his father, despite Hide's emotional distance and muted appreciation, and he tried to impress him—and outdo him—throughout his life.

Bill was known to keep important clippings from newspapers and elsewhere at his desk. One of them may have reminded him of his father: "Nothing is holier, nothing is more exemplary," German author Hermann Hesse wrote, "than a beautiful, strong tree." Hesse continued,

> For me, trees have always been the most penetrating preachers. I revere them when they live in tribes and families, in forest and groves. And even more, I revere them when they stand alone. . . . In their highest boughs the world rustles, their roots rest in infinity, but they do not lose themselves there, they struggle with all the force of their lives for one thing only: to fulfill themselves according to their own laws, to build up their own form, to represent themselves.

Through two world wars, Hide was undeterred in achieving financial stability and having a family. Fanaticism in Japan and the United States may have rustled his leaves, but they failed to uproot his ambitions.

Hide and Fukiye were born into a country that was undergoing a massive shift in culture and economy—Hide on October 1, 1893, and Fukiye on March 3, 1899. Thirty years earlier, they would have been infants in a feudal system, an almost entirely agrarian economy ruled by regional samurai. But Western countries, including the United States, were colonizing the globe—angling for raw goods, for new markets, and for prestige. It was the United States that helped force open Japan's doors. For years, the shogunate had engaged in *uchi harai*, in which approaching ships were shelled and repelled from the shore to keep other countries away. After years of frustration, in 1853 the United States sent Commodore Matthew Perry to force Japan to trade with America. Choosing to bluff, Perry approached the shore of Tokyo (Edo) Bay and then refused to leave, threatening a military response if he was not allowed to deliver the diplomatic papers he carried. Japan's leaders relented and, in 1854, signed the Treaty of Kanagawa, which imposed a port system on Japan the way the Europeans had done in China a decade earlier.

Because of its isolationism, Japan had almost no political or economic power to wield during the negotiations, suffering from inexperience but also having no allies from whom to draw strength. The shogunate's weakness—in reality and especially in appearance—was baldly revealed and deeply shameful to a culture that venerated honor and strength. As a result, the treaties that Western Europe and the United States obtained were one-sided and eliminated Japan's control of its own trade policy. Certain ports were designated as open, leaving Westerners free to come and go as they pleased. Foreign concession areas were created in those port cities, and foreign nationals set up islands of industry, living, and culture, akin to what happened in Hong Kong under English rule. Kobe, a city on Osaka Bay in Hyogo Prefecture—only fifty miles from where Hide and Fukiye grew up—was one of those ports.

Confronted with its impotence at the hands of foreign powers, Japan experienced a seismic shift in almost every aspect of the country, with one goal: Japan would not be shamed again. Japan changed its government, its religion, and its economy to mirror its Western adversaries, a process known as the Meiji Restoration. The emperor was reinstated as the supreme leader, consolidating power in a central government and giving it the ability to force changes at the local level. The emperor's reign was known as Bunmei Kaika (Civilization and Enlightenment), a reference to a deference to modern ways over traditional customs. Japan became an insatiable sponge, seeking out and fully embracing Western learning and culture. What happened in Japan was in stark contrast to what happened in China, which had suffered the same imposition of the treaty port system after the Opium Wars in the 1840s and 1850s. Its response had been to double down and pursue the Chinese way by rejecting Western civilization whenever possible.

Western governments and businesses welcomed the Japanese government's embrace and were happy to share technological advances in the form of investments. China and its resistance to Westernization had been a source of frustration for decades, whereas Japan represented a new trading market and a potential area of influence in Asia, a situation that could eventually force China's hand. London funded a railway in Japan in 1870, the country had its first horse trolley in

1883, and the first electric trolley tracks were laid in 1903. Elementary public school was made mandatory, and European-style civil and criminal codes were instituted. Japanese leaders saw these domestic changes as creating the foundation for international security against imperialism in Western Europe and—its much closer threat—Russia. These economic and political advances allowed Japan to renegotiate more favorable treaties with Western powers in 1894, the year after Hide Naito was born. The new treaties eliminated extraterritoriality, and foreigners could go where they pleased.

But the Meiji Restoration was more than infrastructure change. The oppressive weight of a centuries-old feudal system was thrown off the people's shoulders, as they felt the pervasive vitality of Bunmei Kaika. Before, more than a dozen distinct dialects had caused confusion between people from different regions of Japan. The emperor made the Edo (Tokyo) dialect the standard for the nation, creating universal communication. Japanese citizens were no longer bound to their social standing at birth, and they were free to travel without getting permission from local governments. It was a time of self-discovery, especially for those who lived near the foreign concession port cities. The world was no longer as small as one's village. By the middle of the Meiji Restoration period, in the mid-1870s, focus had shifted from adopting European customs in their entirety to taking Japanese ways and bettering them through Western influences—a reflection of the Japanese becoming more confident in themselves as individuals and as a country. This became known as the "double life"—like wearing Western-style shoes in public while sleeping on tatami mats on the floor in private. At the end of the restoration, the Times of London reported, "With passionate effort the Japanese have ransacked the Western world for its treasures of knowledge, and have vigorously applied what they have learned."

The village of Tarumi (also known as Tarume Ku), fifty miles outside Kobe, was home to about twenty-five families. Both Hide and Fukiye grew up there, but they came from different rungs on the social ladder and did not develop a close relationship until they reached the United States. It was something Fukiye never let Hide forget, and after their marriage, she would refer to him derisively as a "country bumpkin." While Japan did not have formal castes, like in India, class was still an important social marker. Hide's father was the mayor of the small farming village, an unpopular position whose occupant had the job of collecting taxes. The elimination of feudalism meant a switch from an agrarian economy to one based on currency, and rising taxes on farms were necessary to feed Japan's rapid modernization. During the Edo period, farmers had paid land taxes in rice or other crops based on yield, but under Meiji reforms landowners became liable for a 3 percent cash property tax based on potential land value.[1]

Fukiye's family was a major property owner in Tarumi, with enough money to send her to a Christian finishing school in Tokyo. She moved there without her beloved mother, Yukiye, but when her grandfather lost money because of Meiji land reforms, she was forced to transfer to a less expensive school. Her younger sister, Chikaye, was allowed to continue attending the school that she preferred, which led Fukiye to feel ignored and disfavored by her father. Resentment and a sense of injustice would color the rest of her life. Still, Fukiye believed that her education gave her some sophistication, and she grew into a woman with a high opinion of herself. Because of her family's financial troubles, Fukiye's older brother immigrated to the United States and, once established, sent word to his family to join him. Her father decided to go, leaving Fukiye behind with her mother and sister. Although she was a young teenager, Fukiye was responsible for arranging for passports and visas and payment for passage.

After several years of preparation, Fukiye arrived in Los Angeles on the SS *Shinyo Maru* to join her family on August 12, 1918. Little Tokyo, roughly 1,920 acres in the city's downtown, was thriving, with more than ten thousand Japanese immigrants and their families and businesses. The area, south of Old Chinatown, had been established in the 1870s. San Francisco's 1906 earthquake had swelled LA's Little Tokyo population, as many people fled unstable ground for the closest city with an established Japanese community. As more bachelors and then their wives arrived, support organizations proliferated, ranging from what would become the Japanese American Citizens

---

1 This led to farmer revolts, and eventually the government reduced the taxation rate to 2.5 percent in an attempt to get more public buy-in for the new tax system.

League (JACL) to credit unions and prefectural groups. Because many Issei had gone into agricultural work, Little Tokyo became a shopping district for cut flowers and produce for all of Los Angeles. For Japanese immigrants throughout the West Coast, farming offered an entrepreneurial path to economic self-sufficiency and stability.

Hide left Japan for America during his early teenage years, several years before Fukiye; he would not return until 1954. As the eldest son in his family, with younger brothers Hideo and Kazuo, it seems unlikely that Hide would abandon his family obligations without serious justification. Some sons had left in order to obtain funds to pay off family debts to the Japanese government. Others left to make enough money to be able to return and get married in Japan. Although he knew Fukiye as a child, there is no evidence that they were betrothed when he left for America. One thing is certain: leaving Japan did mean freedom from the burden of mandatory Japanese military service, which most people were beginning to see as an undesirable but singular way to get ahead in Japan. So, if you wanted to succeed financially and do it without fighting in Korea or China, then the United States was your best bet. One story, told by Hide's youngest son Albert, was that Hide had seen an Oriental Trading Company flag and thought to himself, "I'd like to do that." Direct steamship service between Kobe and Portland had been available since 1887, so, perhaps a more robust explanation is that living in close proximity to Kobe and its former foreign concession area, Hide became drawn to Western culture, specifically the United States, and its promise of freedom to achieve success based on his own merits.

Whatever his other motives, Hide was like many other young, single Japanese men who were seeking financial possibilities abroad. Initially, many intended to return to Japan, but Hide was not one of them. Instead of going directly to the United States, however, Hide traveled to Liverpool, England, where he hired a tutor to teach him English for six months. The Japanese considered the King's English superior to American English, so he might have gone there in search of learning "proper" English. The family joke was that he ended up there accidentally when he took the wrong train out of Kobe. In 1912, Hide boarded the SS *Celtic* and arrived at Ellis Island in New York City on August 10, 1912. He listed his occupation as student and his intended destination as Seattle, Washington. Family stories have it that he arrived with only an American five-dollar bill in his pocket. For reasons unclear, he went by train to Chicago, and then after some time to Los Angeles. Hide arrived in Portland, Oregon, around 1917, ending more than half a decade of travel, exploration, and learning.

Portland was recovering from an economic slump. The Lewis and Clark Centennial Exposition in 1905, Portland's world's fair, had announced the city's golden age of economic growth. Japan had the largest foreign exhibit at the expedition, which may have been part of what drew its citizens to the Northwest. Business boomed, as rentable space ballooned from 900,000 square feet in 1900 to almost three million by 1920. The 1914–1916 recession severely affected construction, due to the collapse of wheat and lumber prices and the start of World War I, which all but stopped international trade. But entry into the war in 1917 resurrected the economy, as those same commodities were critical for arming and supplying US soldiers.

Hide obtained a job as a houseboy, working in exchange for food and lodging for Solomon Lipman, an owner of the Lipman, Wolfe & Co. department store. He performed household chores, did laundry, and cooked. Many Japanese houseboys also attended school, and, at night, Hide paid fifty dollars for four months' tuition at the Benke-Walker Night School to learn English, typing, bookkeeping, and accounting.[2] He held other odd jobs to drum up capital, including washing dishes at the Benson Hotel, recently built by timber baron Simon Benson. Unlike many other Japanese immigrants, he sent no money to his family in Japan, saving it fastidiously for his life in the United States.

At the time, Portland was swept up in the war effort and led the West Coast in Liberty bond sales. The city also collected paper, tin, scrap, and even food waste for the war effort. But its energetic patriotism also had negative consequences. High bond sales were due, in part, to a threatening atmosphere: a self-appointed committee of concerned citizens would put those who didn't buy bonds on a list of questionable citizens. A teacher was fired for not taking the oath

2 Originally, the profession had begun with Chinese immigrants along the West Coast, but by the late 1900s, young Japanese bachelors represented a large portion of the industry as the Chinese had moved on into other occupations.

of allegiance; despite her love of the country, her Christian faith did not allow her to support the war. There wasn't a lot of gray area in Portland's war patriotism.

Anti-German behavior was not uncommon: police surveilled German-born immigrants, and the Portland City Council changed the name of Frankfurt Street to Lafayette Street and Bismark Street to Bush.[3] German immigrants had been the largest foreign-language group in Portland since the late 1880s and had an established business and community presence, but President Woodrow Wilson made it clear that "any man who carries a hyphen about with him, carries a dagger that he is ready to plunge into the vitals of this Republic when he gets ready." German-born residents had to carry registration cards if they worked near the waterfront, a result of President Wilson declaring German-born immigrants "enemy aliens" when he declared war on April 6, 1917. German-language schools and books were discouraged but not banned in Oregon, as they were in many other states. The Espionage Act and the Trading with the Enemy Act passed that same year, followed by the Sedition Act in 1918, significantly shrinking the freedoms of German-born immigrants.

Henry Albers was one of several German immigrants who were charged with espionage during the war. His family owned Albers Mill, a successful grain refinery business that had operated on the Willamette River north of downtown since 1911. Albers had spent several days drinking in California and was on his way home by train when a deputy marshal who happened to be on board criticized his behavior. Oregon's prohibition law allowed for alcohol to be brought into the state for personal use, so Albers continued his drinking as the train traveled through southern Oregon. As he drank, his lubricated lips allegedly let slip several pro-German declarations, including, "We could never lick the Kaiser in a thousand years!" and he sang "Deutschland Uber Alles," the German national anthem. His drunken pronouncements were taken seriously, and he was charged with violating the federal Espionage Act. In the anti-German environment in Portland at the time, he was found guilty on two counts.

---

3 Country-wide, frankfurters became hot dogs, hamburger became liberty steak, and sauerkraut became liberty cabbage.

Albers wasn't alone. Marie Equi, a reputable doctor, was a "well-known local agitator" for the Industrial Workers of the World, and her speeches in support of workers' rights were interpreted by authorities as obstructing recruiting and enlistment in the United States military. Julius Rhuburg, a naturalized German of thirty years and a successful farmer in Sherman County, was also accused of obstructing recruiting and enlistment for making disparaging remarks about the United States. It would take a dozen US soldiers to take on one German soldier, he said, the sinking of *Lusitania* was justified, and the United States had no business being in the war. Both Equi and Rhuburg were convicted of espionage, victims of war hysteria in Portland.

The conclusion of the war put anti-German sentiments largely to rest, and German Americans returned to their businesses and retail shops, including Henry Weinhard's brewery and the Meier & Frank department store. Immigrants often ended up in business for themselves because non-Germans would not hire them. Chinese and Japanese immigrants, like their German counterparts, also had businesses of their own. When bigotry and prejudice excluded them from traditional channels of employment, resourceful immigrants found ways to compete in the marketplace, opening restaurants like Kohara in Japantown and the Republic Café in Chinatown, and department stores like Lipman, Wolfe & Co. and Meier & Frank downtown.

By 1920, Hide had a job in a small Japanese import shop on Thirteenth Avenue and Washington Street, an area in the western part of downtown that was populated by high-end stores. When the owner decided to return to Japan, he sold the business to Hide, including the lease for the space, and Hide renamed the shop H. Naito Japanese Goods. For a man like Hide, who had traveled by himself for five years, owning his own business was a natural extension of his self-reliance and self-confidence. With his business and financial future secured, he wrote Fukiye's father in Los Angeles to ask for her hand in marriage. How much the pair had kept in touch during Hide's long journey to Portland is unclear. Despite their shared childhood in the village, their relationship appears to have been like many immigrant marriages at the time, less to do with love and more to do with suitability. For many Issei men, their love life was determined by the practice of arranging for picture brides. A Japanese bachelor sent a letter with a picture of himself, which his family would use to secure a fitting wife. The bride often came from the same area as the husband or had some family relationship. Such was the case with Fukiye and Hide.

By the time the Naitos married in Los Angeles in 1920, Japanese immigrants in Portland had created a strong community called Nihonmachi ("Japan town"), in what is now Old Town/Chinatown. There were thirty-seven such communities along the West Coast. The first wave of Japanese immigrants to Portland had been young men who needed little more than a cheap room while they worked in timber or farming. In 1890, only twenty Issei lived in Portland; by 1910, more than 1,400 Japanese immigrants were residents. As time progressed, working in the United States turned out to be more than temporary. Instead of returning to Japan, the young men decided to make America their home, finding its long-term prospects more promising. Beginning in 1910, Japanese picture brides started arriving in Portland, with more than 1,300 of them in the city by 1920, concentrated mostly in Old Town. Once the men were joined by their future wives and started to have children, many Issei families settled into businesses that would provide both income and housing.

In that twenty-block area to the north of the Burnside Bridge, hotels, shops, restaurants, doctors, and dentists shared buildings to create Nihonmachi, with Japanese-owned businesses catering to mostly Japanese customers. By the 1920 census, there were a little over four thousand persons of Japanese ancestry in Portland, with a smaller enclave in southwest Portland. Families developed a close bond, and there was a strong sense of community. As their numbers grew, so did white concerns about their presence. Racism and anti-immigrant sentiment in the city were nothing new, and there were always people to target as the city grew. In 1900, 58 percent of residents had either been born outside the United States or were the children of immigrants. Chinese and Japanese immigrants were considered particularly undesirable because of their "otherness" and entrenched stereotypes. Portland was never as overtly violent as its northern neighbors, Seattle and Tacoma, where violence toward the Chinese population propelled Portland's own Chinese population to grow by 6,100 across twenty years. Portland's middle-westernness resulted in a desire to avoid confrontation, so instead of acts of brutality, laws were selectively enforced to penalize Asian immigrants, and zoning laws were used to cabin them in certain areas.

In 1882, the city and state, including the governor and a state supreme court justice, had cheered the passage of the Chinese Exclusion Act, which prevented the immigration of Chinese laborers to the United States. Their support for the act came from a fear that Chinese workers were taking jobs from white Oregonians. If a Chinese man could prove he was a merchant, however, he was allowed to immigrate and had the additional benefit of being able to travel back and forth to China and bring his wife and family to the United States (with proper documentation). The unintended consequence of closing off the US supply of Chinese workers was increased immigration from Japan. Eventually, Japanese populations along the West Coast started to cause the same overreaction as Chinese populations had previously done, with white populations seeking to exclude Japanese immigrant communities from white arenas.

This led to a significant international incident. In 1906, San Francisco's school board voted to segregate Japanese students, an action that outraged Japan. By then, Japan considered itself an equal to Western powers, with the Meiji Restoration having achieved so much technological, economic, and political advancement. Heated negotiations between the United States and Japan began immediately and resulted in the Gentleman's Agreement, which allowed the United States to deny entry to Japanese immigrants who intended to work in the country, even if their passports had been issued for Mexico, Hawai'i, or Canada. Those already in the United States were allowed to travel to and from Japan, and their wives or children under the age of twenty-one could join them. Picture brides were used to get around the Gentleman's Agreement, as few returned to Japan to seek brides themselves. By 1924, the National Origins Act set the annual quota of immigrants from Japan to near zero.[4]

With these national actions in the background, newlyweds Hide and Fukiye lived their day-to-day lives like most Americans. A

---

4 Technically, the law set the immigration levels to 1890 numbers. For Japan, however, the law took effect less than a decade after the Japanese government began to allow emigration, and the number of immigrants was initially very small.

year into their marriage, in 1921, Fukiye gave birth to a son, Samuel Teruhide Naito, at St. Vincent Hospital west of downtown Portland. While Sam was a United States citizen by birth, Oregon's Alien Land Law of 1923 forbade the new parents, as resident aliens, to purchase or own property, a law that had passed the Oregon Senate unanimously and with only one vote against it in the House. The practical effect was to prevent Issei from ever owning property, as the Naturalization Act of 1790 meant Japanese immigrants could never become US citizens. Portland was also beginning to enact zoning laws that were intended, in part, to cement existing class, race, and religious segregation. When the Naito family moved from a rental house near Thirteenth Avenue and Columbia, Hide established himself as Sam's legal guardian for the purposes of real estate transactions and bought their new family home on Fifty-Eighth Avenue and Burnside in Sam's name, a common scheme used to skirt the land-ownership restriction.

Passage of Oregon's Alien Land Law was the fourth attempt to restrict the activities of Japanese by the Anti-Asiatic Association, which had formed in 1919 and was organized by George C. Wilbur. Wilbur, the head of Hood River's American Legion chapter, vehemently opposed the Japanese immigrants who had settled in the farmlands of the Hood River Valley, about sixty miles east of Portland on the Columbia River. From 1907 to 1910, the number of Japanese farmers in the valley had increased from 71 to 233. Most received marshland and stumpland in exchange for clearing land that was seen to have little value, as it was difficult to cultivate. By 1941, however, Japanese farmers were producing 90 percent of the state's cauliflower and broccoli, 70 percent of its celery, 60 percent of its green peas, and 45 percent of its asparagus.

Japanese men like Masuo Yasui and Shinjiro Sumoge had carved out successful businesses in the valley. Yasui in particular encouraged local Japanese residents to befriend their white neighbors. Like Hide, Yasui had come to Portland first, working as a houseboy and attending night classes at Couch School in downtown, learning US culture and mores firsthand. But many white locals saw Japanese newcomers as a dire economic threat. The animus was seemingly impossible to stifle. Between 1922 and 1925, organized groups kept Japanese immigrants out of Prineville in central Oregon and Medford in the south, and three hundred people violently drove Japanese sawmill laborers out of Toledo on the Oregon Coast. In 1923, the legislature passed an additional restriction—the Oregon Alien Business Restrictions law, which allowed municipal governments to refuse licenses to Japanese who wanted to open pawnshops, pool and dance halls, and soft drink establishments. Grocery stores and hotels run by resident aliens had to notify the public of their nationality by placing signs outside their businesses. The actions were effective, and the Japanese population in Oregon decreased by 30 percent between 1924 and 1928.[5]

---

5 A similar occurrence had happened with Chinese immigrants in Portland, with the population falling from 7,814 to 1,846 in the two decades after the Chinese Exclusion Act passed in 1904.

GREATER PORTLAND AREA

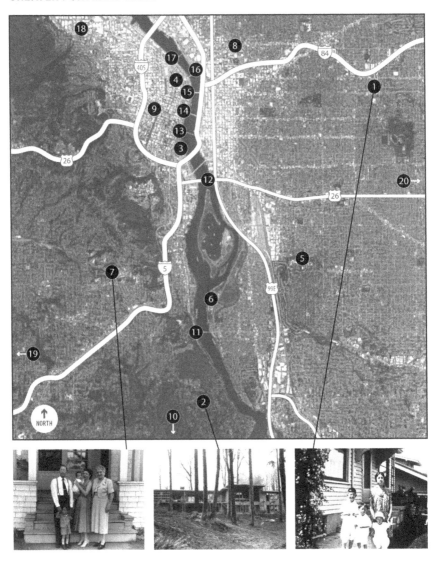

① Childhood Family Home
② Family Home
③ South Waterfront
④ Nihonmachi/Old Town
⑤ Reed College
⑥ Oaks Park

⑦ Hillsdale Neighborhood
⑧ Lloyd Center
⑨ H. Naito Gifts/Downtown
⑩ Tryon Creek State Park
⑪ Sellwood Bridge
⑫ Ross Island Bridge

⑬ Hawthorne Bridge
⑭ Morrison Bridge
⑮ Burnside Bridge
⑯ Steel Bridge
⑰ Broadway Bridge
⑱ Montgomery Park

⑲ Washington Square Mall
⑳ Japanese School

14

CHAPTER 2

Despite the prejudice against Asian immigrants in Portland, Hide's business was prosperous, and his family was growing. Fukiye had intended to have only one child and was happy to have given birth to a son. When she became pregnant again, she hoped for a daughter, but on September 16, 1925, she and Hide greeted a second son, William Sumio. In most Japanese families, to have two sons was considered a success, but Fukiye lamented not having a girl. She dressed little Bill in dresses and Mary Jane shoes, and he did not receive a male haircut until he was five years old. Older brother Sam teasingly referred to him as "the female fugitive from kindergarten." Fukiye cut Bill's hair herself, tearing some of it out in the process, a procedure he likened to torture.

He later referred to himself as Cinderfella, as his mother had him doing chores traditionally done by daughters, like cleaning and cooking. Bill deeply resented being her kitchen helper, but he became a good cook, as a result, as he watched Fukiye cook American cuisine during the week—fried chicken, pork chops, and angel food cake—and traditional Japanese food on the weekends. As an adult, Bill found ways to reject her formalities in cooking, including the way he ripped bread haphazardly into chunks for Thanksgiving stuffing instead of meticulously cutting it into equally sized cubes, as Fukiye required. Hide and Fukiye's third and last child, Albert Teruo, was born in February 1928.

The family lived in southeast Portland, far from Nihonmachi and with no other Japanese families within walking distance. Fukiye could not drive, so instead of going to Nihonmachi for groceries she used a food service that came by once a week. During the day, she sat at the kitchen table, sewing and doing other chores. The table, with a long-hanging cloth, was a place for Bill and Albert to play under, where

Bill in 1926

they would entertain each other for hours. But it also was a place for punishment, to which the boys were banished if they misbehaved. This was often due to violent fights resulting from competitive arguments between them—fights that Bill was expected to prevent. When Bill did argue with Albert, Fukiye would call Bill *moriago*, adopted son. Bill could remember times when he was forgotten under the table and would sleep there through the night, dutifully serving out his punishment for insubordination or for fighting with Albert. He sometimes thought of himself as the "bad child," and he withdrew from the family as a way to cope with his anger and humiliation, leading to persistent anxiety that would take him decades to overcome. His parents saw his withdrawal as "a wretched stubbornness" that needed to be exorcised.

In traditional Japanese households, the eldest son receives preferential treatment because of the role he is expected to play as the leader of the family and the carrier of its legacy. The Naitos were no different. Sam was served first at meals and given every advantage to succeed, including most of Fukiye's attention. She made sure he had everything he needed for school, provided coffee and snacks for his evening study, and gave him extra money even after Hide had refused. Sam was encouraged to work the front of the store and was given access to the account books, showing the intention for him to assume control of the business when he was older. Hide and Fukiye's attention to their oldest son was not based on a preference for one over the other but was expected in a traditional home. But the disparity still stung Bill and Albert, whom Fukiye largely ignored unless their behavior warranted punishment or their physical labor was needed for the business. It was not an easy environment for the brothers to grow up in, and it fostered ill feelings among them that would remain for life.

There is an adage in Japan that cleaning by a mother or wife is often an expression of anger, and Fukiye was *always* cleaning something. She swept the rugs a least once a day and cleaned the bathroom after it was used. She was loathe to allow the boys to have friends over to the house, as they might bring dirt with them. As part of her familial duties, Fukiye maintained Japanese traditions, an obligation Hide did not feel, and she kept a *kamidana* (God-shelf), a small Shinto shrine for daily prayers to gods and ancestors. She prayed for blessings from her older brother, who had died as a young man in Los Angeles, and her mother. She made sure that she prayed beside Bill—an attempt to get him to behave—but he would always peek when he was supposed to have his head bowed. He felt that his dead uncle, great grandmother, and other ancestors were watching him, adding to the pressure he felt from Fukiye's critical eye and leading him to resent the practice. Bill had few positive memories of his mother.

Although she practiced Shinto at home, Fukiye was heavily involved in the Methodist Church, an organization central to Japanese immigrant families at the time. She attended Epworth United Methodist Church, which also served as a meeting place, kindergarten, dance hall, and support association. For Fukiye, it provided a place to connect with other Issei women who she could speak with only on the phone during the week. The Naito boys attended

Sunday school at the neighborhood Mt. Tabor Methodist Church. In Bill's mind, it was one of the ways that the Japanese world was his mother's, and the white world was his. He would later characterize her as a "tormented woman" who had phobias and was obsessed with form over substance. Looking back as an adult, however, he believed that she did the best she could. Hide worked twelve hours a day, and he left most of the childrearing and house maintenance to Fukiye, in a foreign city and culture whose language she never mastered.

Fukiye was proud and hardworking, but she was also emotionally distant and often condescending to Hide. Her criticisms focused in particular on his family's status in Japan, his clothes, and how he ran his business. From Bill's point of view, she treated Hide almost as if he were another son rather than a husband. Bill sought to please his father by doing chores around the house, chopping and stacking wood every day and meticulously weeding the lawn row by row. His brother Albert didn't feel the need to please Hide the way that Bill did, but Bill made him weed the lawn row by row just as he did anyway. In Bill's eyes, his father was a samurai superman, and he wanted to gain his favor—a vivid memory of his father crunching chicken bones between his teeth at dinner stayed with Bill for life. In Fukiye's eyes, Hide was beneath her. Her family had remained in Los Angeles, and every four years she took Sam, Bill, and Albert to visit for several weeks in the summer. Her mother and father worked in a hotel populated mostly by Japanese bachelors in Little Tokyo, where she laundered the sheets and he swept the floor and cleaned the bathrooms. In between visits, Fukiye and her mother corresponded weekly through letters. Living apart from her family and other Issei women, married to a man she felt was low class, and not assimilating to US culture isolated Fukiye and contributed to her harsh and abusive behavior.

Hide was isolated, too, but on his own terms. He was not social by nature and was independent in his thinking, which was probably how he was able to spend five years crossing the United States without any money or knowing people to help him along the way. In Portland, he didn't have any particularly close friends and spent most of his free time working on the Japanese garden in their backyard or fishing

From left to right: Albert, Bill, and Sam with their aunt and uncle, circa 1933

alone. On Sundays, he would drive Fukiye to services at Epworth Church but wait outside. Many Issei participated in local organizations dedicated to Japanese interests, such as the Japanese Association of Oregon (now the Japanese Ancestral Society); recreational groups at Obukan Judo and haiku clubs; and the Japanese American Citizens League, dedicated to civil rights and combating discrimination. Those groups were a way to keep Japanese traditions alive and to have others to lean on as immigrants adjusted to life in the United States. Hide joined the Ancestral Society but did not actively participate in it or any of the other organizations.

It was in business that Hide was his most social, engaging with other businesspeople with whom he had a reputation as an honest, aggressive, and skillful businessman. H. Naito Goods was one of several curio stores in Portland, but he differentiated himself with a focus on collectibles. In the 1920s, many Americans were flush with cash and looking toward an expanding world for distinctive things to buy. At Foreign-Born Day at the Oregon State Fair in 1920, Hide, along with restaurant owner R. Kohara and mercantilist and labor agent S. Ban, ran a Japanese booth with "trinkets made by the nimble fingers of the orientals," according to the *Oregonian*.

"Polly o' Portland," an *Oregon Journal* feature focused on local shopping, often highlighted H. Naito Company products. In 1923, the column suggested that "Japanese paper in all colors splashed with gold and silver and fancy cord to tie up your gifts; insure your friends a real Oriental Christmas." Through connections from the previous owner, the shop offered an array of Japanese goods, including original Japanese prints, which Hide sold at low prices. Another popular product was a line of bobby pins manufactured in Japan, called Suzuran, Japanese for "lily of the valley." Commonly called the invisible bobby pin, these were very small, made in Japan with Swedish steel, and came in a range of colors to match a woman's hair color. H. Naito Goods also sold Japanese cloisonné and porcelain pieces (Kutani, Imari, and Satsuma), incense burners, and god and goddess figures like Buddha and goddess of compassion Kwan Yin (Kannon in Japanese). Hide's business was so successful that he opened a second location in 1926 at 384 Southwest Morrison, which Polly o' Portland urged *Oregon Journal* readers to visit for holiday gifts like decorated candles, haori jackets (traditionally worn over kimonos), lacquer jars of preserved ginger, and garden shears. At Christmastime, demand would be so high that Fukiye had to help in the store. Hide's twelve-hour workdays paid dividends for his business, which succeeded in spite of his introversion and because of his tenacity.

But those heady days were short-lived. When the stock market crashed in 1929 and ushered in the Great Depression, it eliminated the market for almost everything but necessities. Portland's emergency fund, which was used by the city council for charitable and patriotic causes, was depleted by the summer of 1930, and exports and banking activity were cut in half as businesses failed and jobs were lost. By 1933, two out of three small businesses in Portland were in arrears on their property taxes. Hide closed the second store, and Bill recalled a day when his father came home from the store having made only a dollar. For little Bill, that wasn't too distressing, as he could run to the nearby grocery store with ten cents and get a loaf of bread and a quart of milk and have a penny left over for the most important thing of all—candy.

Hide appeared to be unfazed by the downturn as well, but that was because of how deftly he shifted his focus to cheaper products.

H. Naito Goods began to sell ti (*Cordyline*) plants from Hawai'i and redwood burl from California, both of which could be grown from cuttings in water, requiring little money or time from customers. His plant sales proved reliable, and Hide understood that in a time when people felt helpless and hopeless something as simple as growing a plant could buoy their confidence. Part of this insight came from Hide's own green thumb. He had cultivated a traditional Japanese garden with fruit trees and a fishpond in the backyard, and he maintained a Japanese rock garden in the front. He also had a small greenhouse that he built on a lot next door, purchasing the land, like the house, in Sam's name. On Saturdays and Sundays, Hide potted cacti, which he sold on Mondays for 35 cents. He went further and sold agar-agar seaweed, which, when dried, was used in Japan to cure constipation in older people. Most importantly, he maintained a gracious, welcoming demeanor in the shop, regardless of how many customers had money to purchase anything.

Hide also started up a separate wholesale importing business, an idea that came to him when he realized that purchasing giftware directly from Japanese manufacturers would be more profitable than going through middlemen in the United States. It would be worth the cost, he knew, only if he imported quantities far greater than the demands of his single store, so he did not start the business until he could afford to hire salesmen to sell goods to other stores in the area. He began by importing novelties, figurines, and salt and pepper shakers. Ashtrays proved incredibly popular. In 1935, H. Naito and Company moved to 904 Southwest Morrison, across from Olds, Wortman & King. By 1941, he had at least four salesmen, customers nationwide, and a full basement in his gift shop, where Bill worked as a teenager. Hide's diversification and steadfastness not only saved the business but also expanded it, shielding his family from financial ruin.

Hide's adaptability and foresight in business can be seen in his choice of a neighborhood to live in. He appeared most comfortable doing whatever would further progress toward his goals, regardless of the means. So, it is understandable that he chose to locate his family in a white neighborhood. What better way to speed the assimilation and progression of his children's success—or the potential for their success—than to have them grow up without the safety net of the Japanese immigrant community? It is what the Japanese had done during the Meiji Restoration to become the greatest nonwhite power in the world. It also reflected the demographic realities of the early 1900s: 70 percent of westside residents rented, while over 65 percent of eastsiders owned, and almost all Asians and two-thirds of African Americans lived west of the river. If Hide wanted to own a home, then he would have more success looking outside of Nihonmachi.

Fukiye and Hide spoke only Japanese at home, and Sam knew no English when he entered first grade as the first nonwhite student at Mt. Tabor Grammar School. Four years later, Fukiye repeated the process when she shoved Bill through the school doors and pointed down the hall to his classroom. He could not understand his teacher, something she did not realize until she told him to wipe his nose. Through the grace and understanding of that teacher and local librarians, Bill learned English and quickly caught up with his English-as-a-first-language peers. As he got further along in grade school, he spent weekends and summer vacations at the library. The experience rendered libraries sacrosanct to him, and he became a staunch supporter. In 1993, when a library levy was on the ballot, he contemplated what would happen if it failed: "It will be a major disaster, more than an earthquake could create. The library is probably one of the most important institutions next to the public schools."

Bill worked hard to meet his parents' expectations for educational excellence and became a successful student at Mt. Tabor. All three Naito boys attended Japanese School at Modeville in the Russellville School District in a two-room schoolhouse in the middle of a raspberry patch. Russellville was home to successful Japanese strawberry farms, and in 1911, half the land in the area was under Japanese control (the district is now part of David Douglas School District near I-205 and Powell Boulevard). After school on Mondays, Wednesdays, and Fridays, the boys learned how to read and write Japanese. The goal was to give second-generation Japanese children a common language with their parents, but Bill resented having to go after spending the day in school. It meant he couldn't play softball or football in the vacant lot across the street from their house with his white classmates.

As an adult, he never figured out why he hated Japanese school so intensely. Perhaps it was, as Ruth A. Sasaki described in her short story, "The Loom," that the Japanese language represented something shameful in a white world. Japanese was "like a comfortable old sweater that had been well washed and rendered shapeless by wear," she described. "She would never wear it outside of the house. It was a personal thing, like a hole in one's sock, which was perfectly all right at home but would be a horrible embarrassment if seen by *yoso no hito* [foreigners]."

When he was very young, Bill suffered from rickets, which weakened his bones and made it necessary for him to wear leg braces. Hide often had to carry him. The condition was widespread during the nineteenth century, and by the turn of the twentieth century was prevalent in poor and industrial areas of the United Kingdom and the United States, usually the result of not having enough vitamin D or calcium. Bill didn't have the condition from lack of access—his family was middle class and never went without food—but it may have been because he sometimes denied himself food to cope with anxiety. He was cured after his parents took him to a white specialist doctor. For Bill, the incident created an almost paralyzing fear of negative reactions from his parents, especially his feeling of being an inconvenience or a burden on them. "My parents never gave me security," he remembered many years later. "I could never run home if I had a fight on my own because I knew that I would be punished, not supported." It was better to suffer in silence, no matter what that suffering meant. In eighth grade, when a routine eye exam at school revealed that he needed glasses, he was so terrified about the cost that he didn't eat for several days. Hide, working all the time, and Fukiye, absorbed in her own interests, didn't notice. Eventually, one of his teachers told Hide about the eye exam, and Bill got his glasses.

Despite the growing tide of anti-Asian sentiment in Portland and the United States generally, the Naitos were welcome in their neighborhood, perhaps because they were the only Japanese family there and not threatening or simply because they were good neighbors who kept to themselves and maintained a tidy home. It is impossible to know, but what is certain is that the neighbors made all three boys feel at home. Because Sam was the first minority student at Mt. Tabor

Grammar School, he was considered something of a marvel by other students and treated as someone who one was lucky to know. He felt no animosity in Portland, to the degree that he felt "white," as he later remembered. He felt completely accepted, just as American as his Italian American, Polish American, and Anglo-Saxon counterparts. Sam could not recall experiencing prejudice until he was in a high school speech class and was supposed to role-play as a married couple with a female student. His teacher, who didn't want to upset parents who might be offended by the idea of their daughter pretending to be married to an Asian, was visibly flummoxed. It stung Sam with the reality that others viewed him as different *in a negative way*. Bill had felt discrimination earlier and more acutely. He remembered being on the trolley when he was eight years old and having people avoid sitting next to him. The hurt of that feeling stuck with him through the decades, he told his friend Paul Bragdon years later. "You know," he said, "you did not sit easily on the bus when I was a kid."

The difference between the two brothers' experiences probably had a lot to do with how they felt at home. Sam, as the firstborn son, was given every advantage and was held in high esteem by his parents. Bill, because he felt discriminated against by his own parents, was more aware, maybe even overly sensitive, to what could be perceived as discrimination from others. Despite these difficulties, Bill would later say that "those were the best of times and it was a great city to grow up in." They surely must have been, because those years cemented in him a deep and abiding love of Portland. It was a love strong enough to overcome the city's participation in his family's expulsion during World War II and a love deep enough that he spent most of his life in service to the city's livability for others.

CHAPTER 3

By 1935, Sam and Bill were focused on schoolwork and their friends, like most kids in Portland. The world, however, was undergoing an ominous change. Hitler had solidified his power in Germany with rhetoric heavily laced with the language of invasion and domination. Japan was behaving in much the same way, with conquests in Korea, China, Manchuria, and Siberia, and the country had a ravenous eye for more. The Sino-Japanese War in 1894–1895 and the Russo-Japanese War in 1904–1905 marked the beginning of Japan's version of manifest destiny, in which the small island nation would secure its natural role as leader of Asia and the Pacific arena. Japan had adopted the West's colonialist hunger along with its judicial system, technology, transportation, and fashion. Radical nationalism was rippling through Japan, some of it in response to US demonstrations of prejudice against Japanese.

The Meiji Restoration, which had transformed Japan from an isolationist, feudal society into a modern, capitalist one, had been about becoming an equal of the white Western world. By 1912, many Japanese believed they had achieved it. But they were still being treated as inferior by Western powers. At the Paris Peace Conference after World War I, US and European leaders refused to add "all men are brothers" to the Paris Peace Accords, despite Japan's fervent attempts to have the phrase included. Japan's outrage at the decision fueled the nation's belief that the United States was its greatest existential threat. Previously, Russian and Western European imperialism had driven their security concerns. But US action in Hawai'i, Samoa, and Cuba in the 1890s sprouted fears of US imperialism. The refusal to acknowledge the Japanese as equals was further proof, especially among leaders in the Imperial Japanese Navy, that the United States meant their country harm.

Japan's continued military aggression in Asia led to the Second Sino-Japanese War in 1937, which increased fear of an attack on US interests in the Pacific region. That fear led to growing acts of prejudice against Japanese in the United States, which only fueled Japan's increasing nationalism. Cartoons appeared in local and national newspapers depicting Japanese as buck-toothed, slant-eyed, apelike buffoons, often with vampire ears and circular glasses like General Hideki Tojo (head of Japan's army). Bill was confused. Was this what other people believed Japanese people looked like? He had never seen anyone who looked like that, but he started to wonder if that was how Japanese people were perceived by the white world. Was that how *he* was being perceived? For a boy already sensitive to criticism and self-conscious about others' opinions, it was upsetting. Japanese actions abroad and growing prejudice at home were painting him with a brush he could not understand.

In Oregon, picketing against the sale of scrap metal shipments to Japan almost shut down the Port of Portland in 1939. The protest was in response to reported Japanese atrocities in China during the Second Sino-Japanese War. As early as 1935, a letter to the editor in the *Oregonian* decried, "A junk firm or any other organization of Americans who sell scrap metal to Japan for the continued rape of China are putting the dollar ahead of decency." By February 1939, Chinese Americans on the Oregon coast had started protesting shipments, culminating in a mass demonstration on February 24 at the Port of Astoria that featured mostly school-aged Chinese American children. Longshoremen considered the group a picket line and would not cross it. By March 5, the Port of Astoria had agreed not to allow iron shipments to Japan, and the protests moved to Terminal 4 in north Portland's St. John's neighborhood. At two o'clock that morning, the local Chinese community heard about a Greek liner with scrap iron bound for Japan. Within two and a half hours, four hundred protestors had shown up. Six hours later, the crowd had grown to more than seven hundred people. On March 11, more than 2,500 people met to applaud a potential embargo on iron shipments to Japan, including Oregon US senators Charles McNary and Rufus Holman. Governor Charles Sprague had to meet with the Japanese consul to avoid an international incident.

Bill's parents never spoke to him directly about the tensions between Japan and the Western world. Instead, he overheard dinner conversations between them and Fukiye's closest friends, Celia and Newton K. Uyesugi, president of the Portland chapter of the Japanese American Citizens League.[1] Bill was not allowed to participate in dinner except for a gracious hello before retreating out of sight, but he could hear the couples speaking in hushed tones about a potential war with Japan. Hide spoke about his belief that Japan was overreaching and that the country was too backward to achieve so much so quickly. He knew firsthand that many of the changes during the Meiji Restoration period of modernization were made to *appear* Western but had not fundamentally changed conditions. For all its advances, farmers were struggling to afford rice to eat, and few were enjoying the amenities resulting from technological advances. That was one reason that so many men had left Japan to go to America; it's likely why Hide did. Now he had lived away from his home country for more than twenty-five years, and he could see that Japan had yet to grow up. Despite an increasing sense of foreboding, Hide could not believe that Japan would be foolhardy enough to go to war with the United States. Bill took comfort in that notion, as many did.

Then, in the early hours of Sunday, December 7, 1941, Japan attacked the US naval base in Pearl Harbor, Hawai'i, killing 2,403 Americans and wounding 1,178. It was an unspeakable act of violence and an attack on sovereign US territory, which had not occurred since before the Civil War. The United States declared war on Japan the next day. Sam was in his dorm room at the University of Oregon in Eugene and later remembered students screaming and yelling in response to the news. Some students got drunk, some blacked out their windows with paint to protect themselves from air raids, and some burned their books in a fervor driven by shock and anxiety about the future. At home in Portland, Hide read the news and concluded that Japanese leaders had gone crazy. For the duration of the war, he wanted neither side to win, believing that both had acted stupidly, and he hoped for a stalemate. For a man so fixated on business success, a war between his

---

1 After imprisonment at Minidoka concentration camp, Uyesugi changed his last name to Wesley and, with George Jessen, developed the first contact lenses.

adopted country and the country from which he imported all of his goods was a worst-case scenario.

Overnight, everything changed for second-generation Japanese Americans. Ruth A. Sasaki poignantly described what many young Nisei (second-generation Japanese Americans) like Bill and Sam experienced when she wrote, about a character in "The Loom," "[she] recalled how truly she had believed she was accepted, her foolish confidence, her unfounded dreams. She and her Nisei friends had been spinning a fantasy world that was unacknowledged by the larger fabric of society." Bill had gone to bed on Saturday as an American and had awakened on Monday as an enemy of the state. He didn't want to go back to Washington High School that morning, but Hide and Fukiye made him. His experience on that first day after Pearl Harbor was like that of fellow Portlander George Katagiri: "Nobody teased me, but the other kids weren't as sociable as they used to be. Nobody knew what to say." Fifty years later, Bill wrote about the days after the attack: "'A Jap is a Jap,' people used to say. That phrase still echoes painfully in my ears as an anthem of our humiliation." The label and the rejection by white society shaped many decisions for the rest of his life.

The day after Pearl Harbor, Governor Sprague ordered all Japanese immigrants to remain in their homes and wait for instructions from the government. The US Treasury Department closed H. Naito and Company, changed the locks, and put a red sticker across the door. Without a search warrant and with no evidence of wrongdoing, US marshals searched the store for signs of treason and collusion, something they were doing to all Japanese-owned businesses on the West Coast. Hide showed up at his store that day to find himself barred from the premises.[2] The Treasury Department froze the Naitos' bank accounts, and auditors from the Federal Reserve were brought in to review the company's financial records.

On December 9, the FBI searched the Naitos' house without a warrant. The searches were happening all over Portland so quickly that no one was prepared, and Bill came home from school to find

---

2 One of the US marshals who searched the store would later become a US Customs agent involved in clearing merchandise for the Naitos after the war.

Fukiye frightened and in tears. The United States government had been surveilling Japanese Americans long before the attack and had so-called ABC lists, rank-ordering those Japanese who were potentially the most dangerous. The A list included first-generation Japanese Americans who led cultural organizations, the B list identified those who led an organization but were slightly less suspicious, and the C list named members of those organizations and those who had donated money to them. The searches created an environment of extreme fear, Bill remembered. "It's like an Anne Frank type of fear, where any minute, the Gestapo would be there. And the Gestapo did come—or the FBI. And they went through the house scaring my mother, twice. You know, just like the Gestapo." Sam's hobby was building shortwave radios, which he had hidden even though they could only receive and not transmit, and Bill had thrown his BB gun into the pond in the backyard.

Ultimately, the FBI left the house with a toy radio and a box camera. The family had been lucky. In other homes, the FBI slit open cushions and mattresses and left behind damage and disarray. The anxiety caused by the chaotic actions of law enforcement was heaped on the anxiety that every other American was experiencing at the time. There were rumors that the Japanese planned to bomb Portland, Seattle, and San Francisco, and many towns and cities had blackouts in preparation for nighttime raids. The Japanese seemed likely to win, and fear of an invasion was tangible. What could the Naitos do in response to such overwhelming threats at home and abroad? Bill knew the family's livelihood was in jeopardy and Hide's loyalty was in question, so he went to neighbors and the Mt. Tabor Methodist Church asking for letters of support for his father in hopes that authorities would allow him to reopen his store. "I was a little scared because of my youth," he remembered, but he gathered them anyway. Hide was permitted to reopen his store a week after the attack—"a miracle," Bill called it. He would later joke that the success of his family to get the license reinstated taught him that one person could take on the bureaucracy and win. But the victory was short-lived.

Portland Mayor Earl Riley declared, "There ain't going to be no more city business licenses for enemy aliens [Issei] and those [existing licenses] that are, ain't." Bill remained hopeful, however, and assured his parents that the Constitution and its Bill of Rights would protect them from mistreatment. In 1940, 62.7 percent of people of Japanese descent were second-generation US citizens who were not in league with or supportive of the Japanese Empire. How could they be punished for nothing? When you're sixteen years old, he later wrote, "you believe a lot of things." But in the months that followed, the FBI arrested innocent Issei men, some of them Hide's acquaintances, and jailed them at the Fort Missoula Detention Camp in Montana. They were considered security risks and subjected to loyalty hearings that were supposed to determine whether a person was a danger to the state. Most of the men were "community elders," who were considered the greatest threat because they were Japanese nationals and influential members of local Japanese American communities. Questions for those detainees often had to be translated into Japanese to be understood. None were found to be disloyal, but they remained imprisoned indefinitely.

In Hood River, about sixty miles east of Portland on the Columbia River, a scene took place that happened in many households. Homer Yasui, who would become a good friend of Bill's and cofounder of the Oregon Nikkei Endowment with him in 1989, came home from school and found that his father, Mas, had disappeared. No one in town knew where he had gone. Because of his role as a community leader among Japanese farmers in Hood River, he had been taken to Montana. During his loyalty hearing, Mas Yasui was presented with one of his children's school drawings of the Panama Canal. He was ordered to explain its purpose and intent, suggesting that it was part of a plan to blow up the canal.

In 1942, by February, 2,192 Issei like Mas had been disappeared into federal custody. Hide's social isolation helped him avoid the fate of other successful Issei in Portland. Immigrants who were involved in organizations with Japanese affiliations were taken, even if the connection was innocuous, like sporting clubs. Hide wasn't a member of Japanese groups, aside from a membership in the Japanese Ancestral Society, and his relationship to Japan was almost entirely connected to business. Bill remembered that his parents were too busy making ends meet in America to have any money saved in Japan or to have extensive connections there, and most of Fukiye's family had moved to the United States.

The atmosphere was toxic. Newspapers and magazines published false stories about Nisei spies, and the San Francisco *Chronicle* reported inaccurately that Japanese Americans had blocked traffic during the attack on Pearl Harbor, preventing reinforcements from reaching the base. Henry Sakamoto, who would create the Oregon Nikkei Endowment with Homer Yasui and Bill, remembered the racism being more covert before Pearl Harbor. Afterward, it was out in the open, with public sneers and stares. Nisei children were fingerprinted and had to carry notes stating their nationality. Beginning in February 1942, Japanese immigrants were subjected to a five-mile travel limit and had to obey a curfew from nine at night until six in the morning. Vandals knocked over Japanese headstones in the Rose City Cemetery in Portland. An *Oregonian* poll found that 77 percent of respondents favored the forced removal of all Japanese foreign nationals, while 33 percent supported the forced removal of Japanese American citizens. Chinese Americans wore buttons declaring "I am Chinese" to protect themselves.

In late January 1942, Portland City Council held a hearing on Resolution 22113, which would cancel all business licenses to Japanese foreign nationals. Sitting on the commission were Mayor Riley and Commissioners Fred Peterson, Kenneth L. Cooper, and Sam Bowes, all conservative in their politics; Commissioner Ralph Clyde was the lone progressive. Japanese businessmen prepared to argue in front of the chamber to protect their livelihoods, but chances were slim that any of them would be given a fair hearing.

To argue against canceling the licenses, Sam helped his father hire attorney O. C. Rohr, who had done work before for Hide and had a good reputation in the white community. Other business owners testified directly, and the Japanese American community turned out to oppose the resolution. Mike Masuoka, representing the Japanese American Citizens League, testified that the right to earn a living was fundamental and pleaded, "Gentlemen, give us a chance." Nevertheless, the council voted unanimously to cancel all business licenses, leaving Hide devasted. After the vote, council members walked to the waterfront memorial of the *Battleship Oregon* for a ceremonial welcoming of newly naturalized citizens, none of whom could be Japanese by law. The battleship, built at the turn of the twentieth century, had come to represent US exceptionalism and leadership in the world. After the ship was retired from service, its mast was put on exhibit on the bank of the Willamette River, where it had become the scene of many patriotic events. As the new Americans celebrated their citizenship, the Japanese community just up the street was left with nothing.

The council's actions were unconstitutional—the order was based entirely on ethnicity, in violation of the Fourteenth Amendment— but local newspapers either reported nothing about the order or supported the city. *Oregonian* editor Palmer Hoyt and *Oregon Journal* editor Marshall Dana unequivocally urged evacuating Japanese and Japanese Americans out of Oregon; Hoyt warned that it would take only a dozen saboteurs to set the entire state on fire, destroying its timber industry and killing thousands. The United States had been too "lax, tolerant, and soft" toward the Japanese, the *Oregonian* concluded, allowing them to operate Shinto temples, which the paper considered propaganda outlets and centers of spying for Imperial Japan. The paper quoted sources without challenge, reporting that Spanish-American War veterans said it had been conclusively proven that Nisei had shot "thousands of films" of vital infrastructure. Bill was angry and remained so for decades. At a meeting of Portland minority leaders hosted by the *Oregonian* in 1994, he expressed his outrage at the failure of the fourth estate. "I have waited half a century," he said afterward, to be asked whether Japanese Americans and other minorities were upset with the paper. "I finally had my day in court and as I walked out, I felt a great sense of relief and discovered that my anger of fifty years was over."

Members of the Japanese community did what they could to counteract the wartime animosity. On January 23, 1942, local Issei sent a telegram to President Franklin Roosevelt affirming their loyalty. Hood River Issei signed a common pledge: "May we pledge our loyalty to the stars and stripes just as do our children who are patriotic American citizens, with our prayer for a more peaceful kingdom on earth, which is the divine bequest of the American people for future generations." Unmoved by such declarations, the president issued Executive Order 9066 on February 19, 1942, authorizing the Western Defense Command to forcibly remove all persons of Japanese descent from the West Coast. Oregon governor Sprague welcomed what he considered a long-overdue and necessary action. His actions in that moment would guide him after the war to devote his life to civil rights work as atonement, but in the grip of war hysteria he was glad to have "the menace" of Japanese Americans contained.

The method of removal was left to the Western Defense Command. General John L. DeWitt, its commander, was a racist, and there was nothing that moved him from his belief that Japanese Americans were dangerous. DeWitt held firm to that conviction even when Japanese Americans were volunteering to fight in the army in 1943 and when others in the military began to question their continued imprisonment in camps. DeWitt testified before the House Naval Affairs Subcommittee in defense of the imprisonment policy on April 13, 1943: "It makes no difference whether he is an American citizen, he is still a Japanese." The United States, he continued, "must worry about the Japanese all the time until he is wiped off the map." Even though the FBI and the Justice Department disputed his conclusions and intimated that he was lying, DeWitt remained in charge of the fate of almost 120,000 people. He later became commandant of the Army and Navy Staff College.

From the beginning of the war, it was clear to DeWitt that imprisoning all Japanese and Japanese Americans was the only way to protect the United States from sabotage. In April 1942, the Western Defense Command issued Exclusion Orders, numbers 25 and 26 referring to the Portland metropolitan area, requiring the "evacuation" of all persons of Japanese ancestry from within two hundred miles of the western coastline.[3] If families or individuals could prove they had a place to move outside the exclusion zone, they could voluntarily leave before they were forced into concentration camps.

Sam was one of twenty Japanese American students at the University of Oregon, and compliance with the order meant leaving in the middle of the term. He and another student made an appeal to President Donald M. Erb to be allowed to finish their school terms before being forcibly removed. They had already paid their tuition

---

3 "Evacuation" was the term used by the government to hide the severity and illegality of its actions.

and believed that a call to General DeWitt from a university president would make a difference. When Erb refused to help, Sam went to the dean of the College of Arts and Letters, C. Valentine Boyer, who agreed to intervene with the president on their behalf. Erb still refused, and they were forced to leave campus.[4]

Albert was an eighth grader at Mt. Tabor Grade School when Executive Order 9066 went into effect. At the same time, Amy Uchimoto, whom he would one day marry, was being forced out of her senior year at Armijo High School in Fairfield, California. She knew forced removal was coming, but she held out hope that it would come after graduation so she could receive her diploma with a gold seal reflecting her academic achievements. Instead, she was imprisoned in the Gila River Camp in Arizona with her mother and father, sister, and two brothers. Armijo High School mailed her the diploma but without the gold seal, a crushing disappointment.[5]

With the deadline of EO 9066 looming, and as head of his household, Hide had a difficult choice: face the uncertainty of immediate imprisonment or face imprisonment after moving when the exclusion zone was expanded. Fukiye's sister-in-law lived in Salt Lake City, some six hundred miles from the easternmost boundary of the exclusion area, but there were no guarantees. The exclusionary area had been an arbitrary boundary and could always be pushed farther inland, especially as the United States was doing poorly in the initial months of the war. Still, Hide made it clear to his sons that incarceration was not an option. The camps represented the end of his American dream, a terminal stop on his long voyage to financial stability and success. Later, Bill could remember only one other family that avoided imprisonment like his family did. Many Isseis still had their bank accounts frozen and had no legal means of getting their assets out. Most had no family outside the exclusion zone and had stayed close to the coast and in communities like Nihonmachi in Portland, Little Tokyo in Los Angeles, and Bainbridge

---

4 In 2008, University of Oregon awarded honorary degrees to all twenty of the students who had been expelled.

5 Not until 1994, fifty-two years later, when a Fairfield resident brought her story to the attention of the principal, did Amy Naito find out she had been valedictorian. She finally received her diploma in a ceremony and received a key to the city; June 10 was declared Amy Naito Day.

Island in Seattle. Some were married to men who had been in detention in Montana for months, and they were trying to navigate the situation entirely on their own, often knowing little English.

Japanese Americans who could afford to move outside the exclusion zone often encountered resistance. Many states and cities were public in their unwillingness to accept them, a logical reaction given that the federal government had labeled them a dire security risk. Of the 10 percent of affected Japanese Americans who were able to move voluntarily, many formed or joined farming communities in eastern Washington, Oregon, and California, where EO 9066 and the draft had left farms shorthanded. For the Naitos, farming work was never considered. Hide was a merchant and had never done anything related to farming. They had family in Salt Lake City to rely on—not an ideal solution but better than a concentration camp.

Even though the Naitos avoided imprisonment, they suffered the same restrictions on what they were allowed to take with them to Utah. Hide, Fukiye, and the three boys had to fit themselves and their belongings into the family car with nothing more than one suitcase and one duffel bag per person. Bill, a sophomore at Washington High School, tried to clean out his locker without being seen before taking the streetcar home. Labeled as un-American and not to be trusted, he was too ashamed to say goodbye to his friends. His humiliation cut deeply. School was a place to define himself, where he had found genuine support from his first days of elementary school. He was an active member of 4-H, known as the "teenage chicken-farmer and high school honor student." He had raised a rabbit named Taro and fourteen pet chickens, selling their eggs after learning all he could at the Multnomah County Library from its three books on chicken husbandry. The chickens were a source of pride, giving him a sense of independence and the thrill of success. Taro had been a comfort in a house where he often felt alone, but the chickens—"I just loved those chickens, they were my pets, kind of my subfamily." They gave him sanctuary, "another world there, away from the turmoil of the times." He was forced to slaughter them all before leaving Portland.

Once the family had checked in with authorities at the Portland Assembly Center (now the Portland Expo Center), they began the two-day journey to Utah, taking unpaved back roads through eastern

Oregon because Japanese Americans were banned from the highway. Authorities feared that they would blow up Bonneville Dam on the Columbia River. Hide and Sam took turns driving. After staying overnight in a motel in Ontario, on the Oregon-Idaho state line, they arrived in Utah on bald tires.

The five thousand Japanese Americans who remained in Portland received arbitrary identification numbers, and families were assigned to rooms in the Portland Assembly Center, more accurately described as a detention center. The US Army had hastily put up plywood walls in the large building to create "rooms" in what had been the Pacific International Livestock Exposition (now the Portland Expo Center). Detainees slept on gunny sacks filled with straw and ate food provided by the army. The military was unprepared for the operation, a mass imprisonment of civilians that included the elderly and families with young children. The food was often contaminated, resulting in persistent dysentery, and water seeped into the ground below when the floorboards were hosed down. The entire building reeked of manure. In short, it was not fit for human beings. There was no structure for children, who had been pulled abruptly from school. The Catholic sisters of St. Paul Miki school in downtown Portland had a small but loyal cadre of Nisei students suddenly unable to attend school. Named after a man who was martyred in sixteenth-century Japan for his Christian faith, the school had offered free kindergarten through second grade. The sisters tried to continue their classes and masses at the detention center, but the noise was overwhelming, and learning was impossible. Two of the nuns were surveilled by the FBI for potential anti-American activity.

After five months, two-thirds of the population at the center were sent to Minidoka, an American concentration camp not far from Twin Falls, Idaho, a dusty prairieland on dry days and a muddy mire on wet ones. The other prisoners were sent to nine other benignly named "relocation centers." Japanese Americans went peacefully, believing their cooperation would prove their loyalty to the United States, but it was also a form of *ganbaru*—toughing it out—that most Issei had lived with in Japan as part of the peasant/lower class. As one prisoner described it, the Issei "were survivors because they were like soil—they were strong, and they didn't strike back. . . . 'Dish out everything you can. I'll beat you by taking it. . . . You ain't got me beat, because I'm still here.' And that's the victory." Most remained imprisoned for three and a half years, surrounded by barbed wire and guarded by men with machine guns in sentry towers. The US government justified the camps by claiming they were for the inmates' "own good"—to protect them from angry Americans who might attack them.

The Naito family avoided the terror of imprisonment, and they were fortunate in other ways, too. Most of those targeted by EO 9066 had sold their belongings, homes, and businesses to "friends" and neighbors who had promised to look after them. But when most returned after the war, they found that nothing was left. Because the Naitos' house had been purchased in Sam's name and was in a white neighborhood, Hide was able to rent the property rather than being forced to sell it and their belongings for pennies on the dollar. Many who had lived in rented homes faced having their leases canceled and nowhere to store their possessions. Many white Americans, knowing the dire situation of the Japanese Americans in their community, made false promises and liquidated their newly acquired assets as soon as the prisoners boarded the trains. The government offered storage for those leaving for the camps, with a promise that the contents would be protected for the duration of their incarceration, but most of those storage sites were empty by the time the owners returned.

The landlord of H. Naito and Company's space, Betty Lou Roberts, continued to lease the shop to Hide. Laura Saunders, who was white and had worked for Hide for ten years as a clerk, took over the shop, which she renamed Mrs. Laura Saunders Gift Shop in 1943. Hide had left behind a basement full of imported Japanese products, and some of that inventory was sold to stores on the Oregon coast by a salesman who used an agate polisher to remove "Made In Japan" from products like ashtrays and vases. In exchange for a small amount of rent, Hide agreed to let Saunders keep any profits, which proved to be sizable, since the war effort created jobs and increased disposable income. Portland especially benefited as a hub of shipbuilding, which brought thousands of workers to the area to work in the Kaiser shipyards. In the end, the people that Hide relied on to take care of his property and business did not betray his trust. Without them, everything he had built would have been lost.

The Naitos stayed in a motel in Utah before buying a house in the southeast of Salt Lake City. Bill was "more frightened than bitter," he later remembered. But for many young people, including Bill, evacuation and internment had a hint of adventure to it. Never before had he been more than twenty miles out of Portland, and he was suddenly liberated from his daily routine of chores. None of his Washington High School friends were there, but there was a freedom from feeling humiliated in their company. None of them had said a negative word against him, but he felt that being evacuating must have rendered him an enemy in their eyes. In Salt Lake, he could catch his breath.

And Salt Lake City was different from Portland, with a dry climate, high elevation, and the Wasatch Mountains looming above the city. There was an established Japanese American community in the central city—Little Tokyo/Japan Town—with more than three thousand people at its height in 1930, some of them drawn to Salt Lake because of Mormon missionaries. Railroad work and beet farming also had been significant enticements for Japanese laborers. Initially, the newcomers found a general acceptance, in part because Mormons thought the two groups had "similarities with their value systems," one researcher wrote, "especially with their vision, organization, strong family ties, and industriousness." Groups formed to help the immigrant community as it grew, including a precursor to the Japanese American Citizens League. The organization hosted a fall convention with a main speaker who was white. "We wanted to prove we were not what [the whites] thought we were," an organizer said. "We organized these conventions to prove we were Americans. I mean, we were going to be if they would let us." By 1940, the Japanese population had decreased to around two thousand people, largely due to the Great Depression. Segregation of schools was considered but never implemented.

Once the United States entered the war, the discrimination against Japanese became more pronounced. Someone sabotaged the railroad tracks in hopes that Japanese American workers would be blamed, and the railroad laid off all of them to avoid further trouble. Even though Japanese Americans in Salt Lake weren't considered as dangerous as those on the West Coast, they were still subject to illegal searches and surveillance. One man recalled giving his shotgun to a white friend after Pearl Harbor for safekeeping; when the sheriff learned about it, he demanded that the friend turn it in. After Executive Order 9066, the Utah legislature considered incarcerating Japanese Americans in the state but passed an alien land law instead. Utah hosted the Western Defense Command's Topaz concentration camp, which housed around eleven thousand people, mostly from San Francisco. The JACL, forced out of California, relocated its headquarters to Salt Lake City, making the city a center of Japanese American political activity.

The Naitos lived about eight miles from Little Tokyo, and Hide had to find something to do. He was angry and wounded, as all Issei men were. Unable to protect their families, to provide for them and to assure them, they were broken spiritually by the evacuation. In the camps, Issei men tried with what little they had to resurrect their community, fulfilling their traditional roles as patriarchs. Many had their wives to lean on, but it was impossible to be the same person in prison as they had been at home. "I used to do watercolor paintings," Yosh Kuromiya remembered about his time in the camp. "I don't think I ever finished one of them. I don't know whether it was unconsciously deliberate or not. There was always this big question mark. Who are we? What are we doing here?"

The idea of *shikata ga nai*—it can't be helped—had long helped Japanese cope with the difficulties of living in an oppressive feudal society and later in a modern one built on the economic exploitation of its citizens. One should fight only what can be fought and accept what cannot without anger or resentment. For many who endured forced removal, that cultural touchstone was enough, but not for Hide. He had kept his family out of the camps, but he had no way of earning a living in Salt Lake City or any way of ensuring a secure future. He had lost the comfort of one of his few hobbies—his lawn and Japanese garden—and everything had changed for the worse. He needed something to give his life purpose again. Until he could find that motivation, he did what he was prone to do when upset: sulk. It irritated Fukiye, who thought it was childish, and troubled Bill, whose image of his father was challenged when he saw him moping about the house. Hide was trapped by the overwhelming feeling of helplessness.

His sons handled the situation differently. Sam wanted to finish his college degree and applied for admission at the University of

Utah. After Robert G. Sproul, president of the University of California, suggested that forcibly removed students should receive tuition-free admission at universities outside the evacuation zone, a letter of protest appeared in the *Utah Chronicle*, the university newspaper. The letter writer asked, "Why should the bad boy be given quarter after having been spanked for his behavior before?" The author went further, comparing Japanese Americans with "unwanted and unneeded material" dumped onto their front lawn by a neighbor. Sam responded with his own letter, explaining that he had paid his spring tuition and expected no handouts. Japanese American students were US citizens, and he hoped that "you do not believe that our great educational system has failed to make us good citizens." In the end, "all we ask is a chance to prove our loyalty not by lip service but by action, and especially prove that we are not 'bad boys' and 'unwanted and unneeded material.'" The university admitted Sam.

To pay tuition and help the family, Sam used the family car to drive to multiple jobs. He mowed lawns at a country club that banned people of color as members; served as a teacher's assistant at the University of Utah during the school year; and prepared salads at the Hotel Utah (now the Joseph Smith Memorial Building), a few blocks from Japan Town. He tried to get a warehouse job, but the owner told him that he was worried that someone would throw a brick through the window. People were often more worried about other people's reactions to Japanese Americans than about the Japanese Americans themselves. At the university, Sam helped form the Cosmopolitan Club so Japanese American students would have the opportunity to participate in extracurricular programs. "We are trying to foster better understanding and fellowship on social and cultural planes," the *Utah Nippo* reported in November 1942, "as well as making it possible for minority group students to participate in student affairs." He also became active in JACL events, joining the Relocation Aid Committee, which sent magazines, books, and toys to the Tanforan Assembly Center in San Bruno, California, where Japanese Americans were detained before being imprisoned in Topaz concentration camp in Delta, Utah. He was JACL's social chairman from 1943 to 1944, resigning when he was accepted to Columbia University.

Bill enrolled at Granite High School and worked as a greens boy at a nearby golf course. His most important contribution to the family at that time was suggesting that they raise chickens as a way to make money. Together with Hide and Sam, he built two large coops that housed six hundred chickens. None of them knew carpentry, but they managed to pour the slabs of concrete themselves. Every member of the family contributed to make the business work. Fukiye and her mother, who had come to Salt Lake City from Los Angeles, cleaned the eggs, and Fukiye made the candles used to incubate eggs so they could hatch more chickens. She despised having to do such menial work—it was like poison to her, remembered Bill—but she did it all the same. Hide sold the eggs to a local poultry wholesaler. When the hens stopped laying, Hide and Bill slaughtered the birds, cleaned them, and sold them to Coon Chicken Inn, a West Coast restaurant franchise that began in Salt Lake City and had locations in Portland and Seattle. The restaurant had a cartoonish Black man with exaggerated mouth and lips as its symbol, and diners literally walked through his mouth to enter the restaurant. Fukiye cooked mostly chicken for the family to eat—chicken sukiyaki, chicken teriyaki, fried chicken, chicken stew, roast chicken, chicken, chicken, chicken. Bill would forever after refuse to eat chicken whenever possible.

The chicken business gave Hide a sense of purpose and optimism. It also gave him income, which, when added to the rent he received from their home in Portland and the earnings from Sam's and Bill's jobs, provided enough for the family to be comfortable. It was not Portland, but the Naito family figured out a way to make Salt Lake City a productive placeholder as they waited for the war to end.

CHAPTER 4

Many young Nisei men felt an undeniable need to prove themselves as Americans and saw military service as the ultimate way to demonstrate their patriotism and loyalty. Initially, they were not allowed to enlist, but as the war progressed, the US government came to believe that they should serve. Those who wanted to had to respond to a loyalty questionnaire. Two questions required an affirmative response:

Are you willing to serve on combat duty whenever ordered?

Will you swear unqualified allegiance to the United States of America, to defend the US from all attack, and foreswear any allegiance to the Japanese emperor or any other foreign organization?

Those who answered negatively were called No-No Boys and were not allowed to serve. But to say "no" did not mean they supported Japan. In most cases, it meant they believed the questionnaire was offensive, the imprisonment of Japanese and Japanese Americans was unconstitutional, and to fight for a country that ignored its own citizens' rights was a bridge too far. To foreswear allegiance to the Japanese emperor implied a loyalty that had never existed. Being Yes-Yes, however, didn't protect a soldier from discrimination. Oregonian Robert Akio Sumoge was serving in the army in the Midwest when President Roosevelt arrived for a visit. Because of "security reasons," he and other Japanese American soldiers were locked in a garage until the president had left. Sumoge protested and spent the rest of the war in the stockades for insubordination.

Bill Naito later explained that "it was very important . . . to show my friends back home in Portland that I was a loyal American. I'm

Hide and Fukiye with Albert and Bill in uniform, circa 1946

willing to go fight its wars." He was a US citizen and subject to the draft, and he decided to enlist after he graduated from high school. Hide and Fukiye supported his decision, reasoning that they were Americans and the family owed it to the country for giving them a living and their sons an education. So Bill finished his studies at Granite High School with hopes of joining the navy. But only the army allowed Japanese Americans to serve, so, in August 1944, he joined the US Army at Fort Douglas, in Salt Lake City. His active service start date was September 4, 1944, almost two weeks before his nineteenth birthday. He was placed in the 442nd Regimental Combat Team, a segregated outfit. By that time, much had changed in the war. The Soviet Union was proving to be a formidable force, and the Germans were suffering large losses on the Eastern Front. On D-Day, June 6, 1944, on the beaches in Normandy, the Western Allies began the liberation of France from German occupation. In China, Japan was finding military success in the Pacific War, but the United States was making inroads in the Pacific Islands that allowed their bombers to run increasingly devastating campaigns against Japanese strongholds.

Eighteen-year-old Bill Naito arrived for training at Fort Benning, Georgia, as a slight young man—five foot four inches tall and weighing barely a hundred pounds. He shared a shack with four other soldiers, all of whom were married, and they teased him about his youth, his size, and his inexperience. Bill couldn't compete in feats of physical prowess and couldn't force himself to grow, so he did what years of watching his father had taught him: he looked to his own strengths to adapt to a difficult situation. He decided to become a sharpshooter. Reading manuals, listening intently to instruction, and practicing as much as possible, he became the best shooter in the company and won the respect of his fellow soldiers. At Fort Benning, he formed a lifelong friendship with Henry Kato, who was from a farming family in California. Kato had come to basic training from the Poston War Relocation Center on the Colorado River, where his family was imprisoned. Bill and Henry had similar dispositions: neither drank or smoked, and both saved their money. They were also among the few Christians in the regiment and regularly attended Sunday services together. After church, parishioners treated them to lunches in their homes, a generosity difficult to imagine on the West Coast.

The regiment was preparing for war in Europe, where the 442nd and the 100th Infantry Battalion were engaged in intense and bloody combat with German forces in France and Italy. The 100th Battalion was a companion to the 442nd Regimental Combat Team, composed initially of National Guard soldiers from Hawai'i. Although the 100th Battalion joined the 442nd in June 1943, the 100th Battalion infantry unit continued to be identified separately in recognition of its distinguished service. Known as the Little Iron Men in Italy and as Gentlemen Soldiers in France, the soldiers were fierce against the enemy but also compassionate toward civilians in towns they liberated. With a motto, "Go for Broke," the 442nd and 100th earned eighteen thousand decorations for valor and sustained 9,486 casualties, including six hundred killed in action, making it the most decorated unit in American military history. Driven by a desire to prove their worth as Americans and bring honor to their families, the men fought without fear in the face of often overwhelming odds. But Bill was never able to join them in combat, his sharpshooting skills never put to the ultimate test. Instead, he and Kato were selected to take placement tests for eligibility in the Military Intelligence Service Language School.

When Japan attacked Pearl Harbor, the US military was not fully prepared for the intelligence battle facing them. Few officers were fluent in Japanese, let alone Japanese shorthand, known as *gyosho*, a semicursive script with some characters seeming to connect to the next, and *shosho*, the most difficult type of calligraphy with some strokes eliminated entirely. The military had assumed that most Nisei spoke Japanese and would be able to quickly penetrate Japanese military communications. But only 3 percent of the first 3,700 men recruited for Japanese intelligence duty were accomplished linguists, and only 4 percent were proficient in the language. Most Nisei were like Bill, who considered Japanese school to be an unwanted chore. The military solved the problem by creating the Fourth Army Intelligence School on November 1, 1941, outside San Francisco, with fifty-eight Issei and two white students.

Once Japan attacked and the scope of the war became clear, the school moved to larger quarters away from the coast because its Japanese American soldiers were subject to Executive Order 9066. Camp Savage, south of Minneapolis–St. Paul was selected in part because the Twin Cities was relatively unbiased toward Japanese Americans. Nisei soldiers had to complete a sixty-page questionnaire to enter the camp, but the more impediments the government put in their way, the harder Nisei service members strove to overcome them. The first soldiers at the MIS Language School were eager to prove themselves. After seven hours of instruction and two hours of study every day, the night duty officer had to search for unauthorized lights to stop furtive study. The War Department later said that the soldiers' work meant that "never before in history did one army know so much concerning its enemy prior to actual engagement."

MIS soldiers trained as interrogators, interpreters, translators, radio announcers, propaganda writers, and cave flushers (those sent to persuade Japanese soldiers barricaded in hillside entrenchments to surrender rather than commit suicide or die fighting). Despite having Japanese parents, many arrived at the school believing that "every Jap was a savage, maniacal militarist," according to soldier and author James Oda. Like most Americans, they saw the enemy as one-dimensional and less than human. Their beliefs about the Japanese were proof that the Japanese Americans who the US government had labeled as enemies of the state were just as American as their white counterparts. They were also proof of the effectiveness of domestic propaganda about the Japanese Empire. Propaganda instructors had to humanize the enemy before they could teach their student-soldiers how to persuade them.

By August 1944, when Bill enlisted in the 442nd, the MIS Language School had moved to Fort Snelling in St. Paul, where students had six to seven months of training. Most of the soldiers had left families struggling in American concentration camps, but the Twin Cities was welcoming. Local families hosted the language students on weekends and holidays, young women attended church dances with them, and people treated them as welcome guests who were nobly volunteering for their country. Drivers often stopped when they saw Nisei soldiers on the road and offered them rides. The local arm of the American Bar Association donated prizes for their academic achievements.

Bill was assigned to a student company for housing, messing, administration, and basic training. Wake-up call was at six in the morning, with classes starting at seven-thirty. Language instruction, which focused on POW interrogation and document translation, ended at 4:20 p.m. Two hours a week were devoted to theory and tactics. After exercise and dinner, students had supervised evening study from seven to nine, with an additional hour and a half of voluntary study. Lights-out was at eleven. On Wednesdays and Saturdays, they had military training, which often included a five- to ten-mile march. Many of the student-soldiers would end up accompanying troops in battle and were sometimes under fire from their fellow soldiers by accident of skin and adrenaline. This was especially true for cave flushers, who stood alone outside the caves or pillboxes of Japanese troops and, armed with a grenade, would attempt to persuade them to surrender. Bill avoided those dangers because the United States dropped atomic bombs on Hiroshima and Nagasaki in early August 1945.

Bill, around 1946

Japan surrendered on August 15, and the formal surrender was signed on September 2. The United States then faced the sizable task of occupying Japan, which entailed not only physical force but also propaganda control. Bill was among 149 Japanese American men from Fort Snelling who were assigned to Civil Censorship School at Fort Mason in San Francisco. The group was selected solely on Army General Classification Test scores and represented the top of their class, although no Japanese Americans were allowed to become officers. The Civil Censorship Detachment (CCD) was one of four prongs of the military's Civil Intelligence Section, which also included the 441st Counter Intelligence Corps that pursued war criminals. CCD reviewed old and new newspapers, radio scripts, movie scenarios, dramatic productions, books, magazines, and pamphlets to make sure they complied with the Press Code and Radio Code. One of the most violated clauses involved the prohibition of anything that would "invite mistrust or resentment of [occupying American] troops." Mail and telegrams were also monitored, especially because external activists, such as those in Hong Kong, were pressing for a communist revolution.

Bill was sent to Tokyo with the Zebra Platoon. They traveled on the SS *Lurline*, a luxury liner commandeered by the War Department. A directive from President Harry Truman resulted in the platoon being dropped in Manila, Philippines, where they stayed at least a week for what amounted to a vacation. Finally, someone assumed that they were part of the Allied Translators and Interpreters Service (ATIS), and the platoon traveled with ATIS members to Tokyo on the liberty ship USS *Kinkaid*. Although the war was over, their passage was through waters littered with undetonated mines and the wreckage of ships and airplanes. In Tokyo, still with no orders, the Zebra Platoon stayed with ATIS.

After several days, Bill was sent to Fukuoka in southern Japan, eighty-seven miles northeast of Nagasaki, where he worked with Japanese nationals. Each day, two or three members of the unit took a truckload of Japanese materials for review to a warehouse outside town. Bill often got the assignment with Warren Kittell, with whom he formed a lifelong friendship while serving. The two soldiers and other members of the Zebra Platoon went through the incoming and outgoing letters and packages of local people to ensure that none expressed support for the Japanese Empire or against the United States. They were performing a duty that other soldiers had performed in American concentration camps back home—an unsettling irony.

Zebra Platoon member Yosh Ozawa later described the time as hectic, "not knowing what the future held for us Niseis." But Bill found redemption in helping people rebuild lives that had been devastated by the Japanese Empire, helping a student at the naval academy in Kure, south of Hiroshima, enroll in a college in Illinois and visiting Hide's family near Kobe. Bill was honorably discharged on August 21, 1946, at the rank of Technician Third Grade (Tec 3), the same pay grade as staff sergeants but without the ability to issue orders. His work and service were recognized with an American Theater Service Medal, an Asiatic-Pacific Service Medal, an Army of Occupation Medal (Japan), a Victory Medal, and a Good Conduct Medal. The nature of his service, and that of every other MIS soldier, was classified until the 1980s.

Bill visiting his extended family in occupied Japan, 1946

In 2010, all members of the Military Intelligence Service, the 442nd Regimental Combat Team, and the 100th Battalion received the Congressional Gold Medal for their exemplary service during World War II. The award is the highest civilian honor that Congress may confer on a person, group, or institution that "performed an achievement that has an impact on American history and culture that is likely to be recognized as a major achievement in the recipient's field long after the achievement." Nisei servicemen and women had done something extraordinary: they had experienced, in the words of the Presidio Army Museum, a "phoenix-like emergence from the ashes of suspicion and fear to an almost unparalleled position of honor and regard." Bill would in time rise above the pain and shame of Executive Order 9066 and the racism shown by his fellow Americans during World War II, but the progression would not be easy, nor would it happen quickly.

CHAPTER 5

Bill returned to Portland with immense internal conflict. Among the many clippings he saved was an August 12, 1944, *New Yorker* article about the experiences of a white soldier that was similar to his. Joseph Theodore Hallock had graduated from high school in Portland in 1939 and had been at University of Oregon at the same time as Sam. A bombardier during the war, he had received a Purple Heart, an Air Medal with Three Oak-Leaf Clusters, and a Distinguished Flying Cross. The article highlighted Hallock's seeming detachment from the war. His view of life mirrored Bill's:

> Whatever I tell you [about my war experience and accolades], boils down to this: I'm a cog in one hell of a big machine. The more I think about it, . . . the more it looks as if I've been a cog in one thing after another since the day I was born. Whenever I get set to do what I want to do, something a whole lot bigger than me comes along and shoves me back into place. It's not especially pleasant, but there it is.

A lack of agency had dominated Bill's youth and wartime experience. Under the domineering thumb of Fukiye and then the family's forced removal by the US government, he had felt unwanted by his family and his country. But school had always been his safe haven, and he sought solace there by going to Reed, a small liberal arts college in southeast Portland that was relatively close to his parents' home. It was there that he would find his voice and the beginnings of his ability to lead. But it was not simple.

Bill later remembered that when he first arrived at Reed he was "pathologically shy" and deeply skeptical that he would be accepted into US society. He was silenced by that fear. "The 'T' for traitor," he said, "still stung on my face." Serving in the occupation of Japan had only exacerbated his anxiety, and he wanted to turn inward to hide, just as he had done at home. But class participation could not be avoided at Reed, an institution that prides itself on creating thinkers and debaters through intense discussion. "It's the academic and scholarly atmosphere," Reed president E. B. MacNaughton explained. "We specialize in it as much as West Point specializes in a military tradition. The scholar is our hero."

Reed set the tone for the way Bill approached being a parent and a boss, pairing a freedom to fail or succeed with superficially distant supervision. "The theory," journalist Richard Neuberger wrote in 1952, "is that an atmosphere of complete personal freedom, in which the student is on his own, can coax out of any individual the utmost within him, particularly if he will become a hero among his associates by doing so." So ardent was Reed's adherence to high academic principles that in 1935 the faculty rejected having a Phi Beta Kappa chapter, believing that all of their students were of that caliber. They relented in 1938, and Bill became a member upon his graduation with a bachelor's degree in economics in 1949. The honor was partially due to the strength of his senior thesis, "The Experience of the United States in Financing the Two World Wars," which evaluated whether the United States had found better methods of funding war. In typical Reed fashion, the answer was yes and no.

At the same time as he attended Reed, Bill also took night classes in accounting at the Vanport Extension Center (now Portland State University), as did many veterans returning from the war. Unlike Sam, who had learned accounting and basic business skills from Hide, Bill had worked doing warehouse labor. The extension center also held a special summer session to help returning GIs make up for their deficiencies in math and other core subjects. In that way, Bill maximized his GI Bill benefits.

At Reed, Art Leigh—"my hero," Bill called him—helped him find his voice. Leigh, a professor of economics, suffered from poor vision and needed students to read articles, papers, and exams to him. He hired Bill and patiently listened as Bill slowly overcame his shyness and occasional stuttering. The word that Bill struggled with the most was the one that would come to define his life: entrepreneur. As a student, Leigh remembered, Bill was cheerful, full of energy, and brilliant. But like many teachers before him, Leigh did not realize how important he was in influencing the student that he admired. His support allowed Bill to come out of his shell, something that he had struggled with since he was young. Bill later described the atmosphere of his upbringing:

> The one thing that I always sympathize or identify with — Anne Frank type of stories. And, the life that we led during most of my childhood was like Anne Frank. And you've got be quiet, the enemy is outside, but we'll carry on our own feud inside . . . between ourselves, relatives, you know. Within the family you could kill each other or just raise hell, but outside, we can't go outside. If we do go outside we have to put on our masks, our facades, you know, just be very still. And that's the type of devastating kind of upbringing, . . . like the Anne Frank type of situation. . . . It really gets me. Where one is sort of running away.

Leigh buoyed Bill's confidence, strengthened his public speaking abilities, and helped him feel comfortable speaking his mind.

Bill also found a group of men at Reed who validated him and became his lifelong friends: Bill Daw, Orval "Bill" Clawson, Don Morey, and Daniel Momyer. The Reed Bridge Group, as they later called themselves, were servicemen who attended Reed on the GI Bill. All but Bill were white, a tangible acceptance by the white America he wanted to feel embraced by. Bill Clawson had graduated from Grant High School in Portland and served in the navy and became his closest friend. While at Reed, Bill confided to Clawson about his fears that whites would not like him because of his ethnicity. The two talked about it often, which helped Bill overcome some of those feelings. Clawson also graduated with a bachelor's degree in economics, then went to graduate school for a master's degree in education and taught US history in Portland.

At Reed, Bill loved to sit back with a beer and listen to his friends talk about socialism and the need for government intervention to level the playing field. Those ideas appealed to him: he had just witnessed the

Bill's graduation photo,
Reed College, 1949

mass robbery and incarceration of 120,000 people who had received no help from the private sector and, more importantly, no recourse in the courts. During the war, the *Korematsu*, *Hirabayashi*, and *Yasui* Supreme Court cases had validated the imprisonment of Japanese and Japanese Americans despite constitutional violations. Gordon Hirabayashi, who had been a student at the University of Washington, had been convicted of violating the military curfew imposed after the Japanese attack on Pearl Harbor. "If I'm accused of sabotage," Hirabayashi explained, "I can defend myself against that. But ancestry is no crime. I can't defend myself against that." He was found guilty, and his conviction was upheld on appeal to the Supreme Court.

The *Yasui* case originated in Portland. Min Yasui was born and raised in Hood River and graduated Phi Beta Kappa from the University of Oregon. He finished law school and was admitted to the Oregon State Bar in 1939. On March 28, 1942, he was arrested on purpose for violating military curfew in Portland so that he could have standing to challenge Executive Order 9066. The US Supreme

Court upheld his conviction in 1943, deferring to military necessity, and he was transferred to the Minidoka concentration camp for the remainder of the war.

Korematsu v. United States, the best-known of the three cases, involved Fred Korematsu in San Leandro, California, who had avoided forced removal in the hope of having a future with his Italian American girlfriend. She broke up with him, but he remained in his home in violation of Executive Order 9066 and was arrested. The US Supreme Court found that Korematsu's right to due process had not been not violated, because the order was based not on race but on military necessity. Dissenting, Justice Frank Murphy called the decision the "legalization of racism." After the war, the Japanese and Japanese Americans who had been imprisoned in the camps were sent to the cities where they had lived, with a train ticket and twenty-five dollars, as if that sum was sufficient to restart their lives. It was an affront to human dignity.

Discrimination also continued to affect Bill's life. His adviser at Reed told him to give up on his desire to go to law school, not because he wasn't good enough but because no one would hire a Japanese American attorney. "Bill," he said, "you'll starve." Socialism seemed the cure for a society sick with racism and inequality, and, for Bill, economics seemed the subject through which he could effect change. Reed had given him a new perspective, attending as he did during what many considered its golden age, partly because it was the time when the school fully embraced a humanities-centric curriculum. It was also a time when students were especially motivated. "All those veterans wanted answers," remembered Fred Rosenblum, a 1948 graduate.

Bill would later refer to his time at Reed as one of his happiest and most productive, and he was passionate about the college for the rest of his life. In 1996, after Bill's death, Reed president Steven Koblick gave him this tribute: "Bill personified fundamental Reed values: consistency, over time, to uncompromising standards of excellence, intellectual rigor, an unrelenting work ethic, and an insistence on challenging civil discourse." Bill became a trustee at Reed in 1974 after being the alumni association's treasurer from 1965 to 1966, and he focused much of his attention on the buildings and grounds.

Through his work with President Paul Bragdon in the 1970s and 1980s, he played a key role in increasing Reed's endowment by $40 million and placing the college on secure financial footing. In 2008, Steele residence hall was renamed Naito Hall.

In 1949, Bill enrolled at the University of Chicago to study economics with a plan to get a doctorate. He was one of many Nisei who achieved academic success after the war, a way to show that they deserved the pride of their families and their country. That success helps explain why so many of the businesses that their mothers and fathers had started, like hotels and shops in Nihonmachi, remained closed after the war; their children had become professionals. Fukiye, like many Issei women, was pleased. She wanted her sons to become doctors, a desire that came from the traditional Japanese importance of titles. Having the title of doctor was as close as the United States got to being a baron or a duke, but getting into medical school was difficult, as schools often had quotas for the number of minority students they would accept. In response, many Nisei men became optometrists, dentists, and pharmacists. But Bill fell in love with economics, and as a professor with a PhD, he would be called "doctor." That would satisfy his parents and himself.

At the University of Chicago, Bill would find the key to opening himself up to the world. Without his experience there, he likely would have remained an introvert, bright but not driven, expounding the virtues of monetarism to university students and avoiding the family business. Instead, he rejected socialism as a remedy for social ills and participated in a study that gave him an optimism he had never known. "Even if the whole world were caving in around me," he once said, "I'd still be smiling." It was soul-defining.

Bill attended the university when the theory of economics known as the Chicago School was coming into itself. At its core was the idea that freedom was the goal of society and that the individual was its ultimate entity. The Chicago School argued that a free market was critical for a free society and that government was an impediment to achieving it. Accordingly, the size and influence of government should be minimized as much as possible. It was liberalism as economic theory, and Bill considered it a revelation. He came to see that the world wasn't as bad as he had thought it was and that government couldn't solve every problem. When he looked back on the swell of racism in the years leading up to Pearl Harbor, he saw how the free enterprise system had helped Japanese farmers: they could still sell their fruit and vegetables to Fred Meyer grocery stores because no one cared where the food came from.[1]

Bill's belief in humanity was redeemed through a "faith ultimately in the decency of ordinary people in an open society," as Reed president Paul Bragdon described it. It was an optimistic vision of capitalism: the market was not only a great equalizer but also a great motivator, forcing participants to rise to the competition through innovation and invention. People would do what was right when they were presented with the facts, Bill believed, much like English philosopher John Stuart Mill, who believed the working class would stop having so many children when given the consequences (downward pressure on wages). When the Multnomah County Library Trust needed funding through a bond measure in 1993, for example, he argued that Portland voters would voluntarily tax themselves for the greater good of the community. For Bill, economics was not just numbers and percentages. Heavy-handed monetary policy had consequences, including bankruptcies and unemployment, which led to divorce and child abuse.

Oregon US representative David Wu once said without irony that Bill had "the antithesis of the conservative business mind." For Bill, conservative monetary policy did not eliminate dynamic public spending. If the government spent money, then it ought to be used to encourage vibrant public-private endeavors. And limited government didn't mean abdicating the state's obligations to its citizens, including protection of the environment, forward-thinking urban planning, and a robust education system, including libraries. Education was a good above all others; it was how people could learn the best choices to make and, thus, required heavy investment by government. High school students, he advised, should learn at least one foreign language,

---

1 Even though Bill had discovered socialism at Reed, he had gained a foundation for this change in thinking from Blair Stewart, an economics professor who emphasized the importance of banks in the economy. Stewart was part of the Portland Citizens Relocation Committee, a group that helped returning Japanese Americans with housing and employment.

international banking, geography, economics, accounting, and, "above all," English. School should be held year-round, nine to five, Monday through Friday, which would not only increase how much students learned but also ensure that they weren't home unsupervised. In his own house, he buried the television in the yard when he thought his children were watching it too much, and he once jokingly suggested "taxing television watchers as a sin tax for not reading during their evenings." Bill even came to believe the unconventional idea that education could be used to balance the trade deficit by treating higher education as a commodity to sell to foreign buyers.

Bill received his master's degree in economics in 1951 and began work on a dissertation on monetary policy under the National Banking Act. His adviser was Milton Friedman, a founder of the Chicago School and a key figure in the resurrection of monetarism, a theory of economics that emphasized the role of money supply in inflation, consumption, and output. Friedman was Bill's idol, and Bill kept clippings of his mentor's editorials and articles from the *Wall Street Journal* and the *New York Times*.

Yet, despite his enthusiasm for economics and his success as a student, Bill felt adrift. Without his tightknit group of friends and the security he had achieved at Reed to support him, he had reverted emotionally. He was internally at sea, governed by a sense of both uselessness and listlessness. He had dated little up to then, and he felt isolated in social groups, where he struggled to connect with both Nisei and whites. John Okada, who wrote *No-No Boy* in 1957, described a predicament similar to Bill's. It was a matter of attitude, he explained: "Mine needs changing. I've got to love the world the way I used to. I've got to love it and the people so I'll feel good, and feeling good will make life worthwhile. There's no point in crying about what's done. . . . I want to go on living and be happy. I've only to let myself do so." But Bill was unable to change his attitude on his own. Help came in the form of a study on the acculturation of minorities at the Chicago Institute of Psychoanalysis.

Its seminar Personality Correlates of Different Patterns of Response to Cultural Marginality began in 1951 with the goal of creating a comprehensive theory that reconciled anthropological explanations about the cultural marginality of minorities with a psychological cognitive

Bill in his backyard in the Mt.
Tabor neighborhood, around
1930

evaluation of the individuals involved. The hope was to explain why
some people, when uprooted from traditional values and structures,
become hyper-rigid while others become more tolerant. Bill's friend,
Lorne Sonley, a fellow economics graduate student, had suggested the
class to him. As part of the seminar, Bill met with a psychiatrist four
times a week for two years. Even though the sessions were free to participants, he paid a dollar for each one out of a sense of pride.

Bill's therapist noted that he was shy, awkward, ill at ease, and
immobilized in his physical behavior. The muscles on the right side of
his face didn't move, and he had no noticeable nasolabial fold on that
side of his face (the line in the skin from the side of the nose around
the mouth, commonly known as smile lines). She characterized this
as partial paralysis. He spoke to her about his resentments against his
mother and his brother Sam, his feelings of inadequacy and anxiety
and a lack of control. He struggled to trust strangers, including his
therapist—so much so that he would later admit to watching her
leave and enter the building where they had their sessions. He was

Bill at the McCormick Pier
groundbreaking in 1981

diagnosed with passive-aggressive personality disorder with severe overt and covert anxiety.

In Japanese terminology, Bill suffered from *taijin kyofusho*, or anthrophobia, characterized by feelings of inadequacy, fear of meeting people, blushing, and stammering. He sometimes stuttered severely when talking about how his mother rejected him. Fukiye had interpreted his facial paralysis, caused by severe anxiety, as being a crooked mouth, a bad mouth that he internalized as "some act of God for being disobedient" to his parents. The social hierarchy within the family left him feeling inferior and gave him an immediate and negative reaction to anyone around him who acted superior: "A superior eye is terribly hostile," he remarked to his therapist. It was part of his resentment toward Sam, the firstborn. Throughout his childhood, he had learned to turn his negative emotions inward, suppressing them or turning them on himself.

By the end of two years of therapy, Bill could see that he did not have a fatal, irreversible flaw. He could look at Fukiye with sympathy and understanding and was able to forgive himself for what he had believed were his faults and failures. He was not bound to what he thought his family's perception of him was. He later said that when he started therapy, he felt like a passenger on a train; when he finished, he felt that he was in a position to help the engineer but was not the engineer himself. He had found a certain pragmatism to his newfound optimism, and he understood why his family acted the way they did. That sympathy allowed him to temper their influence on his sense of self-worth. There were limits on how much he could control, but that was not a reflection of inadequacy. He had become the man "who knew who he was and what he had," as executive director of Association for Portland Progress and later director of the Port of Portland, Bill Wyatt, recalled years later.

Therapy gave Bill greater confidence in engaging with others, and it left him with a capacity for positive thinking that became his trademark. He saw the glass as half full—and the remaining half was full of potential. Optimism had never been a meaningful part of his life before, but therapy had made it an essential element of his life going forward. Coupled with his intelligence, it created a forceful dynamic. As former Portland mayor Neil Goldschmidt explained, Bill "had the ability to connect things that were complicated. . . . [He] always made them seem so simple because he talked in a way that didn't make things seem impossible or difficult." Therapy had elevated his vision for the future beyond the weight of the past and had given him the capacity to lead others. His philosophy could be summed up by a John LeCarré quote—the underlines were made by Bill on a cutout that he kept at his desk of the 1993 *New York Times* op-ed by the famed novelist:

> In my country, and perhaps in yours, the service industries of criticism have almost drowned the magic of creation. . . . We are poisoning ourselves with malice. Yet we take no risks. We are not brave. Our orthodoxy still gives us no way out. Yet we have never been so free. We no longer need to clip the wings of our humanity. It's time we flew again.

Optimism developed through therapy helped him become the man who could imagine what could be and not fixate on what wasn't.

CHAPTER 6

Lorne Sonley, who had suggested Bill enroll in the psychotherapy seminar at the University of Chicago, was a pragmatic thinker—a man who sought out as much information as possible before coming to conclusions and making decisions. Ten years older than Bill and a Canadian who had become an American citizen in 1943, Lorne grew up in a farming village and was obsessed with finding out why some farms prospered when others did not, despite being only miles apart. He ultimately pursued a master's degree in economics at Iowa State College, which meant he could defer military service during World War II. But watching others who were husbands and fathers leaving to serve, he enlisted and was stationed at Long Beach Army Air Force Base in California. He never made it into active combat.

Resuming his graduate studies at the University of Chicago, Lorne became Bill's closest friend there. He suggested the seminar to help Bill with his emotional issues surrounding the war and his child-hood. Lorne had taken a job in occupied Japan in 1947, reporting to General Douglas MacArthur's office about the country's agriculture. The post was critical, since the war had left the country on the verge of mass starvation. He often felt under serious pressure to produce results, and it was the first job he had that he was truly invested in. "It sort of 'gets one,'" Lorne said at the time, "to feel that his work has a direct bearing on 'how many Japanese are hungry.'" It may have been his affinity for the Japanese people that allowed him insight into Bill's situation. Lorne's suggestion to Bill to participate in the seminar had been transformational, but it was his introduction of his younger sister that opened Bill to the possibility of love.

Micki was short and petite, with wavy brown hair and an English nose. Strong-willed and determined, she was also shy and somewhat reserved. She had grown up in the farming village of Manilla, Ontario, with her brother, nine years her senior, and her parents Edith and Hilliard. During her parents' courtship, her father had driven a horse and buggy to Edith's home every Sunday, passing the day in her parlor. Hilliard often said the long day of wooing exhausted him, and he would fall asleep in the buggy as the horse dutifully returned him home. The couple married in 1917 and moved into a tiny house while Hilliard continued working on the farm. Nine months later, Edith was in a difficult labor with Lorne, and Hilliard overheard the doctor tell the midwife, "Never mind the baby, save the mother." Both survived, and eight years later Edith gave birth to Millicent, named after Hilliard's mother. Lorne later told Micki that she had been planned, in part, because her parents felt that they needed a "heartbeat" once he grew old enough to leave the home.

The family had moved to a larger house before Micki was born. It had a country kitchen, where Micki's mother baked every Friday and where Micki learned from her mother the art of making perfect pie crust for freshly picked berries. There were also potatoes, peas, turnips, lettuce, carrots, and tomatoes from the family garden, and it was Micki's job to pick hornworms (caterpillars) off the tomato plants and squash the pests. Canning fruit and vegetables was an important part of eating during the long winters. She loved helping her mother with the flower garden, and gardening remained a lifelong passion. Micki's room was sparse, with a bed, a chair, and a dresser, but it had a window that looked onto a big maple tree. In the winter, she would watch at bedtime as the snow fell and collected on its branches. But she spent most of her time everywhere but her bedroom, doing chores, attending school, and running around with friends. In the forest, a muddy pond provided hours of distraction, and when the children weren't outside, they often could be found playing Crokinole, a Canadian tabletop curling game.

Her parents gave her cod liver oil every day to make up for any nutritional deficiencies during the winter. She suffered mumps, measles, and chicken pox, but it was a simultaneous whooping cough and pneumonia that caused the greatest concern. When Micki got colds, which she often did in the frigid Canadian winters, she was treated with mustard plasters (mustard seed powder paste wrapped in cloth) on her chest and back, which were hot and painful. She gained a reputation as being "delicate," a label that followed her until she went to college. Only then did she realize she was perfectly healthy. She did not feel close to her parents, who maintained a stoic relationship with her, a product of the rural environment and family heritage. Micki believed that her mother liked boys more than girls, and she saw evidence of that in the way her parents treated Lorne. But they read to her—*Black Beauty*, *Brer Rabbit*, and *The Little Red Hen*—and took the children on summer drives to Lake Simcoe for picnics. She felt a certain closeness with Lorne, but it was mitigated by his persistent teasing of her, which she felt helpless to repel.

The Sonleys were part of a large extended family, second- and third-generation descendants of English immigrants, and the Wesleyan Methodist Church was an important part of their lives. Edith taught Sunday school and was the organist at the church, and Hilliard sat on the church board and volunteered as an occasional caretaker. When Micki was older, she taught Sunday school and was the church pianist and mission band leader. Her favorite memory of church was walking home on winter evenings, under the moonlight, listening to snow crunching beneath her feet. Growing up in the village gave her a deep appreciation for nature.

Micki's childhood was littered with small, but lasting, disappointments. She remembered attending the annual village Christmas celebration in the town church and spotting a large doll on the Christmas tree. When Santa gave out the presents, he called the name of another girl and handed her the doll. Micki stood up and called out, "Oh no, Santa! That's my doll!" Her parents, thoroughly embarrassed, severely berated her, which she later said instilled in her a fear of speaking up. She remembered coveting her brother's bicycle but having little hope of one of her own. And when she wanted to learn tennis and found there were no courts in Manilla, she solicited money from people in town for a net, rackets, and balls, but she came up short and was never able to build it.

When Lorne graduated from high school, Hilliard sold the farm in order to pay his tuition to the Ontario Agricultural College (now part of the University of Guelph). The farm had never made much profit, so it wasn't considered that big a loss, and Hilliard found work transporting grain for farmers, building houses, and cutting trees for firewood. He was elected reeve of the township council and president of the local phone company, and he served on the local library board. Edith was a member of the Ladies Aid Society and the Woman's Institute (now the Federated Women's Institutes of Canada). When the couple moved to Toronto, the community expressed their appreciation: "Few localities have both husband and wife lend themselves in so [self-sacrificing] a manner for the welfare, uplift and interest in everything pertaining to Church and community."

One thing that gave Micki great joy was school, but she believed college was not possible, given her family's financial situation, and entertained studying to be a nurse. Lorne, who wrote her long letters from his various locations in America, was emphatic that she not go to nursing school. The pay was poor for nurses, he warned, and the work was hard. He insisted that she pursue a college education. In a very modern opinion, he told her in one letter, "In the long run, a girl's role in society is to become an intelligent citizen, a social thinker able to evaluate not only personal but also national and international problems and act accordingly. This means that a girl must become either a well-educated career woman or else a well-educated wife and mother or both." He offered to pay her first year's tuition and encouraged her to write to colleges. He had a good-paying fellowship at Iowa State and no marriage prospects, and it was better to see his little sister in college than sit on a pile of money. But his decision to enter the war in 1943 reduced his income considerably, and with regret he told her that he would not be able to help with tuition after all. She planned to work at a menial job while waiting to find a husband.

On the last day of her senior year at Lindsay High School in 1943, Micki's English teacher suggested that she apply for a college scholarship for needy students. Two weeks before classes were to begin at the University of Toronto, she learned that she had received a scholarship. Her teacher drove her to the university and dropped her off with good wishes. It was a quiet beginning to a monumental change. She had never been more than twenty-five miles from home, didn't know how to use a dial telephone, and had never used a flush toilet. Luckily, her dormitory was small—about twenty girls—and she had a friendly roommate from Vancouver, BC. Micki majored in

Lorne and Micki in Chicago, around 1950

economics and political science, the same fields Lorne had studied. Even on her own, she tried to do what he did without thinking about her own interests.

From his post in Long Beach, California, Lorne remained her cheerleader. She sent him her essays and exams, and he answered her questions about relationships and sex. While working in occupied Japan, he wanted to arrange a job interview for her at the Food and Agriculture Organization in Washington, DC, and persistently offered to ask others to write her with advice about careers or boys. After graduating, she found a job with the Ontario government but was soon fired for insubordination, having failed to follow instructions because she believed that she knew a better way. Her next job was in a bank library.

Lorne did his best to come home when he could afford it and could spare the time. On a visit to Toronto shortly after moving to Chicago to resume his graduate studies, he discovered that Micki was dating an

Bill, left, with Susan and Micki, around 1950

Englishman. He was not impressed with the man and wasn't confident that their parents were giving Micki good advice about her future. Micki should join him in Chicago, he said. A suggestion from Lorne was not an order but had the force of one, and so Micki moved there shortly afterward. She found a job as a statistical clerk for Standard Oil of Indiana. Lorne's future wife, Susan Blake, had followed him to Chicago from Alabama, where he'd met her while on air force duties. The couple was often looking for a plus-one for Bill when they went dancing or to the movies. With Micki in Chicago, she could join them.

Lorne would often joke that he had intended for the two of them to fall in love. Bill felt an instant attraction to Micki. "She looked beautiful," he later remembered. "It was love at first sight, and the more I got to know her, the more I liked her." And Micki took to him, seeing a man who valued her thoughts and acknowledged her individuality. They went to movies and plays in downtown Chicago and joined Lorne and Susan for dancing or outings to the country. Micki never had any reservations about dating a Japanese American and later could not remember any negative experiences they had in Chicago. But Bill's mother wanted him to marry a Japanese woman. She was willing to tolerate a Japanese American but found the idea of a white wife for her son repugnant.

But that was what Micki gave him—freedom from the triggers that Japanese culture, specifically aspects that reminded him of his mother, often caused in him. With Micki, Bill could leave behind the anxieties of his childhood, including his feelings of inadequacy, and she understood what it felt like to be the forgotten sibling. Together, they felt free to be themselves. As Bill wrote in an anniversary card more than thirty years later, "Without you, just another voice crying in the wilderness." Their happy times along the Chicago waterfront and in its Old Town would shape many of his later ideas about Portland. After a year of dating, the couple married on November 10, 1951, in the Bond Chapel at the University of Chicago. Lorne walked Micki down the aisle, Susan was her maid of honor, and Bill's younger brother Albert was his best man. Bill wore the only suit he owned and a light blue tie. Micki wore flats so she wouldn't be taller than he was, the three-inch difference between them critical in the wedding photos.

The couple was aware that Oregon's miscegenation law was still in effect and that their marriage would be illegal there (the law would be repealed at the end of the year), but they had no immediate plans to return to Bill's childhood city. He was only in the fifth month of his therapy program, and they were in love; there was no law that would legislate that. None of their parents attended the wedding. Bill didn't want his mother there, who already had voiced her disappointment that Bill had not married a Japanese woman while in occupied Japan, and Micki and Lorne had not told their parents that Bill was Japanese American and were wary of their reaction. The couple honeymooned in New York City and Washington, DC, and moved into a prefabricated house built as emergency housing for veterans and located on Midway Plaisance, opposite the university library. Bill went back to his PhD research, and Micki set about becoming a housewife. They spent their first Christmas in GI-student housing, with a small Christmas tree decorated with silver tinsel. Despite the meagre living accommodations and having little money, Bill wrote his Reed College friend Bill Clawson that "married life is truly wonderful."

Bill and Micki at their wedding reception, November 10, 1951

There were a few surprises. Shortly after moving into their new home, Bill invited a friend over for dinner. To his disbelief and irritation, Micki didn't know how to cook. Bill was a good cook, having been forced to learn by his mother, but he had not planned on having to do it once he married. But Micki learned quickly, and they came to enjoy cooking together. Micki later remembered being shocked when she heard Bill tell a friend that he planned to be a millionaire by the time he was forty, a feat seemingly impossible given their current living situation. The newlyweds spent their first anniversary with Lorne and Susan at a dance hall near the university. Micki described it as the best time of her life. When asked years later why she thought they got on so well, she replied that they were both short, liberal democrats.

A year later, Micki was pregnant with their first child, and on July 5, 1953, she gave birth to William Robert Naito, whom they called Bob. During her mandatory eight-day stay in the hospital, she shared the maternity ward with five other new mothers, including a Japanese woman who nurses kept assuming was Bob's mother. Interracial couples were still unusual, and it was only in 1953 that Japanese immi-grants like Bill's parents were allowed to become American citizens. When Micki's parents finally learned that Bill was Japanese American, they were initially upset, but in July they traveled from Ontario to meet their new grandson. As they got off the train, they came with outstretched arms toward the young family. Micki later recalled how Edith hugged and kissed Bill, and how Bill charmed "the false teeth off" of Hilliard.

Micki always underplayed the decision to marry a Japanese Ameri-can and never saw the Japanese in her children, probably in the same way she never saw the Japanese in Bill. They were the people she loved, and if they were different from her, it was because they were Ameri-cans, not Canadians. For Bill, her attitude was paramount, because he wanted his children to be as American as possible. Like many who had suffered through the forced removal of his family during the war, he didn't want the stain of it on his children, and he sought to distance them as much as possible from their Japanese ancestry. He didn't speak Japanese at home and made no attempt to teach Micki or his children the language or Japanese cultural practices. It was how he assured him-self that his family was protected from America's worst impulses.

Bill was toiling away on his PhD, and life was good. But there were issues that would pull him back home to Portland. Whatever Bill suffered as the second child in the family, Albert suffered as much or worse as the third. Hide and Sam occasionally called Bill, worried about whether Albert was mentally and emotionally capable of con-tinuing to work in the family business. But Bill refused to get involved. Then Albert experienced a brief psychological episode, and Hide and Sam telephoned daily to ask Bill to come home to manage the situa-tion, which he finally did. He arranged for Albert to get psychiatric care, which helped his emotional stability, but eventually the situation became intolerable for everyone. Albert wanted to be more active in the company, and Sam and Hide resisted. The family believed that only Bill could bring calm to the situation. So, Micki and Bill packed their belongings into their new Ford and, with their six-and-a-half-week-old son, drove from Chicago to Toronto to visit Micki's parents and then to Portland in the searing heat of late August. Bob slept in a bag on the floor of the backseat, suffering diarrhea from the heat.

Bill would never finish his PhD, even though all he had left to do was the oral defense of his dissertation. Almost thirty years later, he still struggled to put his finger on why he had never gone back. It was a genuine regret, but he reminded himself, "I'm really over that period now." He told some people that he and Micki had moved to Portland because they couldn't afford to live in Chicago anymore, but in truth he resented Albert for making him leave his contented life and his close friends.[1]

But Bill had his friendships from Reed, which he reestablished as soon as he and Micki arrived in Portland. Those men and their wives and children became as good as family for Bill and Micki. The group spent Sunday afternoons on large family picnics and spent vacations together at the beach. For Bill, it made Portland feel like home. The Reed Bridge Group, as they called themselves, played bridge at the homes of alternating couples every second Saturday of the month, a tradition that continued for decades. Bill was notorious for doubling the bid, regardless of his hand, and earned the nickname The Great Doubler for growling, "I'll double ya!" Bridge nights always went late and ended up cloudy and smoky from Bill's cigar. The group attended Reed's Christmas dinner together, a festive affair during which everyone sang the "Boar's Head Carol." They were a raucous bunch, and it was a rare holiday dinner at which Bill did not lead everyone in a Christmas carol.

When Bill and Micki had arrived in Portland in early September 1953, it was a glorious Indian summer day. When the rains came in October, Micki decided to wait until it stopped to go the store, but "every day it was raining," she later remembered. "My neighbors would garden in the rain. I thought, 'This is crazy. What I have gotten myself into?'" Despite the gray skies, she was happy. Bill was not working long hours, and they had time to spend together with Bob in Forest Park and other parts of the city.

At first, they stayed with Bill's parents, an awkward situation where language was a barrier. Fukiye never got over having a white

---

1 Lorne and Susan would move to Virginia, where Lorne eventually took a position with the World Bank as an agricultural economist. Despite the distance, Micki and Susan remained close friends, and Bill and Lorne maintained their strong friendship.

Naito family portrait in 1953. Back row from left to right: Bill, Albert, Amy, Sam, and Mary. Front row from left to right: Micki, Bob, Fukiye, Hide, Larry, and Ron

person in the family, and she didn't approve of Micki's independent thinking. After three months, Bill and Micki rented an apartment in northeast Portland, but not without difficulty. The city's realtors had an institutionalized housing policy to keep minorities from certain areas, and some people refused to rent to a "Jap." Their apartment was next door to Virginia Sprague, a young widow whose six-year-old son threw water on Bill because the Japanese had killed his father in the war.

Micki's relationship with Fukiye would never be particularly good. Fukiye would come to their home and meticulously point out the dust, eager to find reasons to criticize her daughter-in-law. Fukiye was, by nature, a nit-picking person, and Micki's race heightened her behavior. In the end, the language barrier served as an unintentional obstacle to further conflict, and they managed to be civil. The reality was that their husbands worked together, and they had to make their relationship work as well as they could. The family did whatever was best for the business.

Sometime after Bill's return, Albert bought an expensive conveyor without discussing the expense with anyone, and Sam and
Hide decided to buy his share of the business rather than continue
to force the situation. Albert briefly went into a competing business
with a friend and then moved his family to California, where he
would become a successful computer engineer. He visited Portland
occasionally to see Sam's family and his parents, but his relationship
with Bill never healed, perhaps because Bill resented his brother for
forcing him back into the business or perhaps something personal
happened between the two brothers. Whatever the reason, Bill's life
going forward had one brother, Sam. In his family, Albert was simply
not spoken about.

CHAPTER 7

By the time Bill returned to Portland in 1953, Hide and Sam had revived the family business. Going back to Portland after the war might not have been a foregone conclusion. For many victims of Executive Order 9066, returning to home was not an option, and many of those who had been held in the camps went to Chicago, New York, Denver, Philadelphia, or another city far from the memory of imprisonment and without its vestiges of shame. Almost 75 percent of the Japanese Americans had lost all of their property, and African American workers who had been brought into port cities to feed the war machine had rented their former homes. Aside from the logistical realities, there was also a psychological aspect to the decision to relocate. So much change had been forced on them; perhaps they needed change on their own terms to feel a sense of control.

For Hide, it was never a question of whether to move back to Portland, but when. Portland was his home, where he had made a successful business and a good life for his family. When he and Fukiye returned from Utah to their house on Fifty-Eighth and Burnside around 1946 or 1947, their tenants had kept it in good condition, and there was no opposition from their white neighbors. Still, the neighbors were apprehensive, worried that someone from outside the neighborhood would set fire to or bomb the Naitos' home, creating damage to their own property. Their fears weren't baseless. Anti-Japanese sentiment remained strong in Oregon. The legislature, with the full support of Governor Earl Snell, had passed a second alien land law in 1945, denying Issei from working or living on farmland.[1]

---

1 The 1945 alien land law was declared unconstitutional in 1949 by the Oregon Supreme Court in *Kenji Namba v. McCourt*.

Sam and Hide, early 1950s

In Hood River, sixty miles east of Portland, Kent Shoemaker, who had been a commander of the American Legion chapter there, ran full-page ads in the local papers. Japanese Americans, the ads warned, "are not wanted. . . . If you come back, we will make life miserable for you." The local Legion had already removed the names of sixteen Nisei soldiers from the public honor roll of those who had died in service during the war. Hood River residents greeted those returning from the camps with anti-Japanese placards, and a full-page ad in *Hood River News* suggested that returning internees were fifth columnists (people who secretly work to undermine their country in favor of an outside enemy): "A recent critic said some of the Japs were willing to risk their lives to return. Any good soldier will risk his life to establish a beach head and the Japs had surely established a beach head in Hood River County prior to Pearl Harbor."

The *Democratic-Herald* in Albany, in the mid-Willamette Valley, and the *East Oregonian* in Pendleton fostered fear by claiming that Japanese Americans would "out-breed" white Oregonians. Oregon Anti-Japanese Inc., later known as the Japanese Exclusion League, formed in 1944 to prevent the return of Japanese Americans from the camps. The group advocated for placing them on an occupied Pacific Island or dispersing them evenly throughout the country, and it sought a permanent ban on first-generation Japanese Americans and their descendants receiving United States citizenship.

Prominent Oregonians came to the defense of returning Japanese Americans in response to a series of well-attended meetings organized by Oregon Anti-Japanese in February and March 1945. E. B. MacNaughton had been president of First National Bank during EO 9066 and had hired Nisei students to staff a booth in the bank's lobby to assist Issei customers. He also protected Japanese American assets until their owners returned from the American concentration camps. He and former Governor Charles Sprague arranged a meeting in Gresham on March 16, attended by more than a thousand people. In "probably the greatest speech of his life," an associate at the meeting observed, MacNaughton asked Oregonians to trust in Japanese Americans as they trusted in the Constitution. Governor Sprague, once a fierce and vocal advocate for imprisonment, had come to deeply regret his actions and became an equally fierce advocate for Japanese Americans and their civil rights.

Their efforts were aided by those of the West Coast War Relocation Administration, which worked on behalf of returning prisoners to ease their transition back into mainstream American life. The agency's efforts were largely successful, in time changing the venomous tone of public opinion against Japanese Americans. By 1956, George Azumano of Portland's JACL believed that "on the whole there is very little existing against us, except maybe in the housing field. This situation is much, much better than it was in the years right after the war." Another Portlander, Yosha Inahara, put it differently: "There is some solace that this 'extra hurdle' is not quite as high as it used to be." Despite the positive changes, Hide could not have rebuilt his business successfully without Sam, his oldest son, who was motivated to build on the practical skills he had learned from his father and the business skills learned in college.

While Bill was in the army, Sam had completed his studies at the University of Utah, where he met Mary Shizuko Kawanami. When President Roosevelt signed Executive Order 9066, she was in her second year at the University of California, Berkeley, and she and her family were sent to the concentration camp in Poston, Arizona, on the Colorado River Indian Reservation. Mary was the eldest of eight children, fourteen years older than her youngest sibling. At Poston, the ten members of the Kawanami family lived in one room, which was inundated each day with sand from the constant wind and dust. She was given permission to leave the camp to attend college at the University of Utah, where she met Sam.[2] They married in August 1946, after Sam received his master's degree in business administration and economics at Columbia University.

Sam completed his military service between 1945 and 1947, which had been deferred because of his poor eyesight, by vetting soldiers destined for occupied Japan. When he and Mary moved back to Portland, they initially lived with Hide and Fukiye. When they moved into a house near Franklin High School in southeast Portland, they received calls demanding that they leave the neighborhood. One neighbor threatened a lawsuit, and an anonymous caller threatened to burn their house down. When Sam called the police, they refused to intervene.

In 1949, with Sam's help, Hide reopened his wholesale business under the white-sounding name Thomas J. Jenkins, at 612 Northwest Davis in Old Town. The gift shop remained at 904 Southwest Morrison. Through their connections at church, they hired Mrs. Clark, a white woman who weathered the strangers who came into the store only to say nasty things about the Japanese. Despite the hostility, Sam and Hide were undeterred in their work. The wholesale business benefited from not being a face-to-face operation, with goods sold through white salesmen, and did well in the atmosphere after the war. The trade embargo with Japan in 1947 and 1948 meant the Naitos could not import their usual goods, so they relied on pottery from California and English bone china. Occasionally, Sam traveled to the East Coast for trade shows, where Chinese immigrants were far more common than Japanese. Sam was often mistaken as Chinese

---

2 To qualify for this program, known as the National Japanese American Student Relocation Program, students had to be accepted by the college, welcomed by the community there, and able to afford a year of school and living expenses; the college had to be approved by the War Department and the navy; and students had to supply an autobiography and complete the loyalty questionnaire.

Hide standing outside Northwest Trading Co. building in Old Town, early 1950s

American, a mistake that he rarely corrected to avoid anti-Japanese bias. Expediency in business trumped pride in identity.

White salesmen sold the Naitos' products using non-Japanese company names, like Modern Age Gift Centers and Northwest Trading Company. After moving to the Fleischner-Mayer building on 115 Northwest First Avenue in 1956, the Naitos settled on the name Norcrest China Company. The change reflected the company's policy of emphasizing its successful and exclusive Norcrest line. It would also continue to expand its lines of English bone china, which would become one of Norcrest's best sellers and result in imports from ten factories in the United Kingdom.

When Japanese imports were finally allowed in the United States, the devastation of Japan and most of the businesses that Norcrest had worked with was revealed. Hide was fortunate to discover that Saji Company and Aichi Ken in Nagoya had survived unscathed, and he began importing porcelain and other products from them. All of the products had to be stamped "Made in U.S. Occupied Japan." At the time, Japanese products had a reputation as being cheap and tawdry, and Hide and Sam worked with manufacturers to improve the quality and style of their pottery and woodworking to meet the demands of the postwar American market. They traveled to Japan in 1954 to encourage more contemporary designs, Sam's first visit and Hide's first return since he had left for America. Eventually, twenty factories in Japan produced goods for Norcrest China. Several factories were in Nagoya, a large city in central Japan, but most were in large, barn-like structures in the hills to the north of the city, where dozens of workers made molds for and painted pottery. Hide's work to revive manufacturing in the area proved critical to the area's recovery, and Emperor Hirohito honored him in 1977 with the Order of the Sacred Treasure, Sixth Class, for fostering better business relationships between Japan and the United States.

Both the wholesale and retail businesses required travel and a strong network of salesmen. Only Hide and Sam traveled overseas for several years after Bill came back to Portland. By then, Norcrest was importing from India, an important source of brass goods and incense, and England, the source of its bone china. Over the years, Hide, Sam, and Bill would visit Thailand, India, Greece, Iran, Iraq, Egypt, China, and England in search of products and to meet with sales agents. After 1954, one of them visited Japan every year. Years later, in 1979, Governor Vic Atiyeh appointed Sam to Oregon's Business Development Mission to the People's Republic of China, whose goal was to foster business and trade relations. In 1987, Sam received his own Order of the Sacred Treasure.

At its peak in the late 1960s and 1970s, the Norcrest China Company published seasonal catalogs that featured some three thousand items. Bill secured a lucrative contract in 1958 to make licensed Smokey the Bear products, including salt and pepper shakers, figurines, and, somewhat ironically, ashtrays. Sam took the photographs and designed the catalogs until the mid-1960s, when the responsibility was passed to Dick Lenhart. A longtime employee, Dick had been in charge of the company's IBM computer, a technological advancement that allowed him to process orders quickly and accurately and separated Norcrest from most other giftware companies.

Norcrest and Pacific Orient, a separate wholesale division, also sold coffee mugs and ashtrays with declarations such as "World's Best Boss" or a finger pointing at "#1 B.S.er." There was Blue

Willow china, with a scene in royal blue of a pagoda with birds and trees, along with fans with intricate flower patterns, keepsake boxes adorned with enamel butterflies, and vases painted with herons. Naito's Fortune Candy, a chewy rice-based confection, was packaged with a free toy and a fortune that Bill wrote. There were ceramic incense burners and animals that ranged from chickens and tabby cats to hippos and tigers. Breakage in shipping was inevitable, and Bill responded to wholesale customers with a letter praising the products and a tube of Super Glue.

But Norcrest's biggest seller was the BK102 fuzzy bunny, which was about the size of a baked potato and covered in a thick flocked velveteen. Lenhart suggested making it into a coin bank, and within three years the company had sold more than a million of them. Once, by mistake, Hollinger's Farm Market in Ephrata, Pennsylvania, received thirty-six dozen of the fuzzy bunny banks, many more than it had meant to order. The store manager thought about returning the excess but then decided to try to sell all of them. Within three weeks, the store had sold fifty-seven dozen. If the bunnies arrived at a retailer not fully flocked, the Super Glue from Norcrest came with a patch of velveteen.

A critical part of the Norcrest business was its network of salespeople, both in Japan and in America. Lenhart often made trips to Japan to meet with Norcrest's salesmen there, being presented with potential products and selecting samples to take back to Bill and Sam. Sometimes, he had to take a pass on great products because he knew that neither of them would pay a price so high, no matter how spectacular a product was. The goal of sales trips was to find products that would move quickly but didn't cost that much in case they didn't. Profit margin was a driving force, but the Naitos never spent unnecessarily to achieve it. Penny-pinching was the name of the game. The catalogs were printed in Japan, which saved two to three thousand dollars but required them to weigh no more than sixteen ounces to keep shipping costs low. Every employee and salesperson knew that product orders and expense accounts would be gone over with a fine-tooth comb.

If there was a way to avoid using money, the Naitos would find it. Achieving financial success drove Bill in the way that economist

Joseph Schumpeter's described what motivates entrepreneurs: "There is the will to conquer: the impulse to fight, to prove oneself superior to others, to succeed for the sake, not the fruits of success, but of success itself." It was Bill's proof. "If you are thrown out of a city and you . . . come back," Bill said, "I feel it shows those who threw us out that the Naitos, the Japanese in the community, aren't a bunch of softies and that we are loyal to the community." Few who dealt with Norcrest in money matters would consider them soft, as no one drove a harder bargain, whether it was wages or purchase orders. There was no need for an in-house accountant to tell them where the accounts stood; Bill and Sam knew every detail of the business like the backs of their hands.

The brothers shared a ravenous frugality but were otherwise quite different from each other. Association for Portland Progress executive director Bill Wyatt described them as coming from "different universes." Sam wore expensive suits and maintained the air of an executive, while Bill wore mismatched jackets and pants with a casual bearing. Sam was attentive to his health, carefully choosing what to eat and drink, while Bill could often be found having a nip of alcohol at his desk throughout the day. Consultant Karen Whitman's experience illustrates the differences: after arriving at Norcrest's offices, she asked someone to direct her toward "Mr. Naito's desk." She arrived at a well-organized desk with a beautiful lamp, pen set, and orderly in and out boxes. Then she turned and, on the other side, saw a puff of cigar smoke, a cluttered desk, and a man ordering people left and right.

But the differences also went much deeper. Sam was risk averse, often focused on the negative aspects of a potential deal, and he used detailed analyses to guide his decisions. Bill said that he relied on gut feelings and an optimistic outlook to make choices. Each was a product of his childhood. Sam was raised to lead the business and had grown up a confident, affable, natural leader. He felt and expected to be superior to Bill. Sam had been the apple of his mother's eye and had adopted her attention to formality and manners. If Sam needed to contact someone, he sent a message to be called; Bill called people directly. Bill's confidence and leadership had come after therapy that dealt with his feelings of being belittled and ignored by his parents. There was an air of defiance in how Bill lived, and it was manifested in his being the opposite of his mother.

From left to right: grandchildren Ron, Bob, Verne, Larry, and Steve with Fukiye, mid-1950s

The brothers' different personalities led to arguments over business decisions, which they initially conducted in Japanese, believing that none of the Norcrest employees could understand them. When they found out that a clerk did understand what they were saying, they were embarrassed that someone had been privy to their conversations. Over time, they stopped arguing publicly and most often communicated through written notes. When the company moved to the White Stag building in the early 1970s, it was understood that Sam could hear the conversations taking place at Bill's desk ten feet away. Broker Donn Sullivan later remembered talking to Bill about a potential tenant and feeling that he could tell that it was always on Bill's mind that he was the younger brother and Sam was listening. Another broker, Paul Breuer, assumed that he was making a dual presentation whenever he met with Bill. The one-on-one with him was conceptual, directed toward his creative thinking. Then Bill would direct Breuer to Sam, and they would analyze the deal in an entirely different way.

When Bill first returned to Portland and the family business, he had been apprehensive about reactions to his skin color and had sent

Norcrest's white salesmen to meet with buyers. He held himself back. But his ego eventually superseded his fears, and he became jealous of the salesmen, who were becoming the face of his hard work. A memory from his childhood helped. His father's shop had received deliveries from an Issei man, who picked up cargo at the pier and delivered it to shops in town, including Naito Gifts. As a one-man operation, the man sometimes needed help, and he asked white passersby to give him a hand. He told young Bill, "Never be afraid of anything."

When Bill didn't encounter the public rejection he feared, he threw himself into the work. He was in the office ten to twelve hours a day, six days a week, and his confidence in managing the business grew. His hunger to achieve greater success increased as well. Once that happened, the brothers had to figure out how to balance each other's personalities with the best interests of the business. Financial gain trumped personal animosity, and both brothers knew how damaging discord could be. Ultimately, they reached a détente, in which they suppressed the urge to act on their resentments and frustrations. As much as they had personal issues with each other, they knew that each had business acumen that would lead to success. They could work together as long as they kept things as businesslike as possible.

Part of the arrangement was that the brothers never made business decisions without agreement from each other. That didn't mean they didn't argue to get there. It was well-known among Norcrest employees that the aisle between their desks was a perilous place to be if the brothers were having a pointed discussion. Some called it the Bermuda Triangle, since each would attempt to get support for his position from a passerby, a no-win situation for the employee. The détente resulted in an indirect form of feuding, in which employees were left with Hobson's choices. Once Keane Satchwell, who was in charge of towing for Norcrest's Old Town parking lots, had a Toyota Corolla towed after it had accumulated three months of notices. Much to Satchwell's surprise, Sam got upset. The Corolla was his son Larry's car, and Sam ordered Satchwell to have it brought back from the tow yard immediately. Eavesdropping on the conversation from a couple of desks away, Bill yelled, "Don't do it, Keane!" It would cost $250 to bring it back, an unacceptably high cost for Larry's negligence. But

Bill with Steve (left) and Bob
(right)

Bill was also engaged in a form of teasing, a way to exercise some of
the sibling rivalry in a quieter, less destructive way than an outright
argument. For two weeks, Satchwell was torn between the brothers'
demands. Finally, he cannily found a solution: having five other cars
towed in exchange for the free return of the Corolla. But finding ways
to please them both sometimes proved elusive.

The manifestations of the brothers' sibling rivalry were managed
through a carefully crafted business deal, but their personal relationship was a different matter. Away from Norcrest, the brothers and
their families had little to no contact. That may be how they kept
their business relationship functional, but it had not been the original
plan. When Bill and Micki moved to Portland, there was a recognized
hierarchy in the family: Hide and Fukiye, Sam and Mary, then Bill
and Micki. This structure of deference and obedience was completely
foreign to Micki and grated on her independence and pride. Fukiye
always hosted *o-shogatsu*, Japanese New Year, and Micki and Mary
rotated the hosting and cooking duties for Thanksgiving and Christmas. One Thanksgiving, Mary decided she didn't want to host and
that Micki ought to. Micki bristled at what she considered an order
and refused. After that, the families stopped spending Thanksgiving
together and, over time, drifted apart.

Bill with Anne (left), Bob (middle), and Ken (right)

Bill and Micki were busy with their own family. By the time Bill took his first buying trip to Japan in 1960, they were raising four children: Bob; Steven Lorne, born in 1955; Anne Susan, born in 1957; and Kenneth Christopher, born in 1960. They were more than a handful. Bill explained years later that it was important to him to be a good husband and a loving father—"really a family man," he said. They moved to a house in village-like Hillsdale on the west side of Portland, where Micki eventually met Ruby Shigley, a neighbor who agreed to take care of the children once a week. On those child-free days, Micki went downtown to go shopping at Olds & King, Meier & Frank, and Lipman, Wolfe & Co. She cherished those days of freedom. She had been told by her brother Lorne since she was a teenager that the best wives were the ones that had their own minds, and she was an independent woman at heart. She became a United States citizen in 1962 in order to vote in US elections and volunteered for Eugene McCarthy's presidential campaign because of his opposition to the Vietnam War.

With four children, Bill and Micki needed more space, and in 1961 Bill bought two large plots in Portland's Dunthorpe neighborhood, about fifteen minutes from downtown. The property abutted a large woodland area that would become Tryon Creek State Park in 1970. Bill was able to buy property in the coveted neighborhood because restrictive covenants had been removed from practice in 1960. (They had been declared unconstitutional by the US Supreme Court in 1948, but many realtors and homeowners continued to use and rely on them.) Before that, Dunthorpe and many other areas in Portland were intentionally white neighborhoods where Japanese Americans—or any person of color, for that matter—could not live. Describing the housing market at the time, Bill said, "You could not be a yellow man and live on Vista," a street in a wealthy West Hills neighborhood. But he wanted the success and acceptance that such a neighborhood signified.

Micki wasn't completely comfortable living in the affluent area, but they needed a big house, and the one in Dunthorpe was more than she could have ever imagined. The house was designed by Van Evera Bailey in the Northwest Regional style, an architectural style that he had pioneered with Pietro Belluschi and John Yeon in the 1930s. Bailey had built his own home in Dunthorpe in 1959, and the area was an ideal location for his talents, with large plots of undeveloped land in forested areas. The house blended into its surroundings—on a sloping hill and ravine that ended in the Willamette River a mile away. Bailey set the bottom floor partially into the hill, with large windows facing the woods. The top floor had a deck along the entire north side of the house, where the family could eat summer dinners. Bill loved to barbeque, and he and Micki often sat outside with one of their German shepherds and read. Inside, a floor-to-ceiling curved stone fireplace made of Mount Adams stone defined the living room in dramatic form.

The house in Dunthorpe met Bill and Micki's need to have a forest around them and a garden with blueberries and huckleberries, rhododendrons, maple trees and fir trees, and flowers. Enjoying their garden was a part of their relationship. In time, they bought two adjacent plots, including one above the house with a large field with apple, pear, and walnut trees. The field was on a slope and covered with grass, and Bill bought geese to mow the lawn naturally. Instead, they meandered into the road, scaring unexpected drivers, and were ultimately killed by their second German shepherd, Caesar. Eventually, Bill purchased a large red Gravely seated lawn mower that he used to trim the grass on the uneven field. In that way, he was a novelty in the neighborhood—a millionaire who mowed his own grass.

Moving into Dunthorpe followed Hide's example of choosing a white neighborhood over a Japanese American enclave. Bill made somewhat the same decision when he changed the pronunciation of his name from nye-toe to nay-toe in the 1950s to accommodate American pronunciation. Expediency and pragmatism were guiding principles for Hide and his sons, even if heritage had to take a backseat. At the same time, Bill was proud of his Japanese ancestry. For many, the idea that a person can be both a US patriot and also extremely proud of his or her ancestral heritage can sound illogical—there is often a push to pick one or the other. For second-generation immigrants, that push often came from family and community. Mary Naito, Sam's wife, explained it this way in 1983: "My life is a conflict between our Western culture and Japanese tradition. Having been brought up as a Japanese, I know I should be this way, and yet that's not the way I want to be, so there's a constant problem." Bill eschewed the rigid traditions of Japanese culture, but it didn't stop him from seeing where there was value and strength in the family's country of origin. In a way, being Japanese American meant being able to take the best parts of both worlds. Emphasizing US culture and identity for his children was a way to protect them from the discrimination and pain Bill had endured, and so he picked a white neighborhood, a Western pronunciation of his name, and did not teach them Japanese.

Bill, a true believer in Milton Friedman's free-market philosophy, applied that thinking to his parenting. He let his children navigate whatever harsh roads they were on largely on their own. "Let 'em swim or sink," he said. "If they didn't finish their homework, it was their tough luck." That laissez-faire style, paired with his arduous work schedule, meant that he was rarely at home. As his children grew, they watched as Bill "used to go to the garden at 6, be with us about ten minutes at breakfast, come home late, work six and a half days a week," son Bob recalled years later. It was Micki who drove them to their soccer games and hockey practices. It also meant they received no heavy-handed interventions from their father. When Bob was in a car accident, he was not met with anger or criticism; when Ken grew marijuana in the field above the house, he received intentional ignorance, not preachy condemnation. But Bill's application of economic theory to an extended act of altruism failed to give his children what he thought it did, and they all quickly learned that to have any real relationship with him meant being in the family business.

CHAPTER 8

Downtown Portland struggled during the 1950s and 1960s. The city "has the most beautiful setting of any city in the world," architect Lewis Crutcher told the *Oregonian* in 1959, but it was also "the ugliest city in the world." Retail sales had declined between 1946 and 1960, and a flight to the suburbs had left the city largely vacant after office hours. Automobiles had long been a significant part of city planning, including where parks were located and which buildings were razed to make way for parking lots. Voters repeatedly rejected improvement levies for parks, sewers, and public transit, and workers earned their money to spend it elsewhere. A good deal of property downtown was owned by absentee landlords.

Financial instability prevented long-term planning and killed redevelopment opportunities. When Julius Zell of Zell Brothers jewelry store asked building owners on Morrison Street to steam-clean their building exteriors and upgrade their merchandise, they laughed at him. When he paid for a steam truck to clean a spot on each building to make his point, they threatened him with lawsuits. The Old Town area was in even worse condition. Known as Skid Road,[1] a name derived from roads used to skid logs from the forest to the river, it was an overlooked part of the city, a home to cheap housing for day laborers and jobless bachelors. In 1867, the federal government had located the Pioneer Post Office and the Multnomah County Courthouse nearer the river on Fourth Avenue and Main Street, and since then people and businesses had moved uptown, leaving behind warehouses, cheap hotels, and bars. Old Town had been populated by waves of immigrant groups for decades, relying on the neighborhood's low rents and cheap goods to help them transition

---

1 It was also referred to as Skid Row.

Shoreline Block on the corner of Burnside and Second Avenue in the early 1960s

into American life. By 1974, Skid Road's two thousand residents were 95 percent men, 85 percent white, and 56 percent were older than fifty-five. They were eleven times more likely to suffer alcoholism than other Multnomah County residents. "The basic issue here," urban studies Professor Nohad Toulan concluded, "is that we face a community in which human suffering, social and economic deficiencies, and physical and environmental deterioration are only elements of one problem that only could be solved if addressed in its entirety."

The Shoreline Block on the corner of Burnside and Northwest Second Avenue exemplified the decline. Originally known as the S. P. Hotel, it had been built in 1926 and was one of the youngest buildings the Naitos eventually purchased. The design was in Twentieth-Century Classical Revival style with Italianate features, including bracketed cornices, ornate brick detailing, and arched windows. By the 1960s, it housed a rundown hotel—"A Home You Will Remember," as declared on the sign on the side of the building—and offices of the Department of Employment Casual and Farm Labor. Day laborers and unemployed men milled around the entrance, hoping for work that rarely arrived.

When Hide and Sam moved back to Portland, they reopened the wholesale division of the business in Skid Road at 612 Northwest Davis. In 1956, they moved their warehouse and main offices to the Fleischner-Mayer building on Couch and First Avenue, a block from the Shoreline building, and rented the building for ten years for their Northwest Trading Company before buying it in 1960. The brick Fleischner-Mayer had been designed by Portland architect Edgar Lazarus, who also designed Vista House in the Columbia Gorge and the main building for the 1905 Lewis & Clark Exposition. The five-story Fleischner-Mayer was an example of early Twentieth-Century Commercial style, which emphasized function; it had five floors and little ornamentation. The building, named after a dry goods tenant in the 1920s, became known as the Norcrest China Building. Given the circumstances—having to rebuild the wholesale business almost from scratch—the Naitos thought a building like the Fleischner and a neighborhood like Skid Road were financially ideal.

In 1962, Bill and Sam heard that Cost Plus, a retail import store in San Francisco, wanted to open a store in Portland. Cost Plus advertised that it sold goods at wholesale prices plus a 10 percent markup, but Bill and Sam thought the actual markup was closer to 300 percent. Sam did some investigating and concluded that the Cost Plus model was viable for Norcrest. He was confident that their company could capture and maintain the bulk of the market by opening a store before the competition did, and he suggested the Globe Hotel, across the street from their offices. Even by Skid Road standards, the Globe was cheap, charging fifty cents a night for an open-air cot in a room where the walls did not reach the ceiling. Each of the five hundred cots that were crowded into the hotel was covered with an arch of chicken wire to prevent patrons from throwing empty liquor bottles onto unsuspecting neighbors. It was a "fleabag," Sam said, with a "horrendous smell."

Built at the turn of the nineteenth century, the Globe had been designed by E. B. MacNaughton, who worked as an architect in Portland before entering the banking business in the 1920s. Bill had a personal reason for buying a building designed by MacNaughton, who had been president of First National Bank in the early 1930s. During World War II, he had helped Japanese Americans protect their financial assets in the bank, and when they returned from American concentration camps, he publicly defended them as Americans worthy of respect. MacNaughton was the first president of the Nippon Society of Oregon (now the Japan-America Society of Oregon) and spent his life in defense of civil rights. Because of his support of Japanese Americans, Norcrest did all of its banking with First National (now Wells Fargo).

But for all of McNaughton's successes and significance, he was an average architect. The Globe was historically relevant but not architecturally important. When it was built in 1911, it had 420 rooms and only one bathroom for the entire hotel (a bathroom was eventually added to each floor). Its upper floors were "musty with the smell of too many men and too little plumbing," the *Oregonian* reported in 1963. By the time Norcrest bought the building in the early 1960s, it was still a functioning hotel but only half full. John Haviland, owner of the classy Heathman Hotel downtown, would suggest the Globe as an inside joke if out-of-town friends asked about hotels other than his.

The realtor who arranged the sale—$52,000 for the hotel and $177,500 for the adjacent property—thought the Naitos were fools to open a retail store north of Burnside. "Upper class women would never cross Burnside to shop," Bill was told. They were crossing the river to shop in malls on the east side, such as Lloyd Center, where Naito Gifts had opened a second location. But the Naito brothers had faith in Old Town and looked past the ghosts that made Skid Road undesirable.

Import Plaza, Norcrest's new retail store, was an instant success when it opened on July 23, 1963, attracting customers with its inexpensive prices and unusual products from around the world. "A decaying fleabag," the *Oregon Journal* reported, "has, almost by magic, become one of the city's most colorful stores." Its target audience—women twenty to fifty-five years old   could find housewares for themselves and gifts for others, ranging from hookahs and buddhas from India to toys from Asia to wicker furniture. Dick Lenhart, Norcrest's manager and often the voice of Import Plaza, explained that the layout of island tables and intertwined aisles was meant to create a "festive atmosphere befitting a foreign bazaar." A large blackboard faced the parking lot with the arrival dates of ships and cargo, and Sam's son

Bill outside Import Plaza June 29, 1975; copyright the *Oregonian*

Larry remembered when the Portland Fire Department threatened to close the store for violating the fire code because of overcrowding. Lenhart believed that many products that may not have done well in department stores succeeded at Import Plaza because of its international atmosphere. Dutch wooden shoes, for example, were wildly popular, despite a general agreement among merchants that they would never sell in America. Customers were encouraged to voice their opinions in a suggestion box, which resulted in imported food products like Swedish lingonberries. At its peak in the early 1980s, Import Plaza would have nine locations in Oregon.

Advertising was a key part of the Plaza's success. Norcrest ran two full-page ads in every edition of the *Oregonian* from the early 1960s to the 1980s. Atop the Globe building, a large neon sign with the store's name spun slowly to draw attention from people on nearby Harbor Drive. The year after the store opened, Norcrest chartered a bus during the holidays to ferry customers from downtown to Import Plaza, driving through the streets between one and four in the afternoon with a large banner on its side announcing its destination. The bus was free to customers, who received a free trinket, and Plaza employees often greeted them dressed up as different nationalities to drum up excitement.

The Naitos used the back of the Fleischner-Mayer building to advertise the store with a large arrow pointing to the Globe Hotel and letters spelling out "Import Plaza." The sign was more than twenty-five times the square footage the city allowed, and compliance with code required that it read "Norcrest China Company."[2] In 1964, Portland City Council contemplated enacting S zones, in which stricter rules for businesses would apply to specific areas on the riverfront. The focus was on areas near the eastside Clay Street ramp and the westside ramps from the Steel, Burnside, Morrison, Hawthorne, and Ross Island bridges, with the goal of eliminating hazardous driving distractions and preserving scenic views. The attorney for Import Plaza argued against the new zone, but city council passed the new restrictions. As a result, seven wall signs and seventy-two outdoor signs were identified as nonconforming, including the sign for Import Plaza. Owners had ten years to remove the offending signs, but Norcrest was in no hurry and wasn't too concerned about running afoul

2 Since its inception in 1942, Portland's sign code was a constant pain in the city council's side. The goal was to limit the visual noise of business signs, which usually meant business complaints about their inadequate ability to advertise themselves on their own property. The code was bulky, weighed down by excessive details, and businesses were constantly trying to get around it.

of the city. Old Town was on its way to becoming a series of parking lots and was generally left alone. Bill would not have attempted such a brazen violation in downtown Portland, and it was an example of the benefits the company enjoyed in Old Town.

In the early 1970s, Portland had turned its attention to reviving downtown, focused on the core area south of Burnside. Through their new real estate company, Skidmore Development Company, Bill and Sam had already begun their own "private urban renewal project" in Old Town, journalist Ken Bradley wrote. "Burnside and Skid Row," Bill once said, "have always been an iron wall, dividing the heart of the city." And when the Oregon legislature started to address historic preservation in the 1970s, Skidmore Development had already acquired a number of buildings and surface parking lots in Old Town. In the process, the brothers had become experts on the city. "There's nothing that goes on downtown that they don't know about," John Guernsey wrote in *Historic Preservation Magazine* in 1981, "including how many people use which sidewalks on which days. They study the details of life downtown with the intensity of urban planners."

The Naitos had joined a movement started by others. In 1963, architect Lewis Crutcher and other preservationists had successfully convinced the city to designate the area around Skidmore Fountain as a D zone to protect historic buildings from destruction. The fountain, a block south of the Burnside Bridge and next to the historic New Market building on Ankeny and First Street, had been installed because of Stephen Skidmore, a city council member in the 1870s who had left $5,000 in his will to create a fountain for humans, horses, and dogs. With an additional $18,000 from others, sculptor Olin Warner was commissioned by influential Portlander C. E. S. Wood to honor Skidmore's wishes. The result was a fountain with a large low pool for horses and four smaller pools for dogs. Two women in Roman robes held up a bowl with a fountain spring in the center. Along the base were inscribed Wood's words that would come to symbolize Portland's guiding ethos, "Good citizens are the riches of a city."

Crutcher and others hoped the area, with the D-zone designation, would be transformed into a vibrant retail district like Jackson Square in San Francisco. But while the fountain had been restored, growth remained stagnant, and by 1968 there was concern that buildings would be torn down despite zoning restrictions. In fact, the pace of demolition in the downtown area between 1963 and 1968 equaled the rate of demolitions in the 1930s when the State Highway Commission cleared the waterfront for Harbor Drive. Some attributed the area's struggle to the proximity of Skid Road to the north, suggesting that some shoppers were uncomfortable being close to homeless people. Another issue was parking. While Old Town had numerous surface lots, the blocks around Skidmore Fountain had only street parking. Protecting the neighborhood against demolition hadn't been enough.

In 1972, the Naito brothers organized the Skidmore Fountain Village Association for the Beautification of the Skidmore Area (later renamed Skidmore/Old Town Association), a mouthful of a title but an important factor in securing the historic district designation by city council four years later. The fountain became a symbol of Old Town, a beautiful representation of Portland's past and a reason to protect it for the future. Few who saw the Skidmore Fountain were willing to see it razed, and linking Old Town and Skidmore widened the group of interested property owners.

In 1975, the Skidmore/Old Town Historic District—seventeen complete city blocks and seven partial blocks, approximately forty acres—was placed on the National Register of Historic Places. The same year, the legislature passed a fifteen-year tax abatement for historic property renovation. At the time, the cost of renovation was one-third to one-half the cost of new construction, and tax incentives made real estate in the district an attractive investment. New money and new life began to flow into Old Town.

That experience led Bill to believe in the power of historic designations. At about the same time, he started working with the Simon Benson Foundation Trust Fund to add another historic touch to the neighborhood. Benson Bubblers, originally a gift to the city from timber baron Simon Benson in 1912, had four spigots that bubbled water for thirsty pedestrians and were concentrated in downtown. Bill began working with the city and the trust in 1971 to bring the fountains to Old Town. It took ten years before Benson High School students built the new bubblers, using the school's foundry and original molds from the Bureau of Water Works. Property owners paid for the materials. The bubblers were installed in the historic district, and students gained academic credit, experience, and, as Bill remembered, "pride in their beautiful city." Years later, in 1989, Bill was the lone member of the State Advisory Committee on Historic Preservation to vote in favor of a Central Eastside Historic District, part of the original East Portland townsite. Committee members opposed the designation because of its size and argued over which buildings should be included. Haggling over the details, Bill said, served only to delay getting attention and funds to the area, which was what being a historic district would mean.[3]

A year after securing historic designation for Old Town, Bill had his first project with architect Bing Sheldon, whose firm would handle Norcrest's first full-scale building renovation, of the Merchant Hotel. Sheldon was on the Portland Planning Commission and a driving force in the 1972 Downtown Plan. He was also a founding board member of Central City Concern, which provided social services to homeless and other people who needed help. Sheldon loved Old Town, which he considered the most urban and authentic part of Portland. When he moved to Portland, he had set his sights on a space in the Merchant Hotel for his architectural firm, Design Collective. Norcrest wasn't interested in leasing the undeveloped upper floors of the building because it was having trouble renting the ground floor, but Sheldon made a pitch right up Bill's alley: in exchange for Norcrest paying the tenant improvement costs, Sheldon's firm would let them show the space to prospective tenants. Thus began a long-standing and powerful relationship between two of Portland's most important preservationists.

Their first project was the Simon façade. The Romanesque-style D. Simon building on Third Avenue had been constructed of rough sandstone in 1892. It was operating as the Alco Hotel in 1973 when an arsonist destroyed most of the structure, leaving only the front façade intact. The Naitos bought the damaged building for $20,000, intending to tear it down to make a parking lot for the Sinnott building next door, on the corner of Third Avenue and Couch Street. The Sinnott

<hr>

3 The East Portland Historic District was eventually created in 1991 at a smaller size than the original proposal.

Sinnott building, with Simon building façade to the right

was originally a three-story masonry building, designed in the High Victorian Italianate style, with ground-floor storefronts and lodging above. Its façade had ornamental detailed cornices with human faces and leaf motifs, coupled with arched narrow windows, making it one of the most significant buildings in the Skidmore/Old Town Historic District. But by the early 1970s, the Sinnott's only tenant was the Couch Street Fish House. The Naitos intended to move the front entrance of Sinnott to the north side of the building, fronting the new surface parking lot where the Simon building had been.

Sheldon, then the chair of Portland Planning Commission, saw the large crane intended to bulldoze the Simon building and ran over to Bill's office to ask him what was happening. After hearing Bill's explanation, Sheldon informed him that his plan would violate city code. Bill gave him twenty-four hours to come up with an alternative. After all, he had already paid for the crane, and a fine for creating a parking lot would be cheaper than having a useless building. Sheldon returned with an idea: preserve the façade and place parking behind it. While Bill agreed that demolishing the building would leave the block looking gap-toothed, he balked at the cost. But when Sheldon told him that no one had ever done anything like it before, he jumped on board with the idea. Venturing into the unknown and stamping his name on an innovation was its own reward. The Simon building was reborn for $25,000: $15,000 for support braces, $7,000 for paving the lot, and $3,000 for rehabbing the façade and landscaping.

Colburn, Sheldon, and Kaji was the architectural firm for the project, and George Guins of Portland Wire & Iron Company provided engineering services. Using Guins's innovative design, two 24-inch-thick, 54-foot-long steel beams with steel struts extended wall-to-wall. The lintels (horizontal supports of cut stone across the tops of windows) were left in place, but the remaining parts of the window frames were removed. From then on, Guins was part of a core group of professionals that Bill relied on for other renovations. He had moved to Portland as a twenty-three-year-old Russian immigrant in 1930 and was a dynamic engineer. He was also a bit unusual, visiting Bill with his orange tabby cat on his shoulders. But he was devoted to historic preservation and personally spent hundreds of dollars to preserve the unique brickwork sidewalk outside his home in northwest Portland. He characterized its preservation much the way that Bill did: "If this is the only brick sidewalk in Portland, then to let it go would be like letting the last whale die."

With the combined talents of Sheldon, Guins, and the Naitos, the Simon building was the first known restoration of a building façade strictly for ornamental use in America. And Bill got his parking lot for the Couch Street Fish House, complete with a new entrance with lights, awning, and shrubs. Colburn, Sheldon, and Kaji won an Award of Intent from the Portland chapter of the American Institute of Architects for its influence on preserving the building. For Bill, it was an attraction to draw people to the neighborhood, and with the cobblestones exposed on the sidewalk in front of the façade he realized a small-scale version of his dream of restoring Old Town's streets. Thereafter, Sheldon could be found at Bill's desk at Norcrest's office on many afternoons in long conversations about the future of Portland and how to get there. They shared a vision for a livable city, with historic preservation, public transportation, parks, and care for those in need. Bill thought Sheldon was a genius.

Their success with the Simon building prompted the Naitos to renovate the Merchant Hotel, the first project Norcrest did with P&C Construction, a Gresham firm started by Ray Pettyjohn, Jim Gillilan, and Don Campbell. Campbell, who Bill considered "a real quality gentleman," had gone to Franklin High School and then Reed, although his studies at the college were interrupted by World War II. Their working relationship was what one writer called "a match made in heaven." Bill stayed with P&C because of Campbell's engineering talent for "saving money and not compromising design." Consider his invention of what he referred to as "the clip," an engineering trick of tying floors to walls in reinforced masonry buildings, which satisfied seismic codes without extensive (and expensive) upgrades. With innovations like that, Campbell was able to take Sheldon's dramatic design elements, like the atriums in the Galleria and Montgomery Park, and build them with Bill's frugality in mind.

Bill with Don in the early 1980s

Both Bill Naito and Don Campbell were hardworking, intelligent men with a sense of humor. They often went fishing together, although Campbell was the truer outdoorsman. On the water, Bill would sit with a cigar wedged in the corner of his mouth while Campbell drove the boat puffing on a cigarette. Both appreciated a stiff drink, and both were building family businesses they could pass to their sons, while also creating a legacy with their buildings. They had seen the loss and devastation caused by World War II, and they were determined to leave the world better than they had found it.

When Doug Campbell, Don's younger son, went to work for Norcrest, it was part of an exchange: Bill got Doug, and Don got Bill's youngest son, Ken. Union work had Ken earning $16 an hour, while Norcrest work got Doug, ten years Ken's senior, $6.50. The way the exchange happened is an example of how both men operated. Dale Campbell, Don's eldest son, was in the P&C offices early one morning when he heard a rapping on the door. He opened it and saw Ken Naito. "What are you doing here?" he asked. "I'm not sure," Ken said. "My dad told me to come here." "Really?" "I think I'm supposed to work for you," Ken continued. "Really?" "Yeah," Ken said. "Your brother [Doug] won't be coming here today. He's going to work at Norcrest." The fathers had switched sons the week before but did little to facilitate the moves. Ken lasted four days; Doug stayed at Norcrest for over a decade and a half as its real estate manager.

Working with Bill, P&C would renovate the Galleria, Montgomery Park, Albers Mill, McCormick Pier, Captain Couch Square, the Rich Hotel, Erickson's Saloon, the Shoreline Block, the Dekum building, the Merchant Hotel, and the Fleischner-Mayer building. Don and Bill also worked together on the expansion of Providence Hospital, with P&C as contractors and Bill as chair of the hospital's building committee. Bill gave Don wide latitude in making changes. He "gave us the authority to effect architectural decisions in particular when there was a question of too much money being spent on items," Campbell later remembered. But giving Don wide latitude wasn't the same as staying away from building sites. Bill's approach was different from most clients, Sheldon noted, because "he was very involved in the details of all his projects" from beginning to end. Gary Brayton, P&C's tenant improvement superintendent for Montgomery Park and Albers Mill, said morale was always high on Naito projects. Bill "walks through and talks to everybody," he said. "I've always noticed that with him, some owners don't even look at you, but he comes up, shakes your hand and tells you you're doing a great job, and it really means something."

Together with Bing Sheldon, George Guins, MCA Architects, and others, P&C and Norcrest preserved many historic buildings in Portland, maintaining Old Town's character but also redefining downtown and northwest Portland. "Bill's projects are successful in many ways," Sheldon explained, "because of his ability to capitalize on the efficiencies of a large multi-disciplined team that has worked together on numerous projects. We can work faster and smarter." And they worked as equals, with the shared goals of preserving history while also preserving capital. As broker Julie Schidleman put it, Bill "is interested in working out deals that work for both parties. He's committed to the long haul."

Bill once explained that his criterion for selecting architects was whether or not they were tenants in a Norcrest building. He had relationships with tenants, and who could he trust better than the people that he saw month in and month out? MCA Architects, for example, had moved into the Skidmore building in 1974. They did all the tenant improvements themselves, and Bill checked on their progress every day, leaning up against the glass with his hands around his eyes. He was impressed by the three young men. The firm was a Naito tenant for thirty years and provided architectural engineering services on more than fifty Norcrest projects without a contract. When they were light on work, principal Jack Miller would give Bill a call, and Bill would bring the firm in on a project or ask Miller to pitch him some ideas. That was how Bill's relationships thrived. They were more like friendships, and that camaraderie was built in Old Town.

OLD TOWN

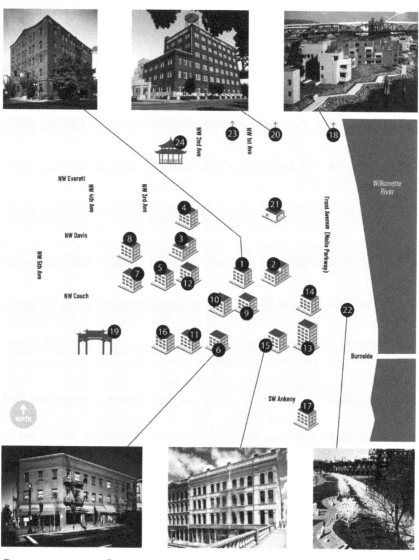

① Fleischner-Mayer Bldg.	⑦ Sinnott Building	⑬ White Stag Building	⑲ China Gate
② Globe Hotel	⑧ Simon Building Façade	⑭ Bickel Block	⑳ Albers Mill
③ Merchant Hotel	⑨ Norton House	⑮ Skidmore Building	㉑ Old Town Parking/Heliport
④ Foster Hotel	⑩ Capt. Couch Square	⑯ Fritz Hotel	㉒ Japanese American Historical Plaza
⑤ Estate Hotel	⑪ Erickson's Saloon	⑰ Ankeny Plaza	㉓ Liberty Ship Park
⑥ Shoreline Block	⑫ Rich Hotel	⑱ McCormick Pier Apts.	㉔ Lan Su Chinese Garden

CHAPTER 9

The Naito brothers formed Skidmore Development Company under the umbrella of Norcrest so they could buy and develop real estate properties for financial gain. But it was also true, as Bill said, that they "fell in love with these old buildings and didn't want them razed." They had a deep love and passion for history. "Walk through the Skidmore-Old Town area with Bill and Sam," John Guernsey wrote in *Historic Preservation Magazine*, "and their eyes sparkle. They point at gilded entryways, rock arches, cast-iron pilasters, fountains and elaborate cornices. They revel in the plainness and sturdiness of the old Globe Hotel, the Skidmore buildings and the Norton House." Historian Chet Orloff described it as Bill's intuitive understanding that "community identity is tied to structures."

That said, there was a less romantic and more pragmatic reason the company bought old buildings. After the Naitos' experience with the Fleischner-Mayer and Globe buildings, it became clear to them just how cheap real estate was in the area. They could buy properties at the cost of the land, sometimes even below cost, because the alternative for owners was the hassle and expense of demolition. Norcrest was cash rich, and real estate investments sheltered profits from immediate tax liability while at the same time putting the money into more stable investments. Deciding to start the real estate company proved critical, as the mercantile side of the business suffered from persistent issues that made it less profitable, such as longshoremen strikes that caused spikes in transportation costs. Then the yen became stronger against the dollar, so the company turned toward China. In 1970, one year shy of the company's fiftieth anniversary, the Naitos had opened a separate wholesale import business, Pacific Orient Imports. The 1973 oil crisis had caused the costs of production in Japan to skyrocket, and the 1974 inflation crisis did the same.

Bill and Sam standing outside of the Merchant Hotel; copyright *Sunset Magazine*, photographer Glenn M. Christiansen

By 1987, Bill admitted that "import prices have gone so high it just doesn't justify our investments. Investments in property management give a better return." The Skidmore Development Company was a protection against those contingencies.

Some of the buildings that the development company bought had a direct link to Bill's past. The Merchant Hotel, in the heart of Nihonmachi, had been built in about 1880 by three brothers—Louis, Adolph, and Theodore Nicolai—who became wealthy through their lumber mills. The building was designed by architect Warren H. Williams using the ornate High Victorian Italianate architecture of the time, with impressive large cast-iron storefronts and ground-level display windows. An alley on the west side led to a small interior courtyard. The building had one of Portland's first hydraulic elevators and took four years to complete. Over time, it became the heart of Japantown, housing professional offices, a grocery store, and the offices of the *Japanese Oregon Weekly*. Bill remembered Fukiye taking him to see a dentist there.

The Merchant Hotel had been slated for demolition when Skidmore Development Company bought it. The roof leaked, and some of the building was fire-damaged. Norcrest converted it into retail on the first floor and offices on the three floors above. Bing Sheldon and George Guins worked with P&C Construction to do the work, including restoring the ornate storefronts using cast iron from demolished buildings. The courtyard was restored with brick walls, a fountain, ferns, and decorative arches.

Bill wanted to honor Nihonmachi by restoring its buildings and making them useful again. Bringing people to the area was a way to remind them of the past and to make history useful to the present in appearance, function, and spirit. At the time, most of the buildings in Old Town met the function aspect, but barely. Hotels like the Merchant had been struggling, and most had a yearly profit of maybe $6,000. At one time, families had lived in the hotels, providing upkeep, security, and labor, but by the 1950s and 1960s, the children had grown up and moved on. It was too expensive to hire outside employees, and the hotels fell into disrepair. Many hotels like the Merchant had to close, and new fire codes in the late 1970s required expensive upgrades that owners couldn't afford.

Merchant Hotel around the time of the Naitos' purchase of it, 1968

By the early 1980s, the hotels that remained suffered from a recession that almost eliminated the demand for day labor, and the disappearance of housing for indigent men in Skid Road was treated as a genuine crisis. In the early 1970s, the city wanted Skid Road to stay Skid Road, where social services were concentrated and cheap hotels provided a fixed address where people could receive benefits. But Skid Road was more than that. Architect Ken Kaji, chair of the Burnside Community Council, described the area as a community and believed there was a "culture among these guys and they'd feel out of place anywhere else." A less altruistic reason for keeping Skid Road a residential area was that it cost less to maintain than paying to address the underlying issues that its residents suffered from.

Some people claimed that the Naitos wanted to push the cheap hotels out of Old Town's buildings to make way for retail and office tenants, but Bill defended himself against those charges. "I have a clear conscience," he said. "I am not a slum lord." He loaned money to some of the hotels in Old Town to help them make rent, and he was never under the illusion that Skid Road would become upscale. The neighborhood's charm was in its seedy character and its rejection of perfection; it was never meant to be like downtown. It was true that Norcrest could charge low rents to fill its properties while doing modest renovations and that Old Town was home for those struggling to find a permanent one. But Bill said that if the next generation of Naitos tore down the old buildings to put up skyscrapers, he would "come out of my grave and haunt them."

Foster Place represented Norcrest's willingness to work with local authorities to provide housing to low-income people. Built in 1907, the Foster had housed Obukan Judo, a laundry, a beauty shop, two hotels, and two trade stores. The Naitos bought the building in 1968, at the same time they bought the Merchant and Martin buildings,[1] with the idea of creating a shopping plaza patterned on Chicago's Old Town, which had similarities to Portland's Skid Road. But that never materialized in Portland. Instead, development came when NW Natural, a natural gas utility, was planning to build its new office in Old Town on Second and Davis, across the street from the

---

1 The Martin was razed to make a surface parking lot of 150 spaces.

Foster Hotel after remodel

Foster. Some existing housing would have to be demolished, and the planning commission ordered the utility to form a task force to find replacement housing.

The task force recommended converting the Foster Hotel into low-income housing, and in 1973 Norcrest agreed to a fifteen-year lease to the Portland Housing Authority at no cost. The housing authority, in turn, subleased rooms in the Foster to low-income elderly people at subsidized rates, between $33 and $35 a month. The federal government helped by paying the city $75 per month for each unit, and NW Natural contributed $13,000 to the project. The initial remodel bid was $480,000, which was paid through a First National Bank twenty-year loan to the housing authority. One hundred and eighty-eight hotel rooms were converted into ninety-six studio apartments, each with a kitchenette and a bathroom. After moving in, one new resident said, "This place is a mansion compared with the foxholes I've been living in." The remodel was designed by Don Eggleston of Colburn, Sheldon & Kaji and constructed by P&C Construction at a cost of $570,000. Housing authority chair Fred Rosenbaum compared the project to making chicken salad from chicken feathers.

That a decrepit hotel could be successfully converted to public housing through a mix of private and governmental action brought hope that the housing crisis could be averted while also bringing shops, restaurants, and businesses into the area. Stan Amy, head of the low-income housing task force, believed the project would turn the tide: "Once a project like the Foster Hotel is completed, the credibility is pushed far more." The arrangement caused a reporter for *Old Portland Today* to call Bill "a rare developer" because he was willing "to sacrifice cash flow from the Foster Hotel." As Bill testified in 1975 before the city council, renovating to lease street-level space to retail businesses allowed him to continue to lease to low-cost hotels for the upper floors, so that pensioners and transients would not become homeless. The success of the project led Bill in 1987 to limit the number of shelter beds in Old Town in exchange for an agreement by area property owners to engage in slower redevelopment and a program to relocate services around Portland. He was always striving to achieve a balance.

Then there was the CHIERS program, run by Central City Concern, which sent a van around the neighborhood to pick up people suffering from too much alcohol and take them to facilities where they could be taken care of. When the program was under threat from defunding in the early 1990s, Bill testified before the city council that eliminating the program would be "unconscionable." At the time, the city implemented drug-free zones to combat the heroin problem in Old Town and gave police the power to exclude individuals from the area if they were suspected of possessing an illicit controlled substance. According to Mayor Vera Katz, the zones were intended to combat an "open drug market." The city banned the sale of fortified wine, and police focused on "street-disorder" crimes, such as aggressive panhandling and loud street musicians. A separate enterprise, the Old Town Nightlife Initiative, sought to prevent people from creating hiding places to transact drug sales. With loans from Portland General Electric and the Portland Development Commission, lighting, trimmed trees, and attractive building facades acted as deterrents, in conjunction with police action. The program resulted in a 50 percent reduction in violent crime between 1992 and 1994.

Paul Richmond of the weekly *Portlander* claimed that the crackdown happened because developers, specifically Bill Naito, wanted to pave the way for large-scale redevelopment. He pointed to Bill's donation of campaign space to elected officials as evidence. Bill's goal was not to drive poor people from Old Town, he defended himself, but "to make them into taxpayers and productive citizens." He wasn't so optimistic as to believe that poverty could be eliminated. "Someone," he said, "has to take care of the downtrodden." Part of his position was the result of him not making moral judgments about a person's economic status. Public drunkenness was not a character flaw, he believed, but most likely due to the lack of affordable housing.

Persistent homelessness in Old Town did mean that fires started where people were trying to keep warm, and they sometimes spread to Norcrest buildings. In the early 1970s, the Naitos bought the Skidmore (Monchalin) Block, built in 1888, and the Bickel (Wexler) Block, built in 1893. The Skidmore had been built because of a death-bed wish by Stephen Skidmore, whose family had made a home in the California Hotel on the site. The Bickel Block, which had T-shaped cast-iron columns with leaflike designs, is considered one of the most

Bickel Block, 1960s

significant buildings in the Skidmore/Old Town Historic District. Both buildings, intended to be used as warehouses, were crafted in the Italianate style with ornate cast-iron pilasters. But between 1979 and 1985, both buildings caught fire, damaging Norcrest inventory. Norcrest held "fire sales," and for a while Bill put speakers under the Burnside Bridge and blasted classical music at night to discourage people from sleeping and setting fires there.

Bill later worked on "Wonderlights under the Bridge," a project meant to dovetail with the opening of a light-rail station under the Burnside Bridge. He suggested installing a grid of colorful electric lights on the underside of the bridge, but there was no funding for the project. Eventually, the city placed lights under the bridge directly over Norcrest's loading dock, with a photocell in place to ensure that the lights would go on only when it was dark. When the city received a citizen complaint that the lights were on during the day, the head of Portland's Street Lighting Bureau sent a foreman to investigate. He returned with a cardboard box that someone had placed over the photocell.

Bill Hughes, head of the bureau, called Bill to ask why Norcrest had interfered with the photocell. Bill explained that it was dark under the bridge even during the day, making it unsafe for pedestrians, so he had had an employee place the box to keep to lights on. The city was trying to save energy, Hughes countered, and the lights would be on only at night. A week later, the light was again on during the day, and again a cardboard box, smaller this time, was found over the photocell. Hughes finally decided that if you can't beat 'em, join 'em. The two men met and worked out a plan whereby there would be a way to manually turn the lights on and off. It was one of many attempts the Naitos made to protect their property from damage without using the police or other security.

The Naitos continued their efforts to provide more housing in the area. In 1981, they replicated the Foster Hotel arrangement at the Rich Hotel on Second Avenue and Couch. Robert Tegen, a German immigrant, had designed the Rich in 1914 in the Streetcar Era style, buildings that flourished between the turn of the century and the 1920s. Retail occupied the first floor, with storefronts flush to the sidewalk and offices or apartments on the upper floors. The Naitos owned the Rich for many years, but it had been vacant for six years until it was reopened in 1980. That June, a fire caused $35,000 in damage to the building and its contents. The Rich was then remodeled into the first single-room-occupancy HUD project in the United States. Norcrest leased the upper floor to the Burnside Consortium for ten years, which charged $95 a month for each of its forty tenants. "The Naitos gave me $45,000," Andy Raubeson of the consortium said, to fill a gap in funding for the remodel. "There's no way they can get their money back from the rent we're paying them." Delbert Dixon, a resident of the Foster Hotel, described living there in 1979: "After I retired I had a house in Kenton for a while, but missed the streets. I came back to Burnside. There's a lot of humor here and looking out of my window is like seeing main street of any small town."

From Bill's point of view, having a community of downtrodden and those that others in society had turned their noses up to was part of the area's core. Old Town had always been a place of questionable character, with opium dens and bachelor hotels, boozy barrooms and sex workers. Bill saw all of that as a facet of the neighborhood to be understood and accepted. And there was no building that encapsulated Old Town's seediness better than Erickson's Saloon, once known as the "jewel of Portland's crimson district." August Erickson, an immigrant from Finland, opened the saloon in the early 1880s as a place to gamble, drink, and enjoy the company of women. It was designed by Aaron H. Gould in the Twentieth-Century Classical Revival style, but its greatest design feature may have been on the inside, where Erickson installed what he claimed was the world's longest bar—684 feet of horseshoe-shaped mahogany separated into five drinking areas. Erickson's was a mystical place that author Kathleen Ryan described as being "free from the greatest of faults—being commonplace—Erickson's breathed the tang of the sea, the scent of the forests, the smell of the sage desert. Here was the flavor of the wilds; the spirit of untamed things."

Fifty bartenders sold sixteen-ounce beers at five cents a pop, with a free lunch, while a $5,000 Wurlitzer Grand pipe organ serenaded customers. For privacy, small pleasure cribs, five by six feet in size, were available upstairs, and private bouncers protected the five entrances, keeping police at bay. Erickson's dedication to

Erickson's Saloon, 1986

alcohol was unbounded. When the Old Town area flooded in 1894, he rented a houseboat and turned it into a saloon, which could be accessed by boat or raft. In 1912, the saloon was remodeled by Fred Fritz and Jim Russell, who purchased it from Erickson and changed it dramatically.

When Norcrest bought Erickson's in 1974, it was operating as the Pomona Hotel, and the Naitos had no immediate plans to renovate the space. "Renovation comes slowly in this neighborhood," Bill explained. "What we do with it depends on the development of the neighborhood." But the Pomona lasted as the main tenant for only a year before a fire claimed thirteen lives and injured twenty-three. The physical damage to the building was extensive, and Bill suggested a full historic renovation, which didn't begin until 1983. With MCA Architects, he looked at historical photos to get Erickson's as close to its original state as possible. Norcrest's goal was to keep historic renovations in sync with the historic character of the neighborhood, and the million-dollar renovation included removing the brick that had been placed over the historic storefronts. "We are interested in the total fabric of the community," Bing Sheldon explained, "and less interested in the individual or corporate symbols. The issue is sharing of symbols, the symbols of the community." Bill wanted to restore as many historic details as possible, no matter how small.

In 1980, the Naitos purchased the Fritz Hotel next door, which had been designed by Aaron Gould, using the same twentieth-century Classical style of Erickson's. But the hotel had a richer flavor, with Italianate features such as bracketed cornices, ornate brick detailing, and arched windows. Its ground floor had high ceilings and wide, arched windows and opened out onto Erickson's main floor. The second and third floors also extended into Erickson's, but the hotel's entrance and frontage were on Third Avenue.

The extensive renovation of Erickson's was completed in 1986, and it reopened with the Advertising Museum, one of three museums in Old Town that Norcrest supported financially by donating space. The Advertising Museum was the first of its kind, with exhibits of more than seven thousand American print, radio, and television advertisements. At the inaugural event, President Ronald Reagan delivered a message from the White House. The Naitos donated $118,000 in free rent and invested $1 million in renovations. Bill believed it was better to have a space attracting people to the area than having no rent *and* an empty space; but he also liked advertising and advertising people, and he was a booster for the industry.

Museums were part of Bill's attempt to make Old Town a diverse neighborhood with a variety of attractions. Norcrest also donated rent for the Police Museum of Oregon, which was also the first of its kind in the nation. Assistant deputy chief of police Ron Still, who was president of the Portland Police Historical Society, thought of the idea. The museum was originally in the Fleischner-Mayer building, but it was soon moved across the street to Captain Couch Square and given a five-year, rent-free lease. The Police Museum's neighbor in the Norton House was the Architectural Preservation Gallery, which exhibited cast-iron fragments and glazed terra cotta artifacts salvaged from area demolitions. Photographs and maps detailed the architectural history of the city, as well as its change and growth over time. Norcrest donated a thousand square feet for the museum with the hope that it would "increase public awareness of Portland's historic buildings."

Bill would cause a minor uproar in 1994 when word got out that he was contemplating leasing space in Erickson's Saloon to Stars Cabaret, a strip club. He defended the idea by pointing out the success of Darcelle XV, a popular drag bar that had been attracting audiences for more than twenty years just down the street. A strip club was consistent with the historical use of the building and the district, he said, and it would help make Old Town into more of an entertainment district, like Bourbon Street in New Orleans. Norcrest did not end up leasing to Stars, but in time, Old Town became a hub of nighttime dance clubs, bars, and strip clubs.

Bill's desire to make Old Town interesting also led him to help set up the first tours of the tunnels that run below Couch, Davis, and Everett Streets, an area at one time referred to as Satan City because of its bordellos, saloons, and gambling houses. Originally, the tunnels had provided access to Portland's terra cotta sewer lines, which broke easily and needed repair, and merchants constructed underground warehouses that connected to each other. Some had used the underground areas as a hiding place from the police who raided Chinese gambling establishments in the district. To drum up interest in Old Town, Bill and others perpetuated the myth that the tunnels were used to "shanghai" inebriated men into ship service in the mid-1800s. Bill urged a tour company to guide schoolchildren through the tunnels to learn the history of their city. He hoped that the district would become like multicultural Vancouver, BC, with cultural gates along Burnside to match the China gate on Fourth Avenue. "Paris has its archways. Rome has its ruins. A city should have gateways for which it becomes known," he said.

One of Bill's more practical projects—one that combined function, form, and style with historical value—was to uncover the cobblestones on Old Town streets. The bricks had been used for ballast on ships traveling from Europe to the West Coast, where they were off-loaded to make way for lighter, profitable cargo such as wheat and timber. The bricks were then repurposed for roads. Cobblestones were pedestrian-friendly, Bill believed, and they discouraged people from driving cars in the neighborhood and encouraged them to walk and explore. He also wanted a "Welcome to Old Town!" sign over First Avenue and Ankeny. He entertained a proposal for a wax museum of Pacific Northwest historical figures and was a supporter of a Will Vinton Claymation theme park.[2] If he had the money, he said, he would buy the New Market Theater and turn it into a farmer's market. None of these projects got off the ground, but they reflect Bill's quest to eschew the mundane or the expected in favor of variety and experimentation in Old Town.

---

2 Vinton, an artist born in Oregon, created the nationally acclaimed California Raisin ads. For more information, visit the entry for Vinton in the online resource, *The Oregon Encyclopedia*.

CHAPTER 10

As historic preservation and renovations spruced up the neighborhood, new tenants moved into Old Town, where rents were low enough that "the potential was too great . . . to ignore," Bill pointed out in 1978. The cheap leases in Norcrest's Old Town properties allowed people to start businesses without much start-up capital, and the Naitos gave tenants the freedom to design their own interiors and often loaned them money to help. Sometimes they went even further. John Tess remembered that, when he started his business, Heritage Investment Inc., in 1982, Bill let his rent slide for a couple of months. He was "one of the fairest people I've known," Tess recalled in 1997. Heritage Investment would eventually take on Norcrest's historic designation research and advocacy.

All of Norcrest's developments in Old Town were speculative, and in the beginning, tenants were not lining up to rent space. Import Plaza had been a huge success, but it wasn't until Norcrest opened its Old Town Emporium in late 1968 that the neighborhood had another significant retail store. That seemed to trigger a shift, and between 1969 and 1971 four non-Norcrest businesses opened: Sinclair's Fine Arts & Old Town Gallery; Daisy Kingdom, a fabric store; and Butterflies Ltd. and Cuckoo's Nest, clothing stores. Because the properties were not fully renovated, the rents were cheaper than could be found in downtown or in the suburbs. Most of the business owners did the improvements themselves.

The businesses were new and often of an unexpected variety. Broker Paul Breuer remembered the first transaction he handled for the Naitos: a potential retailer showed up to meet about renting a space and Breuer's optimism about the deal waned, worried about how Bill would react to a bleached-blonde hippie in a tie-dyed shirt. But Bill eschewed stereotypes and concluded that the man was of good character; the man's ten years as a tenant proved Bill right. Bill believed that young entrepreneurs—he called them "hippie entrepreneurs"—had an esprit de corps that Old Town needed. The owners of Butterflies Ltd., Cuckoo's Nest, and Daisy Kingdom were women in their twenties. Youthful and seemingly foolhardy, they joined together to revitalize the neighborhood. The more merchants were invested in Old Town, the more it prospered.

As long as a tenant was willing to cope with some of Old Town's more colorful aspects, it was a great place to own a business. In the early 1970s, young business owners represented a turn toward a less formal way of doing business. Tenants sometimes had to deal with leaking roofs, which Bill had refused to repair or clean. When the inevitable leaks appeared, he had a simple solution: move whatever was getting wet. If the leak was big enough, he had plastic kiddie pools placed beneath it, believing that whatever amount of water accumulated would evaporate over time. At least once, he rode his luck too long. One year, heavy rain followed snow, and water filled the kiddie pool to the brim in Captain Couch Square. The weight of the pool brought it crashing through the ceiling onto a tenant below. The incident did nothing to deter Norcrest's policy of doing the bare minimum to maintain its buildings, keeping to the goal of minimizing cash output at all costs.

On top of maintenance issues, many of the young tenants weren't fully prepared for the ups and downs of owning a business. The Naitos, a family of entrepreneurs, were there as many landlords weren't, as counselors and cheerleaders. Not that it stopped Bill from running down the sidewalk, yelling at a tenant, "Where's my rent?" in the middle of the day or negotiating harsh tenant improvement terms. Norcrest's compassion was always balanced with the desire to amass cash. Liden Ward Daredevich, who owned Norton House Restaurant, described those days as "an exhilarating time of struggle and setbacks," but "even when things were bleakest, I left [Bill's] office after a chat feeling uplifted in so many ways." Although some of those businesses didn't survive, most of the owners were grateful for the opportunities they had in Old Town.[1]

---

1 One that not only survived but went on to become one of the largest corporations in the world was Blue Ribbon Sports, which set up shop in the Skidmore Building. The company would become Nike, and Bill regretted not investing in the fledgling company when Phil Knight brought him the opportunity.

Bill and Sam Naito were advocates for the neighborhood and all the stores, not just Norcrest's Import Plaza and the Old Town Emporium. They knew that retail couldn't flourish as islands, and Bill started a newsletter that included tips for local shops, including recommending that Old Town merchants recommend other stores in the neighborhood to customers and suggesting how they should use holiday decorations. Eventually, the Naitos held an annual festival called Autumnfest and a Christmas fair to highlight retail in the neighborhood. Bill also hung baskets on the streetlamps, an idea he got from Victoria, BC. He wrote the city for its "recipe" but found that Victoria's moss-covered wire baskets lost water too quickly. Doug Campbell, Norcrest's real estate manager, worked with someone who devised large plastic baskets that retained the water better. Norcrest employees, using a converted golf cart equipped with a fifty-five-gallon water drum, originally maintained the hanging flowers at no cost to other Old Town businesses, property owners, or the city. Their beautification effect on the district was more than worth the cost to create and maintain them.

When Portland City Council planned to light Old Town streets with the same Cobra mercury vapor lights used on freeways, Bill persuaded them to use decorative lamps that mimicked old gaslights and raised the money to make up the difference in cost. He wanted to give the neighborhood "a touch of class." At the time, *Old Portland Today*, a local newspaper, presented an Empty Mickey Award to the person who contributed the most to the deterioration of Skid Road (a mickey was a container of four-fifths of a pint of cheap alcohol, which were often left behind in building doorways). Bill received the first Golden Mickey Award for his contributions to Old Town.

Bill wanted the neighborhood to shed its reputation as being unwelcoming to children, which is why he paved the way for a daycare center at Norton House, next door to Captain Couch Square. Norton House, designed in the Italianate style, had once been a first-class hotel in the 1870s. It was one of Portland's first waterfront hotels, the city's first brick building, and a favorite of lumber baron Simon Benson. The building originally had three stories, but a fire shortly after its construction reduced it to two. The second floor had an unusual semicircular floorplan and fourteen tall, arched windows.

The Naitos bought the building in 1977, when it was used as a storage facility, and none of the original interior remained.

Bing Sheldon's architectural firm SERA was hired for the remodel. The first thing they did was open up the windows that had been bricked up, but they could not resurrect the west balconies on the second floor. The windows without balconies created an odd visual break, and architect Gary Reddick found a simple solution: install awnings that served functional, historical, and aesthetic roles. A catwalk was installed, linking the top floor of the building to Captain Couch Square. In order to lease space to Forest Park Day Care, Bill obtained an exemption from Uniform Building Code regulations that banned day-care centers on the second floor of buildings. Having day care in Old Town was a big deal, countering the perception that the neighborhood was too dangerous for families. Bill subsidized the center with a ten-year, $60,000 loan to help with the lease and paid the $80,000 renovation costs.

Bill also found ways to foster art in Old Town. Bill had an economist's mind but a dreamer's soul, and he had always been interested in art, despite having no talent for it himself. For years he had been a part of efforts to increase support for metropolitan art. In 1976, he helped select the sculpture for the South Auditorium urban renewal area and the bronze animal statues on Morrison and Yamhill Streets. He served on the Metropolitan Arts Commission and the Performing Arts Center Committee and was a board member for the Portland Art Association between 1977 and 1979. With philanthropist Arlene Schnitzer, he was on the board of the Artists Initiative for a Contemporary Art Collection, a failed attempt to create a second art museum on Port of Portland property. In 1987, he argued fervently for a 2 percent hotel/motel visitors' tax that would support arts programs. The arts, he and others pointed out, had been a big part of the turnaround in Portland's economy at the time, bringing $93 million to the city.

When Bill finally decided in 1976 to replace the Import Plaza arrow on the Fleischner-Mayer building with a mural, he worked with graphic designer Joe Erceg, who had been a tenant in the Merchant Hotel since 1971. They settled on a giant butterfly, an image Erceg had used on a previous project. Composed of large, colored

The back of the Fleischner-Mayer building, 1980s

dots of oranges, purple, blue, and green, the butterfly was rendered in a pop art style, in which the totality of the image was visible only at a distance. The mural, which was completed in ten days, lasted for twenty-four years. On another project, salvage cast iron was used to create a public courtyard between Norton House and Captain Couch Square, with a fountain designed by Doug Macy of Walker Macy landscape architects. He was also funded smaller projects, such as an art exhibition by two construction workers in the Northwest Artists Workshop on environments created with poured-in concrete.

Bill hoped to attract artists and photographers to Old Town with its cheaper rents, and he largely succeeded. Some of the buildings, because of their original use as warehouses, were well-suited for studios. Others, because of their general neglect, could be turned into studios with little money or effort. Carl Morris, a singular talent and one of Oregon's best-known painters, had a studio on the third floor of the Merchant Hotel. His space had bare brick walls, a woodstove, few electrical outlets, and worn wooden floors. But it was 3,200 square feet of space, and the rent was low. It also had several windows and high ceilings, which gave Morris an open, spacious area in which to work. He could lay out ten to fifteen canvases along the walls of the large studio, select a color from half-gallon vodka jugs of paint, and apply it differently to each canvas. Instead of paying rent, Morris gave two of his paintings to Norcrest each year. His tenancy in the hotel was a perfect example of Bill creating nontraditional arrangements in which both parties benefited.

In 1979, Bill borrowed an idea from Seattle: an architectural mural to bring artistic character to the blank concrete wall of a warehouse extension, which had been added to the Import Plaza in 1966. The wall was an "eyesore," he thought, and out of character with the surrounding historic buildings. At two stories and 40,000 square feet, the extension had helped to alleviate the space crunch in the Globe Hotel, but it was functional, with no unique or attractive architectural qualities. Bill contemplated a mural of Mount Hood on the building but settled on something similar to what was being done in Seattle. With the talents of Portland mural designer Bill McCabe, painter Julie Mielsen, and architectural historian William Hawkins, the Zeta Psi building (originally the Oregon Railway and Navigation Company building) was resurrected on the wall in a historically accurate mural. The project cost $4,500, a small price to pay to remember a building that had been torn down in 1928 to make way for a parking lot.

Much had changed since Norcrest bought the Globe Hotel in 1962, when "you could shoot a canon down First Avenue on Saturday and never hit a person." Thirteen years later, there were shops and offices, young professionals, and the preservation of several historic buildings. Historian E. Kimbark MacColl, in a letter to the editor in the *Oregon Journal*, wrote, "Bill will not become wealthy out of his restoration efforts, but he is not losing any money. He is having fun, and he is making a real contribution to the present and future development of Portland. There is style and vitality north of Burnside now." Shops like the Funky Skunk and Wildflower Fibres lined the streets, the Pot Sticker and Sizzling Rice drew hungry patrons, and Darcelle XV's drag show left audiences wanting more. Old Town was not "straining to charm everybody," the *Oregonian* editorialized in May 1980. It was the kind of place "where you pay $6 for hamburger and a frosted stein of beer after buying some faked stained glass and a Toulouse Lautrec poster that you'll never get around to having framed."

Sometimes Bill had to resort to slightly underhanded tactics to preserve Old Town's character. In 1980, US Bank wanted to build its tower on southwest Third Avenue and Burnside, and the bank's CEO, John Elorriaga, was desperate to change the area's image. Changing Burnside's name, he thought, would be a good start, and he leaned on Mayor Frank Ivancie. Ivancie didn't have much time for Old Town and was eager to do anything to change it. But Bill told him that he couldn't change the name of Burnside Avenue, because it had been named after Civil War general Ambrose Burnside. Ivancie agreed to drop the idea. When banker Bob Ames heard the given reason, he looked into it and discovered that the name came from a Portland merchant named David Burnside. When he challenged Bill with the information, Bill laughed and said, "I know that, but it doesn't matter because you don't ever have to worry about Frank checking."

In 1975, to signify the end of the old Skid Road and its associated negatives, Bill painted "Old Town" in large ornate letters on the defunct water tower on the roof of the White Stag building on Front Avenue and Burnside. The water tower had not been functional for years but now could be used to prominently promote the district. It was one of four towers that he owned, including one south of downtown in John's Landing on Macadam Avenue. Most water towers had been constructed between 1875 and 1930, when Portland's water system was notoriously unreliable and insurance companies required building owners to have towers on rooftops. Some wanted the water towers taken down for safety reasons, but Bill disagreed: "They're landmarks. I'm not going to let anything happen to them because there aren't many left."

Through all these efforts, Bill Naito became, according to president of the National Trust for Historic Preservation Richard Moe, a "legend in the preservation community." He always made himself available to the National Trust for Historic Preservation, whether to speak to an Oregon senator about appropriations or to lobby for tax credit legislation or to speak to civic leaders around the country about historic preservation and public transportation. Bill provided office space and financial support to the Historic Preservation League of

Bill speaking at the Skidmore Historic District dedication, May 1979; copyright The City of Portland Archives and Records Management Division

Oregon, one of the first statewide offshoots of the National Trust. Bill was eager to share his knowledge, experiences, and optimism. That was especially significant when few people of influence believed that historic buildings had intrinsic value, and there was stiff resistance to preserving them. For many, it was counterintuitive to eschew the new and shiny in favor of the old and drab. But people listened to Bill, and sometimes he changed their minds. "It was beneficial for them," the planning assistant of the City of Albany, Oregon Ruth Rhyne, remembered after a visit in 1978, to learn that "successful business-men considered preservation to be a valid commercial venture."

When Vancouver, Washington, was considering a development called Officers Row in 1987, their city council asked Bill to review the concept and the financing before it would sign off on the project. The area, part of the Vancouver National Reserve Historic District, had twenty-one historic US Army houses—"white elephants nose to tail," according to the project director. The $10.9 million renovation under consideration would rehab the houses and turn the strip into a tree-lined boulevard. Bill reportedly "leaned back and said, 'I've been in the development business for twenty years, and I smell a winner.'" He was right, as it became a successful redevelopment, and that assessment was based on years of his own real estate projects and advocacy for historic preservation that began in Old Town.

CHAPTER 11

Despite his growing success and notoriety, Bill's appearance made him easy to underestimate if one wasn't paying attention. Neil Goldschmidt described him as entering rooms sideways, as if trying to go unnoticed, and Bill Wyatt called it his nutty professor routine. *Oregonian* columnist Jonathan Nicholas described his appearance this way: "He always looked like a guy whose mind must have been on something else the moment he reached into the closet." He wore mismatched jackets and slacks, and many of his clothes looked as if they had been bought at thrift stores. Architect David Soderstrom remembered thinking that Bill's outfits were totally incredible, with "his outrageous choice of ties and sport coats in very conflicting patterns and colors."

Bill was often the only person of color in a group of businessmen or politicians, and, at five feet four inches tall, he was usually the shortest. He could never change his height, but he did take certain measures to alleviate his diminutive stature. While working on the Japanese American Historical Plaza, he would ask his shorter friend and colleague, Nobi Masuoka, to stand beside him at meetings to make him appear taller. But being short didn't deter his confidence in an argument, no matter the opponent. When Bill was elected to the Federal Reserve Bank of San Francisco, he came up against Federal Reserve chair Paul Volker, who stood at six feet seven inches. It was "something to see," Reed President Paul Bragdon reported, when the two went head-to-head about monetary policy.

Bill's smile was crooked and ever-present, and he had an aw-shucks way about him that helped people feel like he was interested in them and what they had to say. His laugh was contagious and sometimes seemed in danger of running away with him. He often reined it in with the wipe of his fingers across his mouth before continuing

Bill fishing in Vancouver, BC, early 1980s

his point, but sometimes he just kept on laughing. He had "mischief so often in his eyes," Reed president Paul Bragdon said. No matter the project, he always seemed to be having the time of his life. But Bragdon also noted, "On the other hand, it was hard to know Bill. He was in a sense a very private person. It was difficult to know whether he was serious or pulling your leg." A stubby unlit cigar was almost always in the corner of his mouth, above a beard that skirted his jawline. Until the 1980s, he would have been smoking it, his words coming out muffled through the stogie's smoke. Bill's offices were an extension of this image.

In 1972, while Old Town was in resurgence and Portland downtown's revitalization was underway, Norcrest China Company—the Naito brothers' umbrella company—purchased the White Stag building on Front Avenue. Sitting across from their successful Import Plaza store in the Globe Hotel, operating entirely as a warehouse, the building was nondescript, its best features hidden by concrete, wood, and brick. It was much better suited to the growing size of Norcrest than the Fleischner-Mayer building, which had been the headquarters for almost two decades. The five-story White Stag had ground-floor picture windows, which had once advertised its name-sake's ski products but were now empty. Under the Burnside Bridge, which it abutted to the south, two loading docks made for easy load-ing and off-loading of retail and wholesale products, but more than twenty support columns made for tricky maneuvering and parking. The White Stag's neon sign still loomed atop the roof.

Despite Norcrest's increasing value and real estate portfolio, the Naitos did little to turn the White Stag building into what most would consider office space. The main door on Front Avenue had a relatively small wooden sign reading Norcrest China Company next to a nondescript door. Inside, a poorly lit, steep staircase wound up to the second floor, with stairs that creaked with each step. At the top, a large, heavy door opened onto a cacophony of sound and activity that was belied by the building's unassuming character. Bill once described himself as a combination of Willie Loman and Captain Ahab, and in some ways the Norcrest office was a reflection of how he presented himself, using a dowdy exterior to disguise energy and activity. The Naito brothers created an open office on the second floor, which never got "anything new more than a light bulb," according to architect David Soderstrom. At the entrance to the cavernous room, visitors were confronted with a wall of fame—dozens of framed certificates, awards, and acknowledgments bragging about the company's success. The room had the energy of a commodities exchange, where conver-sations and the constant ringing of phones encouraged the persistent yelling of names. There was no front desk or receptionist, and desks weren't partitioned, so conversations fell on top of each other with-out ceremony. The three rows of desks and low-lying tables reminded some people of an insurance company. Four wall clocks represented the different time zones necessary for calls with overseas salesmen and vendors, and a money-counting machine loudly sorted change from the company's retail stores.

From six-thirty in the morning until six or seven at night, it was a rare moment when the office was quiet. Bill or Sam opened up in the morning, and employees hoped Sam would get there first. Bill wanted to race them up the stairs, energized by listening to marches and other invigorating classical music on his way to work. Small chil-dren often ran here and there in the office, and it wasn't unusual to hear a baby crying. Mothers brought their children and sometimes their nieces and nephews to work, setting up playpens next to their desks and babysitting for one another. One "Norcrest baby," as the children later called themselves, remembered walking her "dog"—a wheeled stool—down an aisle past Bill, who asked her what she was up to, handed her a stick of gum, and told her to go play. He breathed the business and was always the last to leave, happy to let employees bring children if it meant that they were there alongside him working, too.

The noise and bustle provided an ideal work environment for Bill. "I like an office where everybody says, 'Where did the day go?'" he said. Local radio station KISN dubbed it a three-ring circus, and Bill's wife Micki called it a "zoo." When University of Oregon architecture professor Suenn Ho first visited, she thought she had walked onto a movie set. How could this be the offices of a real estate and import-ing empire? In the middle of the organized chaos, Bill and Sam had their desks, just as their employees did. Bill believed that employ-ees were more productive and motivated when they could see their bosses working just as hard as they were. He wasn't in his office, he explained, "talking to his girlfriend on the phone." Having their desks in the middle of the floor also allowed the brothers to keep an eye on everyone, which they did with strategically placed mirrors on the ceiling.

Bill's desk was famously unruly and was, perhaps, the greatest physical example of the difference between him and Sam. Sam's desk was spotless, while every inch of Bill's was covered in papers, maga-zines, Norcrest products, phone books, brochures, Rolodexes, and a huge adding machine. The piles were sometimes so high that the only evidence of Bill at his desk was a puff of cigar smoke. On the top of the desk sat a piece of unattached glass, protecting a collection of clippings and motivating quotes. A closed-circuit television on the credenza behind him showed what was going on inside Import Plaza across the street. During the 1980s, ceramic replicas of the company's Old Town buildings were lit up like Christmas decorations. The desk was never tidied for company.

The Norcrest offices and Bill's desk served many purposes, including presenting a calculated casualness meant to put visitors

Bill at his desk in the White Stag offices, 1980s. A framed copy of Executive Order 9066 is visible on a column to the right.

off-kilter and give him the upper hand. While people were adjusting to it all, he got their measure. Bill thought a clean desk meant the man behind it had nothing to do, and he admitted that he liked sifting through the piles to find misplaced documents. He also believed that procrastination was a logical method of timekeeping, so there was no need to have everything readily available. "Anything that can be done tomorrow," he said, "I don't do today." No better form of that belief existed than the minutes Bill spent shifting papers from one pile to another in search of a document.

In order to successfully manage the spinning plates in Norcrest's circus, Bill became a multitasker. He could peruse documents and talk on the phone while holding court at his desk. When the real estate part of the business was taking off, Bill maintained that 80 percent of his time was spent on the import business, arguing that properties had modest upkeep once renovations were completed. The truth was that he simply knew how to do several things at once. Don Barney told Portland's City Club what it looked like: "There's Bill in the middle of this sea of desks in this large room, talking to me about the great issues of Portland of the day, shuffling through pink message slips

deciding who he would be able to call next, or signing checks that his
office manager had put in front of him, and at the same time, providing these wonderful insights about the community."

If Bill liked you, he bartended for you at his desk. Five-thirty
was his drinking hour, when all the fluorescent lights were turned
off except the ones over his desk. He served "cocktails," straight gin
or whiskey in plastic cups from half-gallon bottles under his desk, in
the credenza, or from a paper bag on the floor. If you met Bill and he
pulled out the Jack Daniels, he liked you; if he didn't, in the words
of David Soderstrom, "you might as well just leave." Bill's affection
for alcohol was well-known. When the reparations bill for Japanese
American imprisonment during World War II passed Congress, he
and architect Jack Miller mulled over the party they could throw and
calculated how much booze the $20,000 could buy. He occasionally
took a sip during the day, straight from the bottle, and the tobacco
residue from his cigar would often find its way into the jug. If someone noticed a brown swirl in their drink, he would poo-poo their
concerns: "Ahhhhh, the alcohol will kill any of my germs—it's good
for ya!" Bill had learned that a tavern or a drink after hours could bear
just as much fruit as a legislative hall or a formal restaurant.

Bill and Norcrest employees in the White Stag building, 1979

Bill's hunger for ideas and knowledge was matched by his hunger for great company. He liked "upbeat people with integrity, hard workers, with common sense, courage, intelligence, affection." With Norcrest, Bill wanted to do things that were fun, even if they were weighty in substance, and that meant doing things with smart, funny, motivated people—people like him. Few visitors left Norcrest without a smile on their faces, but it was often a trying workplace. The company motto was "Norcrest is not a job, it's an adventure!" for good reason. For all his compassion and cheer, Bill could be a harsh taskmaster and was not shy about getting angry at or firing an employee, especially if someone hadn't followed his orders. Norcrest was a great place to work as long as you were on Bill's good side. But as many people as he fired, he rehired, and he gave many second chances. Norcrest employee Dick English put it succinctly: despite the bluster, Bill was "a softie."

Some employees were a part of the "Norcrest School of Economics," named by high school students that he began to hire upon his return to the family business. Each year, he worked with local high schools to identify students on the honor roll. For a dollar an hour (about ten dollars today), they did a wide range of work: photography, copyright for catalogs and ads, and warehouse work. He kept close tabs on them. On occasion, he would hide inside a box, ride up the conveyor belt, and jump out, sometimes catching them playing chess or cards. The tricks went both ways, including exploding cigars on Bill's desk. Receiving advice from Bill was part of Norcrest School curriculum—they were "paid to listen to Bill's stories," as businessman Sho Dozono put it. Sit at the front of class and ask one question a day. Always study in the library, because "misery deserves company." Despite the meager pay, hijinks, and unsolicited advice, most of his "graduates" were grateful for their time there, and Bill could be counted on for letters of recommendation and even guarantees for student loans afterward.

The White Stag building was the perfect place for Bill to work, reflective of his parsimonious nature and dominant leadership style with employees. But it was also a historical building worth saving and the platform for what became an iconic sign—a fifty-foot-tall neon outline in the shape of Oregon with "White Stag" in large white letters,

"Sportswear" in smaller letters against a red background below, and a leaping white stag above. Every Christmas since 1959, a red nose was lit on the end the stag's snout, an idea Elizabeth Hirsch came up with in reference to the "Rudolph the Red Nosed Reindeer" song. Despite White Stag Sportswear having sold the building to Norcrest in 1972, Ramsay Signs continued to lease the sign to White Stag, who continued to light it. The sign's namesake was also a symbol for Portland in its time.

In 1907, brothers Max and Leopold Hirsch, together with Harry Weis, bought the Willamette Tent and Awning Company, and an advertising firm's suggestion resulted in rebranding as Hirsch Weis Manufacturing Company (*weis* is white, and *hirsch* is stag in German). During the Depression, Max Hirsch's son Harold suggested starting a sportswear and skiing division after Harold had gotten bitten by the ski bug at Dartmouth for college. Harold designed the first skiwear to be produced in the United States. The designs became so popular that the White Stag Sportswear Division became the company's signature brand, supplanting the canvas manufacturing origins as the business's primary focus.

In 1959, the company went public. After merging with an apparel holding company in Connecticut, the White Stag warehouse was left vacant, and in 1972, Norcrest moved its headquarters to it. Bill petitioned the city to have the sign declared a local landmark in 1977. Using his favorite adjective, he crowed, "Portland is a great town and this sign is a great symbol of this town." Receiving protection from the city, however, was not a sure thing. Landmark status was a recent designation, and large electric rooftop signs, regardless of their history, were considered eyesores. The city had been encouraging businesses to eliminate such signs to create a more attractive skyline, but Bill believed the sign had a significance that distinguished it from most of the neon signs that had been taken down. The image of the state and the deer were universal symbols of Oregon, and the sign's position at the west end of the Burnside Bridge welcomed people to Old Town and downtown. And there was the joy the sign brought to everyone who saw Rudolph's nose lit up during the Christmas holidays.

Together with Leo Williams, a preservationist compatriot in the city planning offices, Bill came up with a plan to maximize the odds in

Bill on the Burnside Bridge with the White Stag building and sign in the background, 1989; copyright the *Oregonian*

their favor: they would petition for designation during the holidays, when Rudolph's nose was aglow and everyone was in a festive mood. In addition, Williams had noticed that one city commissioner was more receptive to ideas when there were young people in city council chambers, and so he invited a Boy Scout troop to the meeting when the sign was on the agenda. The strategy worked, and on December 21, 1977, the White Stag sign became the first sign to be a designated historic landmark in Portland.

In 1986, when White Stag Sportswear left Portland after 102 years in the city, there was concern about the fate of the sign. Warnaco, White Stag's parent company, tried to assure Portlanders that it would not eliminate the sign any time soon. Ramsay Signs was still paying to light the sign, and Norcrest China was receiving rent for the space. The bigger concern was the need to replace the sign's enormous wooden support beams, which could become a hazard. So, despite its claims to the contrary, Warnaco opted not to renew its lease with Norcrest, and Ramsay Signs turned off the lights. By September 1989, it looked as if Rudolph would not be lit for Christmas, and the public started to get worried. "I can't stand it anymore," Bill said. "We're going to light the sign again. . . . And I'll pay for the thing myself." He didn't "have the heart to disappoint a zillion kids." With an agreement from Ramsey Signs to pay for maintenance, Norcrest paid the $200 monthly electric bill.

Bill and Sam received dozens of letters from schoolchildren and adults. One wrote, "Just a quick note during this busy time to say 'Thank you' for Rudolph. It seems like a small gesture to most but I think it's a cool thing for you to preserve some of Portlandia just so we can see that cute nose lit up in December. Thanks for rescuing the holiday 'reindeer' of Portland." When it was time to light up Rudolph's nose, Bill took several of his grandchildren to the roof to flip the switch. Sam changed "White Stag" to "Made in Oregon" in 1997, a year and a half after Bill's death, and the City of Portland bought the sign in 2010 and changed it to "Portland, Oregon."

Bill admitted that he was "kind of a kid, too, at heart. I just love Christmas and all the festivities." He put on a Santa Claus hat as he handed out presents for the Norcrest gift exchange and wore the full suit at home on Christmas night for his grandchildren. When he got TriMet (Tri-County Metropolitan Transportation District of Oregon) to allow vintage trolleys to run every day from Thanksgiving until Christmas, he insisted on having speakers inside and out that played Christmas carols, along with Christmas lights along the brim. At Reed's annual holiday dance, he led the crowd in Christmas carols, his enthusiasm making it difficult for anyone not to join in.

Because of Bill, Pioneer Square—an open plaza in the heart of downtown—hosts a seventy-five-foot Christmas tree every year. The original design of the plaza did not include plans for a tree, but Bill was "hellbent" on it, according to the Association for Portland Progress president at the time, Bill Wyatt, so an underground vault was built five feet below the surface of the square. The bricks above could be removed, and the tree set inside without having to use guy wires. The first tree went up in 1984, replacing the city's annual Christmas parade. The Association for Portland Progress paid for the lights and organized the ceremony. A grand tree has been lit in the square ever since.

CHAPTER 12

The Naitos' purchase and renovation of historic buildings in Old Town coincided with a preservation movement that changed Portland. In the 1950s and early 1960s, Portland was married to the status quo and focused on cars, and the character of the downtown was being changed by developments that rarely considered beauty or livability. John F. Kennedy described the cycle of erosion that many cities, including Portland, faced in 1958:

> In a blighted city, economic and social malaise go hand in hand. Industries move out, and so do their markets. The city's core tends to become a community of only the very rich and the very poor. Downtown merchants lose their customers and their ability to match the attractiveness of suburban rivals. As the community deteriorates, the tax base shrinks, the tax burden on those who remain grows heavier—and the community deteriorates further.

Without invested businesses and citizens, most decisions were made in a vacuum by city governments. For example, in 1961, an overpass on Harbor Drive at Ash Street, along the west bank of the Willamette River, was proposed to mitigate traffic. The plan was developed by William Bowes, a Portland City commissioner who was head of Public Works, and was at the suggestion of Mayor Schrunk, after pedestrians were struck by cars on Harbor Drive during Rose Festival in 1959. But Bowes came up with the plan without consulting the City Planning Commission or considering that city council had already designated the Ash Street area a D zone to preserve relics of Portland's gaslight era between the 1890s and 1910s. The ramp and overpass would directly affect the conservation of the area.

A group of preservationists, led by architect Lewis Crutcher, rallied in opposition, and more than five hundred citizens called, wrote letters, and signed petitions to stop the plan. At a city council meeting, Crutcher demonstrated how an overpass would destroy the neighborhood's aesthetic value, interfere with the view of the waterfront, and create a place for homeless people to congregate. Nevertheless, the council voted 3 to 2 in favor of the overpass, and, despite having his plan passed, an angry Bowes attacked "sidewalk superintendents, ivory tower dreamers, backward editorial writers, and misguided architects" for advocating "a return to the horse and buggy, the dirt road and river canoes for transportation."

Crutcher and other progressives were used to this reaction to their desire for historic preservation and city beautification. Beginning in 1950, when Crutcher worked with architect Pietro Belluschi, and nine years later when he opened his own offices, he had earned a reputation as a person who "chided and cajoled Portlanders into being ashamed of ugliness in the center of the city." Relentless in his pursuit of a livable city, Crutcher emphasized eliminating cars as much as possible. He gathered support for ideas like a European vision of Broadway Avenue through downtown with no cars, large shade trees, plenty of benches, and gray-striped awnings. While many in the business community couldn't stomach his anti-car vision, Crutcher's critiques of some aspects of the ugliness in the city took hold: the utility poles and powerlines (Crutcher called Portland the utility pole capital of the world), the large number of neon signs (glorious at night but hideous during the day), and billboards lining the streets (Crutcher referred to the competition among billboards to be each visually louder than the next as 7-Upsmanship).

In 1960, Crutcher was hired as staff architect for Downtown Portland Inc., an organization formed by area businesspeople to improve the downtown neighborhood, and he joined with other architects and like-minded civic groups to form the Portland Beautification Association. It was the beginning of greater citizen engagement in the city's affairs. In 1961, the *Oregonian* noted that "in the past two or three years, Portland has been witnessing among its citizens and leaders a rebirth of civic pride." The civil rights movement and President Lyndon Johnson's Great Society initiatives made top-down planning impossible. Portland's neighborhood associations became vocal and assertive, and by 1974, 21 percent of Portlanders had attended at least one public meeting on town or school affairs. Many voters no longer accepted the status quo, and Portland's government began to change.

Crutcher's time of activism came during the mayoral tenure of Terry Schrunk. Between 1957 and 1972, Schrunk and city planners made all planning decisions for Portland and informed citizens only after the policies were in place. He was not a change agent. The *Oregonian* characterized city council during Schrunk's term as "unimaginative" but also reported that his "team worked conscientiously to solve problems as they arose." In other words, Schrunk's city council had been reactionary, and that had meant it did not slow the steady decay happening in the core of the city. The Portland Planning Commission (now the Bureau of Planning and Sustainability), which had been created before World War II, was largely overlooked by Schrunk and the rest of city council and considered impotent. In 1957, Mayor Schrunk and others had suggested the creation of a semi-independent agency, the Portland Development Commission, to handle large-scale urban renewal projects and long-term planning for the city and also to attract new industry. Part of its purpose was to educate the public about the importance of development and redevelopment to the health of the city.

The city's first urban renewal project—South Auditorium—was imminent and, in 1958, needed a million dollars in funding to secure a two million dollar grant from the federal government. That million dollars had to come from voters. A public relations campaign against what developers called blight and advocacy for "slum clearance"— Let's Perk Up Portland!—worked, and voters approved the Portland Development Commission and passed the South Auditorium levy the next year. The first chair of the five-person bureau was businessman Ira Keller, a strong-willed, dominating figure who saw PDC as an extension of himself. As a member of the Planning Commission with a particular interest in urban renewal, he had not been in favor of a separate agency but was ultimately persuaded that the city needed it to move forward. His first project was South Auditorium, a well-designed, unified eighty-three-acre district.

Centered on a new Civic Auditorium (present-day Keller Auditorium), Keller's idea was to get people out of their office buildings and into the streets. In order to create an environment for what historian Carl Abbott described as "lunch-hour pedestrians," the plan required the elimination of the existing neighborhood, which was considered unpalatable to the plan's target audience of middle- and upper-class workers. As regional planner Karen Gibson wrote, it was "a classic case of 'slum clearance'" that "dismantled an ethnic enclave of Jewish and Italian residents" and displaced 2,300 people. It was a top-down approach to development, with no consideration for the people affected. Similar urban renewal projects changed Portland's African American neighborhoods, first in the Broadway area on the inner eastside to make way for Memorial Coliseum and Lloyd Center in 1960.

There was a real threat that future urban renewal would continue to destroy historic buildings and unravel communities and neighborhoods. "We're simply drifting," architect and civic activist Howard Glazer said in 1965, "and Portland is particularly cursed. . . . We need a 20-year scheme so that urban renewal and other projects can be fitting into something." To achieve a balance between revitalization and preservation, the city passed an ordinance in 1968 that created the Portland Historic Landmarks Commission, and the tide began to turn. Mayor Schrunk appointed seven members to the commission, which held hearings on the potential designations of historic properties and buildings and made recommendations to city council. The council would then accept or reject the proposed designation, demolition, or change.

More advances came at the state level. Oregon's population had been increasing, and so was the rate of development. The result was often ill-planned growth, resulting in unattractive or incongruous buildings and developments that were often too expensive to remove. The legislature passed Senate Bill 10 in 1969, requiring counties to devise comprehensive land-use and zoning ordinances by the end of 1971. The legislation was motivated by both urban and rural interests. Development in cities and counties without clear zoning had led to a hodgepodge of commercial, residential, and industrial development that made areas less livable. Many people in Oregon's rural areas feared that city boundaries would creep into traditional farming areas and lead to the eventual loss of agricultural land in the Willamette Valley. Uncontrolled industrial and commercial developments had created a greater awareness to the threats to water and air quality from pollution, and many feared the effect of pollutants on forests, natural resources, and recreational areas.

In 1973, Senate Bill 100 created the Land Conservation and Development Commission to monitor whether counties were in compliance with SB 10. After the bill passed in the House, the *Oregon Journal* editorialized, "Oregon has been called by some outsiders a land of 'unspoiled splendor.' Those who live here know it is something less than that. Many further have come to realize that it stands to lose its still high level of splendor if its citizens do not act to defend against the damaging effects of unplanned growth." The bill represented a complete shift away from laissez-faire planning, which had largely deferred to the desires of the private market.

A critical moment for historic preservation arrived in 1975, when Oregon created a fifteen-year property-tax freeze on historically designated properties. The purpose of the freeze was to allow owners the cash flow and time necessary to complete expensive renovations without their property being immediately reassessed. The federal tax code changed the following year: instead of allowing new construction costs to be rapidly deductible, only straight-line depreciation was allowed for new construction, and demolitions could no longer be written off.

In other words, the market had not addressed financial risks and uncertainty in renovations, so the government provided the financial incentives to encourage them. An owner could now remodel a historic building, defer the increased property taxes while earning money through rent, and keep a larger proportion of the rent by avoiding higher federal taxes. At the end of the tax freeze, the owner would be in a financial position to pay the property taxes while the community would have a functional, renovated historic building.

During the 1950s and 1960s, activists such as journalist Jane Jacobs were successfully arguing that cities were worth saving and elevating. Cities were places where ideas flourished, and people were forced to defend them. The suburbs were an escape from complex, heterogeneous communities: people could drive to a downtown parking lot, go to work, and drive home without having to engage with anyone that made them uncomfortable. Jacobs and others argued that suburbs created a false perception of the world, where avoiding problems and controversy was more important than confronting and rethinking them. The value of cities came from that conflict, historian Ray Ginger wrote in 1969: "By producing, over and over, clashes between men who embody variant civilizations, a city speeds up innovations." And as Bill noted, cities were not just buildings. They were the crux of human civilization and advancement. "People make a city," he believed.

In response to this change in thinking, Dick Ivey of the engineering and consulting firm CH2M Hill and City Commissioner Lloyd Anderson proposed a structured dialogue among Portland's government, influential business owners, and everyday citizens that would consider these new ideas and lead to a practical plan that Portland could implement. Bob Baldwin, Multnomah County's first planning director, was chosen to manage the process. An exchange between Ivey and Bob Hazen, president of Benjamin Franklin Federal Savings and Loan, illustrates the idea. "Are you saying, 'Here is your city. What do you want done with it?'" Hazen asked. "Yes," Ivey replied.

The structured dialogue was guided by a strategy based on population to create a pedestrian-friendly downtown with open spaces, engaging attractions, storefront windows at ground level, and access to the Willamette River. At the time, Harbor Drive was a busy thoroughfare that separated people from the waterfront, with semi-trucks hauling things between the industrial area to the north and the interstate highway to the south. The proposed shift would make downtown attractive to people who lived in the suburbs but worked downtown, to give them a reason to stay in the city after hours. The goal was also to get them to spend money.

The result was the Downtown Plan, which was intended as "a policy tool to be used by city officials and planners in making decisions on land use, environmental matters, vehicle and pedestrian traffic and other things in the downtown district." No longer would decisions be made in a vacuum; they would be weighed against other aspects of the city. The creation of the plan coincided with a change at the governmental level, with Neil Goldschmidt being elected Portland mayor in 1973. His tenure, which lasted until 1979, when President Jimmy Carter named him US secretary of transportation, gave Portland a believer in livability ideals with the will to implement them.

Adopted in December 1972, the Downtown Plan, in Gold-schmidt's words, was "a collection of good ideas that were generated by a lot of different circumstances and a lot of different people." In essence, several factors came together in a perfect storm. Between 1969 and 1973, city government acquired new blood, as the average age of city council members dropped by fifteen years. There was a similar turnover in the business community, as civic-minded business leaders who thought long term became more influential. For example, there was only a 30 percent overlap between Portland's "most-powerful" lists in 1969 and 1975. At about the same time, the number of motivated and informed citizens grew, as citizen advisory committees increased from twenty-seven to fifty-six and task forces from five to twenty-five between 1960 and 1972. Also significant was that Portland city government was free of the large-scale corruption and backroom-dealing prevalent at that time in larger cities like New York and Chicago.

The Downtown Plan and those who implemented it stopped the city's decline. A new Nordstrom store and the Galleria mall helped keep people downtown outside of work hours, and an investment in infrastructure in older neighborhoods (coupled with inflated sub-urban housing costs) helped keep middle-class families in the city. Mayor Goldschmidt formed the Office of Planning and Development to coordinate the major arms of redevelopment—the Portland Development Commission, the Housing Authority, the Planning Commission, and the Bureau of Buildings—and the Urban Conservation Fund was created to provide low-interest loans for renovating historic buildings. Goldschmidt also brought neighborhood associations into the process by creating the Office of Neighborhood Associations (now the Office of Community and Civic Life), creating a process and a structure through which people could voice their opinions to City Hall.

Private sector buy-in was critical to the success of the plan. In 1969, the business community had created the Portland Improvement Committee "to meet the need for Downtown business involvement in the preparation of the Downtown Plan." The forty-member organization had raised $120,000 to fund CH2M Hill's study, which formed the backbone of the plan. Goldschmidt went a step further and created the Downtown Committee, a thirteen-member board made up of business and civic leaders. As Planning Director Bob Baldwin later remembered, "Anybody who was a leader who wasn't in this group felt left out."

Bill Naito was one of eighteen members of a separate Citizens Advisory Committee, formed "to generate community interest in the Downtown Plan, solicit citizens' suggestions on various phases of the plan, and offer advice on goals, priorities and alternatives." Meetings were open to the public. One of the goals was to allow Portlanders to tell planners what they wanted, and the planners would design based on those preferences. It was a direct reversal of Portland's approach to planning in the 1940s and 1950s and represented chair of the Citizens Advisory Committee Dean Gisvold's goal of making Portland "a place where, in years to come, 'people can be free to be people.'" Still another group of business leaders, including Bill, met informally with Goldschmidt to talk over city hall's issues. That group was expressly not political and was formed "strictly in the spirit of what is best for our community."

When Bill spoke about Portland, it was as if the city deserved to be successful because of its intrinsic value, and he made a personal commitment to do what he could to make that happen. At the beginning, when Bill talked about Portland's quality of life with planners and city officials, his was "a voice in the wilderness," as Goldschmidt put it. Bill was picking up where Lewis Crutcher had left off in 1968. Crutcher had spent two decades urging Portland to save its historic buildings and trees, to embrace a European aesthetic, and to turn its back on concrete and convenience. The heart of his argument was summed up in the words of architect Gary Reddick, a member of Skidmore/Old Town Advisory Council:

> The quality of the streets dictates the quality of the neighborhood. Streets—the exteriors, sidewalks, trees, etc.— are so significant; they affect quality more than open space does. It is most often in streets that people meet face to face, interaction occurs shopping, visiting, eating, and festivals occur in cities. It is in city streets in fact that community life is carried on, where young and old contact each other.

To that end, Crutcher got bridges painted different colors and potted trees placed on the sidewalks. He also turned businessmen, including Bill, on to historic preservation through his advocacy and his persistent pestering of city council and business leaders.

It is likely that Bill met Crutcher because of his efforts to protect the area around Skidmore Fountain in Old Town. Beginning in 1961, Crutcher and others sought to have close to fifteen blocks around the Skidmore Fountain designated a historic preservation zone. The area stretched from the Willamette River to halfway between Second and Third Avenues and from Burnside to Oak Street. The idea was modeled on Jackson Square in San Francisco, which had preserved almost all of its commercial buildings from the 1850s and 1860s to create a pocket of history in the city.

Despite eventually securing the zoning designation, Crutcher still thought of Portland as a "cultural disaster area" in 1965. The success with the Skidmore Fountain had been a minor victory that "triggered a revolution toward keeping and maintaining the city's older buildings." But by 1968, two years before Goldschmidt was elected to the city council, Crutcher had had enough of Portland's "Mickey Mouse" form of government. "The thing I've been trying to do for 20 years," he concluded, "just can't exist in Portland," and he left to become director of planning and research for the Minneapolis Park System. Bill took up Crutcher's mantle as persistent pesterer for a livable city.

He spent much of his time at the planning offices at City Hall, speaking to the staff, an exceptional group of professionals who had been recruited to effectuate a progressive direction. Ernie Bonner, as director of urban planning, had recruited Doug Wright and Ernie Munch to focus on transportation. Don Mazziotti was head of policy, Jim Griffiths was head of buildings, and Dave Hunt and Robert Holmes joined PDC as staff members. They were all motivated and talented and represented the government's turn from the status quo. And they formed strong relationships with Bill, enjoying having someone around who was genuinely interested in what they were doing and why they were doing it.

In 1970, Bill went to the Portland Planning Bureau offices with a mock-up map of a park to replace Harbor Drive. His vision was a reminder of John Charles Olmsted's 1904 plan for Portland, which

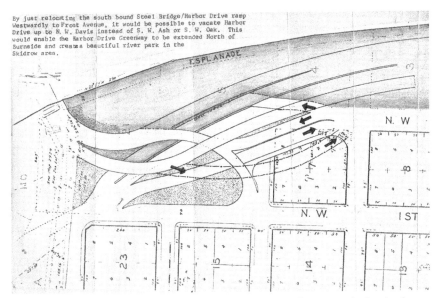

By just relocating the south bound Steel Bridge/Harbor Drive ramp
Westwardly to Front Avenue, it would be possible to vacate Harbor
Drive up to N. W. Davis instead of S. W. Ash or S. W. Oak. This
would enable the Harbor Drive Greenway to be extended North of
Burnside and create a beautiful river park in the
Skidrow area.

Bill's drawing of the waterfront, if Harbor Drive were removed, given to the Portland
Planning offices, 1970

had city parks along the Willamette River. Bill wanted Portland's
waterfront to be more like the one in downtown Chicago that he had
enjoyed so much while in graduate school. But he was not telling
the planners what to do—he was asking a collective question of what
could be done. Rodney O'Hiser was the only member of the planning
team from Mayor Schrunk's administration, and Goldschmidt credited him with being able to take ideas and quickly assess their viability.
"He could take a Bill Naito idea," Goldschmidt remembered, "and he
immediately could understand whether it fit easily into what we were
thinking or whether he needed to pull the brakes on and think a little
bit more about what we were doing." It was O'Hiser who kept Bill's
rendering of a waterfront park.

Bill was also building strong relationships with the business community, and he could count on fellow businessmen to make calls to
council members on his behalf. Bill cultivated those relationships
through encounters at the University Club and at banquets and
lunches. He created friendships, not just business relationships, with
bank presidents and coffee shop owners alike. By having strong public and private relationships, he came to wield considerable power.

One example occurred during Goldschmidt's first term, when the young mayor had O'Hiser look into awnings downtown as a way to protect people from the rain. After a survey of the awnings that already existed, O'Hiser devised strict guidelines requiring them on all storefronts and gathered corporate support for the plan from Meier & Frank and other downtown businesses. When the proposal went before the city council, everyone believed it was going to be an easy vote, but O'Hiser hadn't passed the idea by Bill. In chambers, Bill successfully argued for flexibility, claiming that Portlanders didn't need or want protection from the rain. In fact, the awnings that did exist were almost all on the north side of buildings to provide shade from the sun. The proposal failed. O'Hiser learned that it was always better to talk to Bill before bringing things to a vote.

That was the level of detail in the original Downtown Plan, addressing minutiae in order to reverse more than two decades of decline and create a city with successful retail, entertainment, and housing. But the plan was too broad, lacking in specific rules but also being so complex that developers and city planners were left in confusion. It had been a good first step, but it needed refinement. Goldschmidt and the city sought to take the goals of the original plan and make them more practical. Businesses responded by reactivating the Portland Improvement Committee, established four years earlier to fund the original Downtown Plan. It was a continuation of the symbiotic relationship between businesses and city government, ensuring that city planning had the business support it needed to succeed.

In a way, the Portland Improvement Committee was a precursor to what would come six years later, the Association for Portland Progress. Goldschmidt and Bill independently concluded that the city's downtown needed its own advocacy group, which would act as a neighborhood association for downtown businesses. The downtown core needed more of a focused voice in city council, as Bill thought it still looked "sick" in the late 1970s. Although the Galleria and transit mall had started downtown's resurgence, the district hadn't fully recovered from the neglect of the 1950s and 1960s. To that end, Bill helped incorporate the Association for Portland Progress (now merged with the Chamber of Commerce as the Portland Metro Chamber) and became both a founding board member and its president in 1979. The focus of the group was on strengthening the central business district, roughly the downtown core and the close-in eastside area around Memorial Coliseum and Lloyd Center. Membership in the nonprofit was to be limited to no more than a hundred members from the upper echelon of Portland's business leaders.

Bill's advocacy for the Association for Portland Progress did not signal his rejection of the city's Chamber of Commerce, which dealt with a broad range of business interests and issues and where he was on the board of directors. APP served a different function, keeping a finger on the pulse of downtown business and acting as a tidy way to get issues before city council members. If the mayor was at an event and someone brought up a problem, he could point them to APP, confident that the issue would get to him in the right forum. APP conducted surveys on businesses, pedestrians, workers, and consumers, and the results were delivered to property owners, brokers, and interested businesses.

The results were a revelation for city council. They learned that many of the concerns of downtown businesspeople could be easily addressed and that some issues that the council assumed were important, like keeping taxes low, were actually much less concerning to businesses than, say, accessible parking. APP was forward-looking and proactive, working with the city and private organizations to promote the downtown area to businesses, customers, and potential investors. The organization's interests ranged from marketing and promotional activities to crime prevention and parking. In the early 1990s, for example, at the behest of Mayor Bud Clark, APP started Portland Downtown Services, which used funds from area property owners to pay people who were homeless and recovering from substance abuse to clean up and maintain city streets. At Bill's suggestion, APP also bought the Portland Police Bureau mountain bikes and initiated the Alder Street Task Force, which placed brass plaques on historic buildings, repainted light poles, and hung banners at Christmas.

Although all of the Naito brothers' business interests at the time of the Downtown Plan were located north of Burnside, away from the center of the commercial district, Bill believed that a healthy downtown was vital to the health of the city and also the state at large.

A city could not survive without a strong downtown core, he argued. At a dinner with a Housing and Urban Development representative in the 1980s, city council member Mike Lindberg remembered that Bill orally "drew a total picture of downtown," pointing out how it was connected and that what was good for one section was good for all of it. If one part of Portland succeeded, then everyone benefited.

CHAPTER 13

Despite spending so much time working on Downtown's revival, Bill remained committed to continuing Old Town's resurgence. From attractions to transportation to attempts to bring in large-scale projects, he spent years seeking out multiple avenues to continue to develop the area and bring more people and businesses into it, some of which took decades to come to fruition. In 1974, in the middle of the district's rebirth, Andrea Scharf and Sheri Teasdale were looking for a home for a weekend open-air market. They had been driving to Eugene in the summer to sell their shish kebabs, and they admired the outdoor market there, which featured local craftsmen and artisans selling a range of products from food to woodwork to pottery. But when the two women asked parking-lot owners in downtown Portland and Old Town to provide space, they were turned down time and again. Most didn't want to lose parking spaces on summer weekends, and Bill speculated that they worried the vendors would be hippies who would ruin the neighborhood.

Scharf and Teasdale then pitched the market to Bill, meeting in his White Stag office where they competed with the interruptions of phone calls and employees. Before they could even start the conversation, Bill cut them short, saying he didn't have time to talk. With the next breath, he offered them the Fleischner-Mayer parking lot on Saturdays for $100 a month. He hoped the market would bring people into Old Town on the weekends. The women asked the Metropolitan Arts Commission to help cover the costs of liability insurance, cleanup services, and rent. In the end, they secured a $1,000 grant, a small amount, but enough for the endeavor to go ahead. When Saturday Market opened that year, it had seventy-five vendors; a year later, between 160 and 200 booths filled the parking lot every weekend. Both the city government and the Arts Commission supported the undertaking, and Norcrest advertised the mart in its Import Plaza newspaper ads.

By 1976, Saturday Market had outgrown the Fleischner-Mayer parking lot and moved under the Burnside Bridge, spreading out on the White Stag parking lot and the Ankeny Plaza to the south. Merchants had already been moving under the bridge when it rained, so it was a natural transition. Bill likened the market to a small town and thought it was a beneficial addition to the district. Vendors were people like Sandy Leibrock, who made a living as a basket weaver and owned Baskets from OZ; and Don Theissen, who built wooden toys and traveled to Saturday Market every week from Dallas, sixty miles up the Willamette Valley. By its twentieth anniversary in 1994, Saturday Market had eight hundred vendors and a $650,000 annual budget. It brought 750,000 visitors into Old Town every year and enjoyed over $4 million in gross annual sales.

A year later, the city installed staircases to the market from the top of the Burnside Bridge. Ornate signs announced "Saturday Market/ Old Town," a result of Bill's work. He hoped that Saturday Market would have a seven-days-a-week, year-round outlet near the mass-transit train stop under the Burnside Bridge. Three days before he died, in 1996, he told the market board that he would sell them the space the next year when he could take a tax write-off. That never happened, but in August 2009, Saturday Market received a permanent installation in Waterfront Park through the Parks Bureau, next to the Burnside Bridge. The Bill Naito Legacy Fountain was installed nearby in 2009, a memorial spearheaded by Bill's daughter Anne to honor his support for the market and his desire to attract children and families to Old Town.

Norcrest's most enduring retail success relied on Oregon artisans, craftspeople, and farmers similar to those at Saturday Market. In 1975, the Port of Portland put out a request for a proposal for a store at the airport to sell Oregon products. Bill, Sam, and Norcrest manager Don Pendergrass came up with the winning store concept—Made In Oregon, selling products made, grown, or caught in the state. Initial brands included Dickinson's jam, Tillamook cheese, Jantzen clothing, and Blitz beer, and its best-selling products included myrtlewood bowls, marionberry jam, and smoked salmon. By 1990, after Don

USS *Oregon* smokestacks
in the Fleischner-Mayer
parking lot, early 1970s

Pendergrass's wife and two daughters had assumed management of
the store, Made In Oregon had expanded throughout the Willamette
Valley and to the coast, with 1,400 local vendors producing over $5
million in products and Norcrest employing 250 people for Made
In Oregon. Sam credited the Pendergrasses as the key to its success.
Saturday Market had provided a sampling of the breadth of Oregon's
small-business creators, and Made In Oregon amplified them.

Patrons of the Saturday Market when it was operating in Fleischner-Mayer's parking lot could not avoid two twenty-foot-tall
smokestacks in the center of the lot, remnants of the battleship USS
Oregon. Bill once referred to himself as a "frustrated history professor," and he had preserved the smokestacks as a labor of love. Their
presence in that parking lot was unexpected and a classic case of Naito
whimsy, which often led Bill to act without a clear plan but often
ended in something unexpected and wonderful.

The USS *Oregon* had made news in 1898 when it completed the
15,000-mile voyage from Bremerton, Washington, to the Philippines,
where it joined the Spanish-American War in the Battle of Santiago.

The ship was later part of President Teddy Roosevelt's Great White Fleet, circumnavigating the globe in a US show of force. The ship was decommissioned in 1919 and was moored as a memorial and museum at the end of Southwest Columbia Street on Portland's Willamette River waterfront. But World War II brought an intense demand for scrap metal, and in 1943 the US Navy took the ship apart for salvage. Its hull became an ammunition barge, then a breakwater in Guam, and ultimately chunks of metal in a scrapyard in Japan. The smoke-stacks survived and were left on a property in southwest Portland. Standing twenty-three and twenty-four feet tall, each smokestack weighed three tons.

Twenty-two years later, in 1966, Norcrest employee Dick Lenhart bought the surviving smokestacks on behalf of the Naitos for a hundred dollars. They hoped to place them at the Battleship Oregon Memorial Park on Harbor Drive, near the mast that was already there, and they offered the stacks to city council. The council accepted the "gift of historical significance" and had the stacks taken to a city-owned shop on the east side to be sanded, repainted, and placed in a suitable base. But city council couldn't find the $26,000 needed to pay for the work, and despite a plea from Mayor Terry Schrunk to local organizations to underwrite the project as "a gift to the citizens of Portland," no one stepped up. The stacks sat in storage until 1973, when the Naitos paid $6,000 to restore them, relying on donated services from local businesses to complete the work. Norcrest placed the stacks in the Fleischner-Mayer parking lot, where they stood for years.

In 1986, Norcrest purchased a 1.25-acre parcel from Zidell Explo-ration in the hope of winning a bid to construct a new Port of Portland building on the Willamette River. But the company lost the bid and decided to turn the land into parking for their Albers Mill office build-ing. As construction crews began to dig, they discovered blocks of dense concrete encased in steel, the bows of Liberty ships that had been built during World War II.[1] The ships had been built to haul cargo, and their rapid production symbolized America's industrial prowess.

---

1 Liberty ships had been part of Portland's World War II economic boom, when Portland was known as the "Liberty ship capital of the world" thanks to the efficiency and speed of its ship-building yards.

In the 1960s, Sam Zidell, whose company constructed ships, had about a hundred of the Liberty-class ships that he intended to dismantle for scrap metal, but their hulls were made mostly of concrete, so he used them to fill his swampy land along the river instead. By the late 1980s, the cost of removing the hulls was exorbitant, and Norcrest was left with a useless piece of property, so Bill turned the small plot into a maritime park. With the USS *Oregon* smokestacks, Liberty ship bow pieces, a Victory ship anchor bought at an auction, and a wheat weight from Albers Mill, Liberty Ship Park was dedicated to the Liberty ships and Merchant Marines on July 2, 1991. On National Maritime Day, May 22, veterans gathered at the park to honor those killed while serving on Liberty ships.

Liberty Ship Park was in a neglected area north of the Broadway Bridge and Union Station, Portland's central railroad station built on the west bank of the Willamette River in 1896. The "little gem of a building," as Bill called it, was part of Old Town and was often on his mind. Sometime during the 1970s and mid-1980s, its "Go By Train/Union Station" neon sign had been turned off. Bill heard about a fundraising effort to restore the sign and got in touch with Richard Carlson, who was spearheading the effort on behalf of the National Railway Historical Society. Carlson was selling cloisonné pins for five dollars each, with twenty-four pins to a board. Bill bought an entire board and offered to reach out to other businesspeople who could help out. The campaign was successful, and the sign was restored; it is now an iconic image and symbol of Old Town and Portland.

In 1986, the Portland Development Commission considered buying Union Station and the thirty acres that surrounded it as part of a bid for the new convention center. The plan was to tear the station down and build the convention center in its place. A new central train station would be constructed on the east side of the river. But when the three railroad companies that owned the station were reluctant to sell, most members of the Regional Committee on Convention, Trade and Spectator Facilities believed the proposal was dead in the water. That left three options for the convention center: Lloyd Center property, the South Waterfront, and property near Memorial Coliseum. Even without the ownership issue, there was also a cost gap, with the Lloyd Center property on Holladay Street and Union Avenue (now

Martin Luther King, Jr. Boulevard) coming in $17.6 million lower than the Union Station estimate.

The displacement of tenants from Memorial Coliseum—the Trailblazers and Winterhawks—removed that site from serious contention, and most considered it a lock for the Holladay-Union property. But right before the vote on the convention center location, the reluctant railroads gave PDC an eighteen-month option to buy the station for $18 million, "a very definite 180-degree change of position," the *Oregonian* reported. Bill, "more than anybody," according to Metro's executive officer Rick Gustafson, was responsible for getting the railroads to sell. It was trademark Bill, Gustafson remembered, "a classic case of hanging in there and continuing to drill on them until the last minute." What happened to the area around Union Station mattered to him, and the convention center proposal was part of his argument that the northern Old Town area needed a master plan with a convention center as its southern anchor. Its companion to the north could be the old Centennial Mills property along the waterfront. With that, Bill envisioned a Portland version of San Francisco's Ghirardelli Square. But when Lloyd Center Inc. said the city could have almost a third of the property for the convention center at no cost (a value of $3 million), the committee voted to accept the offer.

PDC exercised its option to purchase Union Station anyway, and Bill and PDC chair Don Magnusen wrote an op-ed in support of a comprehensive redevelopment of Union Station and the surrounding area, advocating for an extension of the transit mall with available federal funds. They also wanted to increase density in the area, especially around the station, and called for social services to remain a presence in the neighborhood. Bill also thought Union Station would be a good location for a rail museum and could become a transportation hub like Union Station in Washington, DC. It was part of his expansive view of Portland's future. But nothing happened to those proposals until 1992, when a consortium of private business owners, bankers, and developers presented a billion-dollar, twenty-year plan to develop the area to bolster Old Town's image. The group realized it needed to broaden the scope, and Bill agreed, believing that Old Town would benefit from any development that happened around it. Six months later, the group presented its ideas to the city council, which put forward funds to prepare a master plan for the newly established River District. The group raised a matching $500,000, and Greg Baldwin was hired to craft the plan. The River District name was intended to highlight the benefits of the area's proximity to the Willamette rather than industrial areas.

"Here's a grand opportunity," Bill said at the time, "of giving a planner or architect a blank sheet of paper." In the original design for the River District, streets ended at the river, creating a series of basins, and water taxis ferried people downstream. The historic trolley line would be extended and become the primary mode of public transportation, and several streets would be turned into pedestrian walkways. Union Station would be remodeled to include housing, conference rooms, and a restaurant. Port of Portland's Terminal 1 would be redeveloped into mixed-use housing, and Bill had an idea for transforming the Centennial Mills building into a conservatory and butterfly museum. But, as with Bill's grander ideas, it was hard to find funding in the City of Portland.

Another ambitious idea that he strove for was another world's fair, either in 2005—the centennial of Portland's first one—or in 1992, the bicentennial of Captain Robert Gray's entrance into the Columbia River. Instead of investing millions of dollars in constructing new buildings, as was often the case with world's fairs, Bill suggested that Pacific Rim countries and others anchor large boats along the waterfront. "It's about time we had a big, big party and celebration," he declared in 1987. While a preliminary report was adopted by the city council, the idea went nowhere after that. But whether an idea succeeded or failed, Bill was persistent, exuding optimism and a love of history to press for it. Consultant Karen Whitman described him as having the ability to put form around an idea, to be tenacious in how he moved it forward and persistent in holding onto the values surrounding it. And that was how he often made things happen. When Bill heard the word "no," he didn't hear a final rejection but a need for a better explanation for why someone should have said "yes." Even when he wasn't successful, he was content to know that he had planted seeds that opened minds.

His persistence is exemplified in the long road he took to get trolleys back on Portland streets. The city's first trolleys had been mule-drawn hand-me-downs from San Francisco, but fewer than twenty years later, in 1893, Portland became the first city in the west to have electric trolleys. Tracks were laid along First Avenue through downtown and Old Town, and trolleys became the primary mode of transportation for many Portlanders. Bill had strong memories of trolleys. His first experience with racism was on a streetcar when he was eight years old and white passengers deliberately avoided the open seat next to him. The trolley was how he got home on the day he was forced to clear out his locker at Washington High School because of Executive Order 9066. But he also had wonderful memories of using the streetcar to get around Portland as a boy. By the time Bill moved home to Portland in 1953, the trolleys had stopped running and the tracks had been covered with pavement to make way for cars.

Twenty years later, Bill Failing, whose family lineage reached back to the beginning of Oregon Territory, cofounded Willamette Traction to find a way to bring trolleys back to the city. It was a way to show pride in and promote Oregon's heritage, he thought, and to showcase Portland's current success. When Failing first spoke to Bill about the idea in 1972, Bill's reaction was a glazed-over look. But when Failing returned with a rendering of a trolley running under the Burnside Bridge along First Avenue, Bill was sold. They joined the Downtown Trolley Task Force and often walked together from City Hall to Old Town, sharing their visions of Portland's future. Bill ceaselessly advocated for Portland trolleys for seventeen years, never missing an opportunity to talk up the idea. City council member Charlie Hales said there were "all kinds of good reasons not" to have a vintage trolley, but they didn't matter because of Bill's passionate resolve for it.

Part of the reason for Bill's eventual victory was his early success in advocating for light rail to connect downtown with Portland neighborhoods and suburbs. That had been an uphill battle. In 1975, there seemed a chance when the city received a federal transportation grant of $150,000, earmarked for Old Town improvements. The grant required a realizable project by June 1976, a tight turnaround for a municipal project that required a lot more than $150,000 to complete. Subscriptions could be sold to property owners along the route to drum up funding, Bill argued, and even the creation of just 200 feet of track and a trolley park would get enough public support to force city council to find the rest of the money. But there simply wasn't the funding or political will.

Sometime later, Bill called Roger Shiels and said, "I can either buy a Mercedes or four trolley cars from Portugal." Shiels suggested he buy the Mercedes, but it was trolleys that were shipped from Lisbon — six American-made trolley cars worth about $175,000. Part of the urgency was that the revolution in Portugal in 1974 could cut down on the number of vintage trolleys available. Bill also bought a 1920s Birney-style Australian trolley, which he kept on display in an alley in Old Town until it was destroyed by arson in 1981.[2]

Bill always said that his forte was adaptive use, which was true, but his true talent was shameless persistence. The executive director of the Association for Portland Progress, Bill Wyatt, described the creation of a vintage trolley line as "Bill Naito making it happen through the force of his will." If he didn't hear what he wanted at the first asking, he just kept asking. He also believed in forging ahead to the extent you can, making a project appear to have momentum. He understood the politics of the situation, and that's what prompted him to buy those trolleys in the first place. He was a "marketing genius" who saw the value in having trolleys to display, US representative Earl Blumenauer explained. By getting people to make the historical connection and get excited about the idea of vintage trolleys, TriMet would be the bad guy if it said no.

Portland's light rail — known as Metropolitan Area Express, or MAX — was approved in 1978, but it would take several years for the details and funding to solidify. Part of the plan required an agreement between the Portland Historic Landmarks Commission and TriMet to operate in the Skidmore/Old Town Historic District. There were concerns that the streamlined, modern look of the MAX trains would clash with the historic appearance of the neighborhood. When vintage trolleys were suggested as a form of mitigation, Bill seized the opportunity and went to Rick Gustafson at Metro. Gustafson was big on transit and had worked at TriMet, helping to plan the transit mall on Fifth Avenue. He arranged a lunch meeting with representatives

---

2 Birney trolleys were the first mass-produced trolleys in the United States, made to be economic commuter cars.

of TriMet and the Lloyd Center mall to talk about a trolley running
to the east side of the river and connecting the mall to the downtown
core. Bill thought that was a great idea.

By agreeing to allow trolleys to run along the MAX line, TriMet
secured an agreement from the Portland Historic Landmarks Commission that the new line would have no adverse effect on the Yamhill
Historic District. That meant TriMet could avoid costly environmental
impact studies that would have delayed the project by several months.
In September 1986, when the first MAX lines opened, Vintage Trolley Inc., with Bill as president, received a two million dollar grant
from the Urban Mass Transit Administration. It came courtesy of
lobbying by Senator Mark O. Hatfield, who had worked on multiple
projects with Bill over the years. At the opening celebration of the
first light-rail route in Portland, Hatfield cornered a UMTA official
and kept him from going on stage until he agreed to fund the vintage
trolley. Gustafson remembered that it took Hatfield "half an hour to
convince the UMTA director of the importance of the Vintage Trolley
grant to the future of the national transportation system."

Dick Schmidt and Vic Rhodes in the city's Office of Transportation managed to get another million dollars by diverting lighting
district money to the project. TriMet had agreed to pay for the lighting on Morrison Street and gave the unused money to the Vintage
Trolley endowment. Additional funding came from one of the first
local improvement districts in Portland, in which a tax was assessed
on all businesses fronting the trolley's route. The money covered the
cost of tracks, the overhead wire system, a maintenance facility, and
other necessary changes to the existing light-rail system. The city
had hired Roger Shiels to form a local improvement district, which
required agreement from 51 percent of affected property owners, but
Bob Bouneff, who owned Ike and Tina's bar and other properties on
the east side of the line, refused to sign on. At Shiels's suggestion, Bill
promised to pay the assessment on Bouneff's behalf, between $3,000
and $5,000. Despite his frugality, Bill supported every local improve-
ment district that came his way, from the Convention Center to the
Yamhill Historic District. In this case, it turned out that 52 percent of
property owners along the trolley line approved the district and that
Bouneff's support was not needed.

While the Portuguese trolleys that Bill bought fit on the tracks, they were not viable. Without steel frames, TriMet would not allow them on the line because of potential collisions with MAX cars, which would decimate the wooden trolleys. Despite the financial investment that Bill had made, he readily put the trolleys aside. He could always turn them into pizza parlors or hot dog stands, he joked, or run them along Montgomery Park's old rail lines into the building, where he would open a restaurant. Ultimately, he put them on display outside Montgomery Park, adding a green double-decker trolley car from the Vancouver, BC, Expo 86. It had been relatively cheap at auction and was visually interesting, with a bold color and Chinese advertisements. By 1989, he was claiming that he was considering a streetcar museum. It was around this time that Bill was pushing for the redevelopment of Union Station, and he likely kept the trolleys in the hope of having some use for them there.

But where to find vintage trolleys with steel frames for the light-rail line? He finally found GOMACO, a company in Ida Grove, Iowa, that manufactured highway paving equipment and made trolleys in its down time. TriMet had paid consultants $600,000 to come up with a detailed list of specifications for the cars, and GOMACO said each car would cost $800,000 to meet them. With a budget of only $2.5 million, the outlook wasn't promising.[3] But Gary Godbertson, who ran GOMACO, told TriMet and Vintage Trolley that his company could make them for half as much if TriMet's onerous specs were removed. Bill agreed and worked to get TriMet's approval. Once that was obtained, Vintage Trolley could order two trolleys immediately, but it needed two more to make the service work. The Vintage Trolley needed a negotiator to persuade Godbertson to lower the price further.

The board persuaded Bill to go to Iowa with Gustafson and Shiels. Negotiations took place over drinks in the Speakeasy, Godbertson's bar, with numbers being traded back and forth on pieces of paper. Bill held out until Godbertson finally agreed to make two more cars for $395,000, but only if they were ordered within ninety days. Vintage

---

3 Some thought that TriMet's unspoken goal had been to prevent the trolleys from getting on the tracks by making it financially impossible.

Bill at the Vintage Trolley grand opening, November 1991

Trolley didn't have the money, of course. But as a longtime ally and advocate for public transportation, Bill persuaded Bruce Harder, Tri-Met's finance director, to pay for the cars with a promise that Vintage Trolley would pay it back. Harder even gave Vintage Trolley the title to the cars prior to repayment. Bill was never shy about asking for money for causes he loved, even though he loathed being a donor himself.

Using a model of a trolley, Bill persuaded US Bank to sponsor a car for $100,000 as a way to draw attention to its hundredth-year anniversary. Lloyd Center came on board as a second corporate sponsor. The third took more guile. Portland General Electric was experiencing financial difficulties at the time, and despite being a supporter of the idea, board member Gerry Frank told Bill that the company would never be a sponsor. Undeterred, Bill went to PGE's advertising department and asked for $20,000 for each of the next five years for marketing. The amount did not require corporate approval, and Vintage Trolley got its money.

GOMACO's trolleys, pale yellow with red accents and gray-lined roofs, were replicas of the cars that had traveled to Portland's Council Crest from 1904 to 1950. Wooden doors admitted passengers at the front and back, and large oak-lined windows allowed for views of the city as the trolley moved along. TriMet agreed to run the trolleys on Saturdays and Sundays year-round. Passengers rode for free, with a suggested donation of a dollar. On every ride, volunteers acted as hosts and conductors, pointing out historic points of interest along the way. During the inaugural ride in 1991, Bill, sporting a conductor's cap, proudly showed off his "new family car" in the company of Gerry Frank and Portland Trailblazer Maurice Lucas. Bill would later relish seeing children laughing and enjoying a ride on a trolley through his beloved Old Town. "That's the quality of life we want for the city," he said.

DOWNTOWN PORTLAND

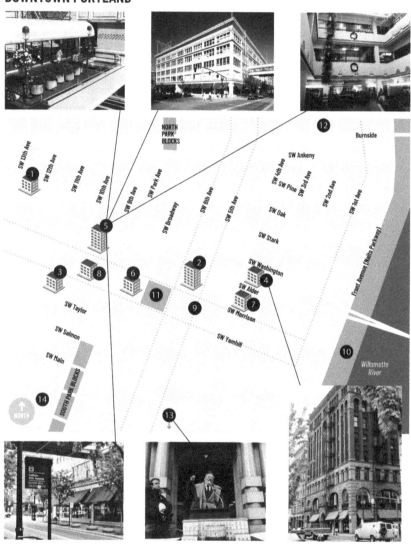

1. H. Naito Gifts
2. Meier & Frank Department Store
3. Multnomah County Central Library
4. Dekum Building
5. Galleria
6. Nordstrom
7. Park East
8. Park West
10. Waterfront Park
11. Pioneer Square
12. Old Town
13. City Hall
14. Portland Art Museum

..... Light Rail

▨ Parks

CHAPTER 14

Successes in preserving and promoting Old Town, coupled with the Downtown Plan and the rebirth of Portland, resulted in the Naitos' first large-scale renovation. Flush with cash earned from wholesale and retail successes and fervent penny-pinching, the company had bought distressed properties in Old Town to shelter its tax liability and stabilize cash flow. No one believed Old Town buildings were worth much, so buying many of them wasn't groundbreaking. But the Rhodes Department Store building was a different matter. It was the first high-profile real estate project for Norcrest, and the purchase elevated the Naito name in the public consciousness.

For fourteen months in the early 1970s, the stately building had been sitting vacant on the block between Ninth and Tenth Avenues and Morrison and Alder Streets. Bill had childhood memories of the 1910 building, which had been designed for Olds, Wortman & King by Charles Aldrich in the Twentieth-Century Commercial style, with help from A. E. Doyle. The building had five floors of terra cotta tile exterior on a steel frame. Inside, a grand stairway to the second floor was bathed in natural light from a 33-by-53-foot skylight. Sam remembered Fukiye taking him to the restaurant in the basement of the building: "I recall vividly the sparkling marble floor, the iron cage elevators with the neatly uniformed operators . . . the lush atrium." By 1925, Olds, Wortman & King was the largest department store in Washington and Oregon and the epitome of class, where floorwalkers had flowers in their lapels and customers rested their elbows on plush red pillows while trying on gloves. A remodel by Portland architect Pietro Belluschi in 1947 closed up the atrium with a false ceiling and removed the central stairway, replacing it with escalators to the third floor—changes intended to make Olds, Wortman & King one of the most modern department stores in the west. The name of the company was changed to Rhodes in 1960.

In 1973, when Mayor Goldschmidt and banker Bob Ames approached Marriott Hotels about opening a new hotel in the city, they were met with a blunt assessment: the downtown area was busy only five days a week. Goldschmidt couldn't disagree. "You could roll a bowling ball through downtown on Saturday or Sunday, and you wouldn't hit anybody," he remembered. The president of the Meier & Frank department store, Ed Steidle, went further: "A national retailer wouldn't touch downtown Portland with a ten-foot pole!" When Rhodes closed the next year, it was considered "a great defeat" and triggered fears that Meier & Frank on Fifth Avenue might be next. There was good reason to worry. Lloyd Center mall, which had opened in 1960, had siphoned off retail business in the downtown core. In fact, Naito Gifts had been one of the inaugural shops at the mall, a statement location designed by George Guins with slate floors, a large stone column made of Montana travertine, and a pond with a revolving fountain.

By the early 1970s, Lloyd Center was the place to shop, and downtown was the place to work. Then Washington Square mall opened in 1973, siphoning off more downtown shoppers to its upscale shopping mecca in the western suburbs. Downtown merchants struggled to attract customers against the lure of the malls. Some believed that the Naito brothers took a foolhardy gamble in 1976 when they bought the Rhodes building for $565,000. Valued at a million dollars, it was costing Rhodes $10,000 a month to sit vacant, and there were no other offers. But even at a bargain price, buying the building was a risk—the nation was in the midst of a recession and investment had largely dried up—but for Bill and Sam the building was a diamond in the rough waiting for the right owners.

Albert R. Bullier, whose firm brokered the sale, characterized it as "a matter of finding someone with faith in the future of downtown Portland." The Naitos could see that the Downtown Plan and the planned transit mall on Fifth Avenue made the building an important part of renewing the city's downtown. And without a healthy downtown, Bill often said, Old Town—the main area of their real estate interests—could not survive. Equally as important, Bill and

Sam knew the west end. As Bill put it, they had "seen change" in the neighborhood and "weren't afraid of it."

Bill and Mayor Goldschmidt had become allies in promoting downtown, with the mayor creating the bureaucratic environment—and the freedom—that allowed Bill to make progress in the private sector. The two men went to Seattle to pitch the Rhodes building to Nordstrom, a department store chain that already had stores in Washington Square and Lloyd Center. Downtown Portland could offer what shopping malls couldn't, they told Nordstrom executives: "the library, the professional people, the large department stores. All the buses run downtown." Nordstrom had no intention of putting a store in downtown, but Goldschmidt "shamed" them into it, the *Oregonian* reported. In the end, Nordstrom decided to construct its own building on Sixth Avenue and Morrison, the first new retail space in downtown Portland in fifty years. Goldschmidt later said he believed that part of the reason Nordstrom made the investment was because they knew "Bill would be there" reviving the downtown with them.

Three buildings were razed to make room for the new Nordstrom block: the Royal, the Orpheum, and the Simon. There was some dismay over their demolition, as both the Royal and Orpheum held significant Portland history, but Nordstrom wanted a block-sized building and the location on Broadway Avenue was ideal. Originally known as the Tull & Gibbs building, the quarter block was renamed the Royal in 1911. As time passed, it became the center of the city's clothing sales and manufacturing industry for decades. It was known as the Seventh Avenue of Portland, a comparison to New York City's Seventh Avenue garment district, and housed almost fifty clothing manufacturer reps who sold most of the women's and children's apparel in Oregon. As Bill told a group of city planners several years later, "You have to be flexible and innovative. If one old frame house is standing in the way of bringing in a major department store such as Nordstrom, surely you can do something. There are exceptions."

A few blocks west, in the old Rhodes building, the Naitos recreated their success in Old Town by encouraging small stores and professionals to populate one of the first vertical malls in America. They named it the Galleria. Forty-two local retail shops occupied the first three floors, with offices on the fourth and fifth floors. Bill and

Sam hired Colburn, Sheldon, and Partners and told them to create a
unique design for the space. Bill's stated goal was to preserve the "1900
flavor" of the building while creating spaces that gave tenants "broad
latitude in choosing their own motifs." The architects gave them a
design that had the look and feel of a European open marketplace.

But when Bing Sheldon suggested that the skylight be reopened,
Bill snapped at the idea. "Look, son, I pay architects to make space,
not take it away." It was one of the few times Sheldon could remember that Bill was short with him. Then the city notified the Naitos that
expensive structural upgrades were required to meet building codes,
which had changed dramatically in the sixty-five years since the building was constructed. If the weight of the building was lessened, however, the upgrades would be unnecessary. Removing the false ceiling
and opening up the center of the building would accomplish just that.
So, the false ceiling was removed, and the skylight was reopened. The
building's interior was flooded with natural light, ducts and overhead
lights were left exposed, and three-story escalators operated in the
center space where ferns hung overhead. There was no building like
it in Portland.

The cost of the renovation was $3.2 million, borne largely
by Norcrest. The "recycling" of the building, as Bill called it, was
accomplished by P&C Construction. To reach the Galleria bid, Don
Campbell of P&C and Bill walked through the building and wrote
numbers on the back of their business cards: Bill wrote $1 million,
Campbell $1.3 million. When Bill asked if P&C could do it for a
million, Campbell replied that he would try, and that was good
enough. Sam described the recycling as a twofold benefit—saving the
original materials and saving materials that would have been needed
if the building had been torn down. Sam also emphasized how much
energy, natural resources, and effort were saved by fixing up the original building rather than constructing a new one.

More than sixty-five clothing manufacturers moved into space on
the Galleria's upper floors, many of them displaced by Nordstrom's
demolition of the Royal building. Dubbed the Portland Mart, it was
the city's first centralized wholesale clothing market, with more than
150 sales representatives and ninety independent showrooms representing three hundred clothing lines. They took up 70 percent of the

fourth and fifth floors and provided stabilizing income. Professionals and nonprofit organizations filled in the rest of the office spaces, creating a constituency for the shops and restaurants below. Each space on the three retail floors had partition walls that stopped short of the ceiling, allowing conversations and sounds from one store to filter into those next door, much like an open-air market. The first floor resembled a plaza, with trees, benches, streetlamps, fountains, and sidewalk-style cafes. Musical entertainment and community events helped create atmosphere.

To everyone's surprise, the Galleria opened with 100 percent of its space leased. The retail stores were locally owned, paying rents below shopping-mall rates and in spaces small enough that they didn't need a lot of startup capital or employees. Paper Parlor featured handmade cards and stationery, and Chown Showcase sold specialty hardware and interior design pieces. Jarring Note sold jars, bottles, and containers, while Cookery sold pots, pans, and gourmet ceramics. Surprise Package offered music boxes, and Sensuous She sold lingerie. Coffee Ritz was the second-floor meeting place for young professionals in the offices above.

The Galleria represented opportunity. Josephine's Dry Goods was one of the stores that benefited from the Naitos' help in the Galleria that inaugural year. "Without your faith in novice entrepreneurs," owners Judith Head and Bonnie Harris wrote Bill years later, "Josephine's Dry Goods might have never become a fabric store with a national reputation." There was also Galadriel's House Plants, the Toy Chest, Downtowner's Gallery, Jewelers Bench, and, of course, an Import Plaza. Pier 101, a seafood restaurant in Lincoln City where Bill and Micki had a beach house, opened on the first floor. Bill's older sons, Bob and Steve, opened their first business in the Galleria, Roberto's Ice Cream (originally named Gelati Roberto), with a large ground-floor window where passersby could watch gelato being made.

The grand opening of the Galleria in 1976 demonstrated how important the enterprise was to the community. Mayor Goldschmidt, jewelers Martin and Alan Zell, Bing Sheldon, and Bill headed a parade through downtown, followed by the Lincoln High School band, fire engines, and vintage cars, including an Olds, Wortman & King delivery truck named the Garford. Sam's and Bill's childhood stories of Olds, Wortman & King resonated with Portlanders, and several older women told Bill how happy they were to see the building come alive again. The Galleria announced how Portland's downtown was becoming attractive and interesting again. That night, Bing Sheldon and Bill looked out over the atrium from the third floor. "This is the first time I've realized what this is all about," Bill told him. Sheldon later remembered being shocked that Bill had taken such a risk without a clear vision of the outcome, but Bill had trusted that the professionals he worked with would deliver even if the outcome wasn't clear to him at the time.

Journalist Maggi White described the scene a little over a month after the Galleria opened: "All these people, the hustle bustle, the hum of activity, the organist playing, the restaurants full, people eating ice cream, and a mailman drinking coffee and watching people go by." In order to attract office workers in the downtown core, the Naitos instituted a groundbreaking schedule, staying open on Sunday afternoons and until nine at night on weekdays. The demand for space was so strong that Norcrest contemplated turning the underground garage into more market space. The next year, the Galleria won a national award from the Downtown Research and Development Center of New York. Sam gave credit to "the citizens of Portland who supported us."

To say that the Galleria was a success for Norcrest China would be an understatement. "For the first time since Lloyd Center opened some 17 years ago," Bill beamed in 1977, "we have the lowest retail rate in the center city." A little over a year later, only 1 percent of retail space downtown was vacant, despite a 93 percent increase in available square footage. Pete Mark, president of the Building Owners and Managers Association, called it a "modern renaissance." Between 1970 and 1976, $5.2 million was invested in rehabilitating Portland's commercial buildings; between 1977 and 1986, that number rose to $217 million. The numbers rose from $20 million to $437 million for public buildings and improvements during the same time period.

In 1982, Bill Naito and Louis Scherzer, working with Ruth Scott, established the Oregon Downtown Development Association (ODDA, later Livable Oregon) to support central business districts throughout the state. The organization was intended to prevent residents from fleeing to the suburbs and to reinvigorate city centers by taking advantage of the Main Street America program, which focused on the revitalization of historic commercial districts. Scott was a city planner in Albany, a small city in the mid-Willamette Valley, and the National Trust for Historic Preservation had approached her to get the Main Street program started in Oregon. She needed funding, and the trust directed her to Bill, who was on its board. He was the first business leader to tell Scott that he would support the program not only verbally but also financially. "Frankly," she said later, "if he hadn't given me that thousand dollars, I think I would've given up, because I hadn't done fundraising before. . . . His encouragement was just essential." Banker Louis Scherzer, who chaired the Portland Development Commission in the late 1970s, helped craft the fundraising plan. In its first six years, ODDA's work resulted in almost a thousand new businesses in downtowns in Albany, Grants Pass, Hillsboro, La Grande, and Astoria and the renovation or construction of more than six hundred commercial buildings. Oregon was the first state organization in the nation to create a nonprofit private-public partnership. One of his significant contributions was his retail recruitment seminars, which were offered through ODDA to Main Street managers—skills he honed in Old Town and with the Galleria.

More than a decade after the Galleria opened, Wally Hobson, an industry analyst, concluded that "Bill Naito is intuitively a genius at putting things together. The key with the Galleria was he bought a building at a very good price and made creative changes in the structure." But the Galleria also represented something personal. Hide Naito had been banned from owning one inch of property in the city, and his sons now owned an entire city block. "It does kind of make me smile," Bill admitted. To own a building that was a part of his childhood, which had been taken away by the exclusion order during the war, had been a significant motivation for him. The opening of the Galleria also signified his realization that complicated, creative real estate developments were where his mind and pocketbook could thrive. It was his most significant accomplishment to date, and the success would lead Bruce Nordstrom to refer to him as *the* Bill Naito as his public notoriety grew.

Micki and Bill, 1980s

But Bill always told people that it was his most significant *business* accomplishment. His greatest achievement was marrying Micki, who he said he would be "sort of lost without." She was a steadfast presence that gave him the freedom to chase his dreams. "She encourages me." he said. "Without a good wife, it is hard to get things done. You have to have the right frame of mind to take on risk." The Galleria couldn't have existed without her. For Bill, their marriage was proof that business success was tied to marital success. For during all the countless hours he spent working, Micki was at home, raising their children and keeping a space for him to feel secure in himself.

And it was clear to him that society needed married people with children to achieve any greatness. Once, when Michael Burgess was at the Norcrest offices interviewing Bill for *Metro: The City* magazine, a warehouseman interrupted them to talk about Albers Mill, the company's latest historic renovation. Inevitably, Bill asked the employee about his personal life, and the man admitted to being in divorce proceedings. Burgess quoted Bill's response after the employee told him he had tried to make it work: "Try some more. You can't have everything in a marriage, but on the whole it's a plus. Take the plusses and the minuses and you come out ahead with marriage. . . . Don't let pride get in the way. It's hubris. Pride will kill you . . . especially men. Pride and men . . . that's probably why we have so many bloody wars. Swallow some pride, that's just my humble opinion. . . . Look at happier days. . . . Give her a break, give her the benefit of the doubt." Then he added, with typical wit: "It's cheaper to see a marriage counselor than a lawyer."

Bill was speaking as someone who wasn't the easiest person to be married to. That he worked such long hours was Micki's only strong objection over the years. "He works all the time," she complained in an interview with Oregon Public Broadcasting in 1985. "If he's not working, he's thinking about work. I think he dreams about work." Bill admitted that same year to the *Oregonian* that Sundays were difficult for him: "There's nothing to do. I can't wait to get back to work and get going again." His schedule meant that the couple often forgot to celebrate their wedding anniversary in November, in the middle of finishing wholesale orders for the year and bulking up retail inventory for the holidays. Micki had begrudgingly accepted that he needed to do this, for his business and Old Town and the city, in order to exist—it had become fundamental to his happiness, and she didn't challenge it.

Bill, on the other hand, challenged her desire to return to work in the late 1970s, when her children were grown and the Galleria was in need of a part-time special events manager. But she felt that "if I wasn't working in the company, I wasn't even part of the family." (All of their children worked in the business at some point.) And she could be just as stubborn as he could, so he relented. Originally, she was paid minimum wage, $2.65 an hour, but Bill complained about having to pay social security taxes on her income. So, for twelve years, she worked without pay, eventually becoming the building's full-time manager. She enjoyed working with the charities with offices on the fourth and fifth floors, especially the Oregon Peace Institute, and she acted as an adviser to all of the tenants of the building, many of whom were first-time business owners. Part of the arrangement with Bill was that dinner would always be ready when he came home, which it was.

Competing with the family business was frustrating, but so was his iconoclastic attitude, which made for some embarrassing moments. From being chronically late and his style of dress to his extreme parsimony and rebellious attitude toward social mores, he did not look or act like a typical businessman. He had a penchant for falling asleep and loudly snoring at the symphony and the theatre, both of which they held season tickets to. On occasion, when Micki made him leave because she couldn't stand the embarrassment any longer, he could be found in the lobby, sleeping on a chair or bench. She often had to fight for him to spend money on things that most would consider standard for an upper-middle-class lifestyle, but he knew the wholesale cost of most goods. Norcrest was the biggest source for her home furnishings and décor. But for all his faults, that was Bill—her Bill. And their union allowed him to be Portland's Bill, too.

CHAPTER 15

The changes in downtown Portland corresponded with a renewed focus on public transportation. Transit projects were always on Bill's to-do list. If you got fewer people to drive, he argued, there would be less need for parking or parking lots. And it would be more likely that people would want to explore a walking district like Old Town, which would lead to fewer historic buildings being razed. Bill also supported transit projects because he was cheap. Unlike buildings, which appreciated in value over time, cars depreciated the moment they were driven off the lot. That was one reason he rode an old Schwinn bike—"a piece of crap," as he called it—and recommended that others do the same. Andy Raubesen, director of the Burnside Consortium (now Central City Concern), described Bill's pitch: riding an old bike is "sensible transportation; after a while someone will steal it, but it cost so little that all you have to do is buy another."

As early as 1973, Bill was advocating for shuttle trains to make five-mile runs from Union Station in Old Town to downtown along Harbor Drive. From there, he argued, the shuttles could continue eleven more miles to John's Landing, a retail and office complex near the waterfront in southwest Portland. The Portland Development Commission could buy up a dozen blocks around Union Station for a parking center and eliminate all parking lots from the downtown core. Trolleys could use existing tracks on those streets, and the waterfront could be developed into a tourist attraction. The idea for the shuttle didn't fly. Politicians and business leaders were concerned that people would be unwilling to walk or ride that distance, and the point of the 1972 Downtown Plan was to draw people to downtown, not to push them away. Besides, most Portlanders were attached to their cars, and convenience and close proximity to a destination were critical to patrons of stores and shops.

But the love affair with cars meant that air pollution had become a serious concern in the city, with air quality levels violating federal health standards one out of every three days in 1972. A livable city had to have clean air, and that had been one of the reasons for creating the Downtown Plan. So, in 1974, ground was broken on a transit mall, ten blocks on Fifth and Sixth Avenues that would serve as the hub of Portland's bus service, known as TriMet (Tri-County Metropolitan Transit District). At the time, only 22 percent of people traveled to downtown on public buses, but the hope was to double that number by attracting people with pleasing bus shelters, information kiosks, and works of art. The city borrowed the idea from Minneapolis, where architect Lewis Crutcher had escaped Portland's bureaucratic intransigence to run the city's parks bureau.

Most of the arguments against creating the transit mall came from businesses that feared they could not withstand the two years of construction necessary to complete it. As Downtown Plan manager Bob Baldwin explained, even stores with downtown locations had bigger and better stores in the Lloyd Center, on the east side of the Willamette River. "Everybody was scared," he remembered. "Yeah, there was real panic." Then there were others who found the idea of closing two primary downtown streets for so long to be inherently ludicrous and foolhardy. But Bill wasn't worried. He was looking ahead to the long-term benefits of a healthy bus system that would encourage pedestrians to explore downtown and put less demand on parking spaces. If livability was the goal, then there had to be less traffic and extensive, accessible public transportation. To ease the disruption caused by the construction, Norcrest purchased a London double-decker bus that shuttled customers around downtown and invited riders with a sign that read, "Follow Me to Old Town."

A vital aspect of the transit mall was the placement of shade trees on the sidewalk, intended to mitigate the presence of buses and to make those blocks more pedestrian friendly. Bill and TriMet chair Bill Roberts, who shared a desire to make the city more beautiful and prosperous, pushed hard to plant London planetrees, a type of syca-more, along the transit mall. Many opposed the fast-growing trees. In 1976, both Lloyd Center and Seattle had to remove planetrees because their roots routinely broke through sidewalks. Using them on the mall would cost tens of thousands of dollars to dig into more than thirty basement extensions to prepare for the trees' disruptive root systems.

But Roberts wanted trees that would grow quickly and give the mall an established appearance faster than other trees could, and Bill believed the planetree was "the most beautiful street tree nature has produced." Using anything less, he said, would be like putting a "beat up spoon" on a "nice table setting." The city forester didn't want them, but both Bills were adamant. The result was a rancorous fight, with Bill, as chair of the Urban Forestry Commission, tipping the result in Roberts's favor. The relative unpopularity of the mall was one reason why Bill pushed so hard for London planetrees, which he believed would help get public buy-in. It was a trade-off, he argued, between paying maintenance costs in the future and selling the public on the mall now. In the end, the money was spent, and the planetrees were planted.

The transit mall opened to accolades in September 1977, accomplishing the city's goal "to speed service, facilitate transfers, and tie together downtown through efficient but pedestrian-friendly design." The opening celebration was called Artquake, named after the seventeen works of art the city had installed along the transit mall. It was the brainchild of Karen Whitman, who had been charged with creating a grand opening. Early on, she had met with Bill because someone suggested that he could help gain support from the business community. She recruited him to chair the event, and he was involved in every aspect of the planning, which took more than nine months to prepare and required over five hundred volunteers.

Eleven downtown blocks were given over to Artquake, with seven performance stages for seventy-three acts and dozens of booths for a hundred artists and fifty artisans. Twenty downtown restaurants sold food, and there were multiple beer and wine gardens. Entry was free, and the costs were covered by the city, the Multnomah County Metropolitan Arts Commission, private donors, and participating merchants. TriMet offered free rides, and there was a ban on parking in the area. The festival drew 100,000 people; many of them hadn't been in downtown Portland for years.

Artquake was Portland at its best: a public-private endeavor, "like a village barn-raising," Bill said. The traffic department stayed until two in the morning to help clean up, and volunteers used borrowed brooms to sweep each block. Bill worked through the night before the event to help with setup and, the next night, the massive cleanup. Whitman remembered him asking for a knife to scrape gum off of the street. When she replied that it wasn't their mess, he said, "If we don't give it back clean, they won't let us do it again." In Artquake's second year, for which Bill was also chair, a half million people showed up over the festival's three days. By the third Artquake, some food vendors were running out of food and thousands of people wanted to continue their fun at closing time.

The first Artquake on the transit mall had been a celebration of the bus system, but thereafter many considered it a disruption, with delayed buses and confused passengers. TriMet and the Police Bureau wanted the festival moved to Waterfront Park, but Bill argued against the move. Artquake was a celebration of downtown, he said, and to move it off the transit mall would make it too much like Neighborfair, an annual event on the waterfront. Besides, without disruptions, people wouldn't think Artquake was a big deal, and a twenty-minute delay was a small price to pay for the arts. He prevailed. In 1980, he was named director emeritus. The festival took place almost every year until 1995.

Mayors and officials from throughout the country came to Portland to learn from its transit mall, and the new system was touted in *Woman's Day* magazine and the *New York Times*. Vice President Walter Mondale visited the city in 1977, and Bill took the vice-president's wife, Joan Mondale, on a tour of the mall and Old Town. He also got city council to name the transit mall in honor of Bill Roberts in 1991, when car traffic remained at 1972 levels and 43 percent of commuters were riding the buses. Sometime later, when TriMet asked Bill if the Bill Roberts Transit Mall could be referred to as, simply, the transit mall in its customer information, Bill replied: "The transit mall is a sanctuary. It can only be changed by God."

The transit mall set the stage for Pioneer Courthouse Square, on Sixth Avenue between Morrison and Yamhill Streets. The block, which had been the site of the Portland Hotel, had been slated for a behemoth of a parking garage, but in 1979 Mayor Goldschmidt persuaded the block's owner, Meier & Frank, to sell it so the city could create a plaza. Pioneer Courthouse Square would finally address one of Lewis Crutcher's most damning critiques of Portland: "Every city needs a heart, a place where things happen, an identification point. . . . Europe has parks and squares, Portland a parking lot."

The design process was contentious, with most businesses arguing for a plaza that was enclosed to keep out homeless people. But Goldschmidt knew it was important to purchase the block while he had Meier & Frank on his side,[1] and he had secured a US Department of Interior land and conservation grant for an urban park. That meant it had to be an open design. A national design competition in 1980 was won by a local group led by architect Will Martin, and a detailed plan was drawn up under Mayor Connie McCready, who had replaced Goldschmidt in 1979.

By the time Martin's design was before the city council in 1980, Frank Ivancie was mayor, and he was concerned that transients and other "undesirables" would cause problems in an open downtown plaza. Ivancie was a formidable opponent, and he pressured Bill Roberts, then head of the Portland Development Commission, to scrap the open plaza plans. In truth, Roberts was already against the idea and needed little convincing about the dangers posed by an open square. He suggested that there was inadequate funding and that a temporary parking lot be placed on the space in the interim. His own idea was to build an aviary on the plaza, a proposal he argued for until the day of the city council vote.[2]

Commissioners Charles Jordan and Mike Lindberg organized Friends of Portland Square to advocate for Martin's plan, but their efforts weren't enough to persuade Ivancie. In the summer of 1981, Pat LaCrosse at PDC called Lindberg and told him the straight dope: if they couldn't raise $100,000 in ten days to show public support for the idea, the plan would be scrapped permanently. Lindberg called property developer John Gray, who liked the idea of the plaza but equally disliked Ivancie's tactics. He offered $50,000 for the project. Lindberg turned next to Bill Naito, who he remembered drawling

---

1 Meier & Frank ultimately donated $500,000 to the creation of the plaza.

2 He did secretly donate $50,000 for Pioneer Square's original fountain, which was publicly described as an anonymous donation.

out, in response to his ask, "Ahhhh, the people want this square. They want to play on this square. It's the right thing to do." Norcrest gave a guarantee of $50,000, which would be due should the organization fail to raise $250,000 by the end of the year. The agreement expressly stated that the guarantee was made in order "to induce the Portland Development Commission of the City of Portland, Oregon, to proceed with the Design Development and Construction Document phases of the Pioneer Square project."

With that kind of money and power behind them, Friends of the Portland Square prevailed over Ivancie, who finally felt enough public pressure to go through with Martin's original design. Roger Shiels was hired to manage the project, and PDC created a citizen's advisory committee to make recommendations on how to use the plaza. Bill was a member. A campaign to sell fifty thousand bricks for a tax-deductible $15 apiece began, with donors' names etched into the clay. Bill and Sam ultimately gave $20,000 to the effort after the terms of their guarantee were met. Ivancie helped find the $600,000 needed from the city to complete funding, declaring, "We're all part of a team now."

Portland's Living Room, as Pioneer Square came to be known, opened on April 6, 1984, Portland's 133rd birthday. A cascading fountain occupied the west side of the block, with office space behind it for TriMet. There was office space below the plaza and a glass pavilion for a restaurant above. To mollify the concerns of people like Ivancie, the square hosted events and programs year-round. As Pioneer Square Inc.'s first executive director, Molly O'Reilly, explained, "The nature of the square 'lends itself to intensive activity.'" In the end, everyone got what they wanted.

Pioneer Courthouse Square was built on the idea of downtown as pedestrian-friendly, and public transportation was a critical part of the plan. City Hall was never going to eliminate cars from downtown, but it could emphasize and encourage alternatives to cars. Beginning in 1975, TriMet instituted Fareless Square in the downtown core to encourage ridership, reduce air pollution, and reduce traffic. When Bill first proposed the idea, everyone thought "it was the dumbest idea," remembered entrepreneur Sam Brooks. Eliminating a source of funding for TriMet seemed imprudent. But in 1973 Seattle had created its own fare-free area, and Congress had passed a transit package that included $20 million to cities to experiment with fare-free areas. After a public hearing in July 1974 with TriMet and the Citizens Advisory Committee, of which Bill was a member, TriMet approved a fareless two-hundred-square-block area. It proved incredibly successful, increasing ridership and encouraging people to explore downtown. A decade later, TriMet was facing a $2 million budget shortfall and considered removing the program. Bill argued that the fareless zone contributed to the health and vitality of downtown and had a "therapeutic effect" on businesses. TriMet agreed to keep it in place.[3]

Transportation was a public good, Bill believed; the more it was used, the more society—and business—benefited. Public transportation should be free everywhere, subsidized by gas taxes, payroll taxes, parking taxes, or a combination of all three. "We don't charge people to use roads in Oregon," he argued. "Why should we charge them to ride a bus?" He championed relentlessly for a free system, never letting too much time pass before rapping on politicians' ears about it. The most TriMet would do was to announce Pollution Days, when all fares were free on days when air quality was predicted to be poor. Rick Williams, a member of the Association for Portland Progress, believed that they should have been known as Bill Naito Days in honor of the man who had advocated so tirelessly for them.

But Portland still remained in danger of breaching the "no growth" air pollution ceiling the city had established in 1974. The ceiling limited industrial growth but failed to improve the city's air quality. As chair of the Clean Air Alliance Committee, Bill advocated for smog alerts to encourage drivers to stay off the roads and bought over thirty bicycles, painted them yellow, and placed them around downtown for people to use. One antidote to unhealthy car attachment, Bill believed, came in 1986 with MAX, a fifteen-mile light-rail line. It had taken over a decade to get light rail into Portland, starting in 1973 with Mayor Goldschmidt requesting a survey of its potential use. Bill sat on the Downtown Plan's Citizens Advisory Committee that heard TriMet's ideas for light rail.

---

3 The fareless zone remained until 2012, when TriMet ended the program after thirty-seven years, saying that it cost $2.7 million a year and contributed to $1 to $2 million in losses from fare evasion.

One light-rail car carried the equivalent of six buses, and an argument for light rail was that it would reduce both labor costs and traffic. Because the cars were powered by electricity, pollution concerns would also be addressed. But many critics were concerned that light rail would be noisy and that its construction would displace homes and businesses without actually reducing traffic. Some members of the public considered it a boondoggle and suggested enlarging existing freeways instead. Supporters pointed to San Francisco, Buffalo, and Atlanta, which all had successful light-rail systems. As an added incentive, TriMet was facing a funding crisis, and light rail was seen as a way to significantly reduce its costs. The tide had turned in its favor.

After the Banfield Light Rail project was approved, a hearty debate began over the route through downtown. There were two options: on First Avenue through Old Town—the "cross-mall alignment"—or on the transit mall. The First Avenue route would create the least disruption to businesses in the short term and would be easiest to construct. The transit mall would be best in the long term, assuming that other light-rail lines would be built at a later date (this was despite the short-term cost of tearing up the recently completed mall). Bill fervently argued for the First Avenue route, while many of the city planners believed light rail should be placed on the mall to create a transit hub for the future. Bill bent any and every ear about how First Avenue was the most pragmatic choice and, thus, the better option. In the end, according to Portland Planning Bureau staff member Rodney O'Hiser, Mayor Goldschmidt "caved to Naito."

It may have seemed counterintuitive that Bill favored looping light rail through the Yamhill Historic District, which he had fought so hard to preserve. The Portland Historic Landmarks Commission opposed that route because it believed the streamlined look of MAX cars would detract from the historic ambiance of the district. It would mean adding overhead electric lines to downtown streets after years of efforts to eliminate them. And light-rail cars would add noise on their constant runs through the district. But these concerns led to a natural pivot toward vintage trolleys, which Landmarks believed would mitigate the "damage" caused by MAX's jarring modernity. In the end, Bill got everything he wanted—development in Old Town through light rail and vintage trolleys on its tracks. Portland got a solid foundation for its light-rail system and a tourist attraction.[4]

In 1994, when plans were being made to run a new MAX line along the transit mall, Bill argued against the plan. The line should run along Tenth and Eleventh Avenues, he argued, bringing new development and businesses to the neglected west end of downtown. He envisioned another successful revitalization, with trees, fountains, artwork, brick sidewalks, and new businesses. The new line could do for west downtown what the original line had done for Old Town, he argued, and construction on the transit mall would be like "dropping a bomb on Downtown Portland." But Bill also had a decidedly pecuniary interest in placing the line there: the Galleria would be at the intersection of south–north and westside lines. At the time, Pioneer Place mall, next to Pioneer Courthouse Square, had drained away most of the Galleria's retail businesses and customers. It was a vertical mall like the Galleria but a brand-new build, part of a $180 million development that included an office tower and parking garage. The Galleria had become an outlier. When all else failed, Bill resorted to hyperbole and threatened to stand in front of the bulldozers "like the student at Tiananmen Square" to prevent the placement of light rail there. Metro located the new line on the transit mall.[5]

As light rail expanded, transportation bonds appeared more often on November ballots. Bill always supported them. If they failed, he warned, "the cars are going to get us." He also understood that cars were not going to disappear and that parking was a large part of what made retail districts attractive to shoppers. That meant expanding parking in whatever way possible. In 1975, the city council had adopted a lid of 39,000 parking spaces to help curb air pollution and encourage people to use mass transit, but by 1980 Bill was arguing that the lid needed to be raised to fifty thousand. More people in the downtown core meant more cars, and they needed places to park. Otherwise, they would go back to the suburbs to do their shopping.

---

4 Placement of MAX on First Avenue made the Sunset Corridor extension easier to implement.

5 In 2001, however, the Portland Streetcar was placed along the track that Bill had championed.

But there were only so many parking garages and surface lots the city could have and still be livable. Street parking had physical limits, too, and Bill became obsessed with rotating the water outlets on fire hydrants to allow for additional parking spots. He had calculated the increased revenue to the city and determined the precise number of spaces that would be created. For Bill, it was a straightforward solution, and he pushed the idea for years. When he failed to find support, he altered his argument: How many fires were there every year, he asked, and how many times were fire hydrants used? What would be the cost to reimburse a car owner if firefighters had to break windows to attach hoses to a hydrant? His solution was obvious: allow cars to park in front of hydrants and empower the police to break two car windows so they could run a hose through them. The cost of repair would be far less than the revenue generated by additional parking spaces.

More practically, he was involved in the creation of two parking structures, one across from the Galleria on Ninth and Morrison and another across from Import Plaza on First and Davis. In 1976, the city told the Portland Development Commission to develop plans for two new parking garages. Transit mall construction was due to begin, and a significant amount of street parking would be lost. In addition, Meier & Frank had agreed to sell the city its parking garage on Sixth and Morrison for a public park, but only if the city replaced the parking with a new parking structure nearby. City council also wanted a parking garage on the west side of Morrison, near the Galleria. The east parking garage would meet current demand, and the west would meet future demand.

The Morrison West block had a surface parking lot and some retail but was otherwise unremarkable. It would not take much to condemn the block and demolish what was there. But the Morrison East block had around thirty businesses, including the Blue Mouse Theater, from which the block gained its colloquial name. The Blue Mouse was one of two theaters on the block, along with a delicatessen, two taverns, a defunct nightclub, a steam bath, a smoke shop, an art gallery, a dentist, an optometrist, and a violin maker. It was, the *Oregon Journal* wrote, one of the places "that make the block a downtown neighborhood of its own." Although the Blue Mouse Theater was "the only motion picture facility remaining in downtown Portland built in the age of motion pictures," it was demolished with little fanfare.

When PDC released its plan for the Morrison West Garage, the structure was only going to be five stories tall. Bill believed that another floor, with 133 more parking spaces, should be added to demonstrate belief in the future of downtown. The cost of the garage was $4.5 million, and PDC was not willing to pay more. The downtown area was still struggling to recover from decades of stagnation, and it was already an act of faith and foresight to invest in any garage in upper downtown. PDC was willing to expand the footings, but only if Bill could raise the $42,000 for the additional floor. Despite a hearty attempt, he failed, but he was able to build a skybridge connecting the third floor of the parking garage to the third floor of the Galleria. Funded by Norcrest, it was the first public skybridge built with private funds in Portland. The result was a seating area where people could look east down Morrison Street and see the Willamette River and Mount Hood. Bill called Galleria's skybridge a "park in the sky."

Bill's second parking garage project, in Old Town, took six years of negotiation and often antagonistic conflict. For more than twenty years, parking in the district had been a problem, and it had gotten worse as buildings had been renovated and the area gained more retail shops. Norcrest had surface parking lots for each of its buildings, but Bill could see that the area needed a parking garage. In the late 1970s, he suggested that the city establish a parking district in Old Town, similar to one in Gastown in Vancouver, BC, where businesses guaranteed a public bond to pay for it. He had to wait until 1995 to see it happen. After a two-year struggle to reach community agreement over where to locate the four-hundred-space parking garage, it was built on Front Avenue across from the Globe Hotel.

The Pacific Square Corporation, Norcrest China, and Hillman Properties Northwest contributed $50,000 each to the $9.5 million project; PDC planned to raise around $7 million using revenue bonds. In order to get a $1.1 million grant from the Federal Aviation Administration, the garage had to include a heliport, which required the city to pass an emergency ordinance by the end of the federal government's fiscal year. Otherwise, the grant would expire. Four votes on the city council were needed. Three commissioners were on board, but Commissioner Bob Koch, who had secured promises for matching funds from local heliport users, was on his way to Florida when the vote came. Commissioner Dick Bogle, the other potential fourth vote, was in the hospital preparing for an operation. In a first in Portland City Council history, his vote over the phone was deemed valid, and the heliport grant was accepted. SERA Architects designed the garage with brick exterior and arched windows and doorways to mesh with the character of Old Town, and the building was designed to provide a helicopter flight path that would limit noise pollution. It was the first federally funded helicopter facility on the West Coast. The Old Town garage was one of the last physical ways that Bill tried to solve transit and parking issues in a city that he had spent a lifetime making more livable.

CHAPTER 16

Bill once told the *Daily Journal of Commerce* that he and Sam took on projects "where people fear to step. I always figured we are more creative, more innovative—we're a little crazy." He was a visionary who was single-minded and refused to follow conventional thinking, and his penny-pinching in a relentless pursuit of success meant that he completed many of the real estate projects he envisioned. He didn't go to Las Vegas, he once quipped, because he found that kind of excitement "in Portland as an entrepreneur." Andy Raubeson of the Burnside Consortium considered him a novelty: "He's willing to take chances, which is rare among those who have [money]." Norcrest's marquee developments reflected that—transforming buildings that others dismissed as teardowns or useless except for their original purpose into iconic Portland structures. The Galleria was the first such project. McCormick Pier was the second.

As early as 1975, Bill talked about trying his hand at developing mixed-use housing in Old Town. "There is no conflict between having retail space on the first floor and apartments on the upper stories," he said. "This would be tremendous." It is easy to forget how revolutionary the idea was at the time. Banks were skeptical of the viability of housing developments, especially in downtown neighborhoods where few people apparently wanted to live. Most people considered housing of any kind in the downtown area to be next to impossible, given the costs, the limited demand, and the general malaise in the local economy. "Housing cannot be built in downtown Portland," city council member Mildred Schwab said in 1976, "unless it is subsidized."

When Mayor Goldschmidt announced that same year that he intended to rezone everything west of Park Avenue and Ninth for housing—requiring that development in a designated apartment zone be at least 60 percent residential—there was near universal disbelief. The area was bordered by Interstate 405 to the west and contained parking lots and office buildings but little housing, and the plan required the consent of building owners to downzone their property. It was also the headquarters of Evans Products, a Fortune 500 rail car and forest products firm that also owned a surface parking lot and another building in the neighborhood. Goldschmidt met with its CEO Monford Orloff to explain his reasoning. Orloff's advisers had told him the plan was bad for business—an agreement to rezone for housing would restrict the company's future developments—but he was willing to hear the mayor out. When he asked who in the business community supported the idea, Goldschmidt was able to point to one person—Bill Naito, who believed it was in Portland's long-term interest to have people living in the central business district. Residents would have a vested interest in the neighborhood's well-being, which would be manifest in everything from crime prevention to support for bond measures. Orloff agreed not to oppose the rezoning, and Goldschmidt later said he wasn't sure he could have gotten his cooperation without Bill's support. His reputation as a trusted member of the business community meant that some ideas that would have been dead on arrival had a chance of success if he supported them.

And that was how Norcrest got funding for McCormick Pier Apartments, its own housing project in Old Town. There were obstacles, including the lingering effects of a recent national recession. Portland's economy was technically in recovery, but it was not robust, and prospects for growth seemed grim. But Bill believed that positive thoughts resulted in positive outcomes and that a sense of humor was powerful in a bad situation. As he said in 1980 to the *Daily Journal of Commerce*, the economic outlook is "not gloomy from a business standpoint, maybe it's gloomy because it's raining outside." Bill often stretched the truth to give something mundane an aura of serendipity, which made things seem more hopeful. He also used luck as his straw man: "There is no substitute for good luck and a little help from the Almighty."

Bill spun such an explanation for how he got the idea for McCormick Pier Apartments. For years he had made illegal U-turns on Front Avenue to get into the White Stag parking lot under the

McCormick Pier apartments under construction

Burnside Bridge. One day, when a police officer pulled him over and forced him to drive the legal route, he saw a narrow strip of land, 1,500 by 180 feet, next to the Willamette River to the north of the Steel Bridge. "What a great plot of land for apartments!" he claimed to have thought to himself. In truth, he already knew there was a plan for the property—the McCormick Dock project. For years, Ole J. Lilleoren had been looking for financing to build a $10 million center with shops, offices, a hotel, and moorage on the property—a bold plan for an area where China-bound square-rigged ships had once loaded grain from Union Pacific elevators.

But McCormick Dock never got off the ground, and Lilleoren's option to buy the property from Union Pacific lapsed. Bill was not unaware of these developments when he had Norcrest buy a one-year option on the property. It would be "kind of a scary project," Bill said, "but really a fun one." McCormick Pier Apartments would become the first project the Naitos built from the ground up, the first workforce housing downtown, and the first housing development on the waterfront. The Portland planning office considered it the first step toward realizing the 1972 Downtown Plan's vision of a twenty-four-hour city.

But government approval was not easily earned for the project. Recovery from the national recession had not stopped a major restructuring of the Oregon economy, from timber and steel toward technology and service industries, changes that put many older laborers out of work and made the recovery like a damp squib. Even by 1983, Oregon's unemployment rate was still at 12.5 percent (compared with the national rate of 8.1 percent), and the metropolitan area lost both population and jobs as a result. Some of the people out of work ended up on Burnside and in Old Town, seeking social services and inexpensive housing. Would they be good neighbors for the young professionals and families that the middle-income apartments would target?

Even architect Bing Sheldon, who had turned the white elephant Rhodes building into the Galleria, thought the project would fail. The Portland Development Commission was concerned about the development's proximity to Union Station, whose trains cut off access to the Steel Bridge and Front Avenue many times a day and ran at all hours, making considerable noise just across the street from the planned apartments. One day, when the Urban Land Institute convention was in town, Sheldon took a group on a bus tour of the city. When they stopped at the strip of land planned for McCormick Pier, the developers lamented: "I feel so bad for the Naitos. This will never work. I've never seen a worse location for housing." But Bill believed it would work, and Sheldon went along for the ride.

Bill thrived on putting such transactions together. While making money was paramount, he loved difficult deals that required him to outthink problems, and his extensive and precise knowledge of the McCormick Pier project overcame all objections from the city. More than forty individual agreements were necessary to complete the deal, which also required permission from the harbormaster and soil engineers. Three of the twelve acres were classified as submersible by the state and required approval from the State Land Board, requiring both a lease and a quitclaim deed. The Portland Design Review committee approved the project, emphasizing that being on the waterfront would be a significant draw for renters to counterbalance the inconveniences. In the end, Norcrest granted three public easements on Front Avenue to the city, including an extension of the Willamette Greenway Park with public access to the waterfront.

The company also agreed to dedicate 5 percent of the apartments to tenants with disabilities.

The Naitos received a $1.8 million ten-year property-tax abatement from the City of Portland (the land continued to be taxed but not the improvements), contingent on the apartments remaining rentals for that decade. Bill said that it "gall[ed] him to ask for the tax abatement," especially since the Naitos had received no public funding for the Galleria renovation, but he believed that affordable housing would not pencil out without some form of public assistance. The abatement was also required by the Department of Housing and Urban Development for approval of a $16.2 million FHA-insured, forty-year nonrecourse mortgage, which also required over $2.6 million in equity. Under HUD's Government National Mortgage Association Targeted Tandem program, Norcrest qualified because the McCormick Pier project would bring middle-income families into the city, a stated goal of the program. The tax abatement was necessary to meet the "public benefit" standard of the mortgage, and with the HUD loan the interest rate would fall from a whopping 22 percent to a more manageable 7.5 percent. Bill believed that support from the government was due, because so little investment had been made north of Burnside, which had been "really kind of unfair." In a way, he said, he was doing the city a favor by taking an area that would likely be a blight along the waterfront and turning it into a functional, attractive housing community. It would also meet almost one-sixth of the city's goal for new downtown housing units and create a hundred construction jobs.

Mayor Connie McCready and City Commissioners Charles Jordan and Mike Lindberg voted in favor of abatement (Mildred Schwab was absent). Frank Ivancie voted against it, saying it was offensive to low-income people to fund middle-class housing. Commissioner Jordan suggested that if they didn't help middle-income people today, they could become low-income people tomorrow. Because of the high cost of land and few existing subsidies, Mayor McCready cautioned, middle-class housing was actually the hardest housing to get into downtown. McCready and Ivancie were in the middle of a bitter mayoral campaign, so there was more politics than policy involved. Ivancie repeatedly implied that Bill had bought a tax exemption for McCormick Pier

Apartments by being a contributor to her campaign. "The only thing
I've told my contributors," he said, "is that you're only going to get a
fair hearing. . . . You're not going to get a tax exemption." Ivancie was
elected mayor, but Bill won the argument by securing the exemption.
Not one to hold grudges, he waited eight years for his I-told-you-so.
By then, Norcrest had gotten the Port of Portland to agree to a pedestrian bridge from McCormick Pier to Albers Mill under the Broadway
Bridge. Without consulting the port, he had plaques placed on the
crossing naming it the Frank Ivancie Pedestrian Bridge.[1]

But Ivancie hadn't been the only one contesting the abatement. Stan
Terry, a Portland businessman, sued the city and McCready, Jordan,
and Lindberg personally, charging that the three commissioners had
received campaign contributions from Bill and that the project was a
private endeavor and ineligible for the abatement. Terry had some personal animus against the Naitos that stretched back to 1972. Norcrest
had bought the downtown Dekum building for a song at $45,743.55
(its estimated value was at $305,290). Terry's arrears on another prop-
erty had resulted in an indemnity suit by Norcrest (perhaps related to
Terry's ownership of the Fleischner-Mayer, which he had sold to Norcrest), since he had used the Dekum as a security interest in a separate
agreement. After a judge's ruling, Terry had a year to come up with
$54,837.55 to regain possession and failed to do so.

The Dekum was a beautiful building on Washington and Third
Avenue, one that anyone would be upset to lose. Frank Dekum, a
German immigrant with a confection business, had been the founder
and president of the German Songbird Society, which introduced
goldfinches and nightingales to Portland. When he had the building
constructed in 1891–1892, he demanded that architects McCaw, Martin & White use only native Oregon products, which cost a reputed
$300,000 for the timber, sandstone, and clay. The building, Dekum
said, was "a monument" to his life. The result is one of the most
attractive Richardsonian Romanesque buildings in Portland. When
it opened, it housed the Lipman, Wolfe & Co. department store on
the main floor and doctor and dentist offices on the floors above. The

---

1 In truth, he did admire Ivancie, who had worked to build up trade with Pacific
Rim countries.

success of Lipman, Wolfe would result in Hide Naito's employment as a houseboy when he arrived in Portland in 1917.

Stan Terry's ownership of the Dekum had gone beyond property ownership and was a matter of pride, and he obtained some good press when he agreed to have five artistically decorated planters placed outside the building. Putting trees in tubs on city sidewalks had been one of Lewis Crutcher's successes, but Terry thought they looked like septic tanks. Architect Will Martin, who would design Pioneer Square, had been Terry's architect for his modest Dekum restoration, and he supervised the five Museum Art School students who decorated the planters with mosaics of glass, tile, and broken pottery. Martin lauded the project as reflecting Mexican and South American street art, and Terry hoped to replicate it on the other planters in downtown. The reaction from the Portland Association of Building Owners and Managers, however, was an emphatic demand to remove the decorated planters. Terry refused and sought an injunction to prevent the removal, which failed, leaving Terry bitter over the whole affair. Then, in 1972, the Naitos assumed ownership of the building after he failed to keep the Dekum. He maintained a grudge toward the Naitos after that and used the tax abatement to seek some satisfaction.

And it was true that Bill was a supporter of Commissioners McCready, Jordan, and Lindberg. Because of all the property Norcrest owned, it was easy for him to donate campaign space to candidates, which allowed Bill and Sam to be supporters without spending any cash. The company gave space in the Dekum building, for example, to Jewel Lansing, who was running for state treasurer in 1976; to Gretchen Kafoury in 1981; and to Don Clark and Ted Kulongoski when each was running for governor. In 1992, Montgomery Park was known as Campaign Row, where Earl Blumenauer (mayor), Phil Keisling (Oregon secretary of state), and Gail Shibley (Oregon House of Representative) had their offices. Mayor Vera Katz was in the Norton House that year, and Bill let the Norcrest offices be used for after-hours phone banks. But there wasn't any evidence that the donations were illegal, and Terry had no standing. The suit was dismissed, the abatement awarded, and the apartment project went forward.

McCormick Pier cost $18 million and created 302 apartments. The design, by Sheldon Eggleston Reddick Associates, featured a series of bright burnt-orange interconnected units, jigsawing along the waterfront to create more units with a view of the river. The design integrated the nearby railroad freight station warehouse sheds, constructed in 1909, which were turned into protected parking areas, the main office, and an amenities building. McCormick Pier was an opportunity for one of the first public-private partnerships in Portland that linked energy grants to a development. The development had the first solar hot-water system in the Northwest, using solar panels and 500-gallon, gravity-fed, rooftop water tanks. Bill considered it their "toughest project yet" because of the tax abatement and the need to get government approval. It was their first experience in residential real estate, and there were many places where the company could have tripped up along the way.

Not the least of which was the difficult economic environment in which to draw tenants, given that the Portland metropolitan area lost residents between 1981 and 1985. When P&C finished the initial construction six months ahead of schedule, Norcrest had secured only five tenants; but within a year after opening, the project had a $16.5 million positive cash flow. Within three years, it was fully leased. "This kind of turnaround is miraculous," Bill boasted in 1985, "especially during a recession." Bill envisioned people living at McCormick Pier without cars, walking or biking to work and renting cars on the weekend to drive to Mount Hood or the coast. It became a community, an oasis of mostly young professionals—and a place for Bill to take trash from home to avoid garbage fees. The $16.5 million was nice, but so was the $16.50 he didn't send to the trash collector in Dunthorpe.

McCormick Pier was also an example of Bill's belief that nothing was impossible and that conventional thinking was often the greatest impediment to growth. His point of view came "from a different angle" with a "different sense of urgency and opportunity," as Congressman Earl Blumenauer put it. Bill thrived on risk and ventures into the unknown, deriving joy as much as financial success from the challenges posed by complex projects. If the Naitos could succeed on McCormick Pier when so many had doomed it to fail, there was no limit to what they could accomplish.

CHAPTER 17

Having had his appetite whetted for bigger endeavors, Norcrest submitted a bid in 1983 to the Portland Development Commission to develop South Waterfront, a seventy-three-acre area that stretched from north of the Marquam Bridge—the freeway conduit that signaled the beginning of the downtown area—to the Hawthorne Bridge. On this undeveloped land, sandwiched between Front Avenue to the west and the Willamette to the east, the river was accessible only to pedestrians, and the city saw it as a prime spot for improvement.

As chair of the citizen advisory committee for the 1983 Waterfront Park Study, Bill was already focused on the waterfront on both sides of the river. He wanted the city to develop a master plan for the east bank, which he described as having "a small park there, and the rest of it is a bunch of spaghetti freeways." Portland's riverfront could be like Paris, he argued, with fully developed left and right banks, each with their own character. He wanted the pedestrian and bicycle bridge on the lower deck of the Steel Bridge, north of downtown, to connect the east and west sides and a newly developed eastside riverbank. It was always his hope that civic leaders would do better to incorporate neighborhoods on the eastside with the city's development plans, an area that he argued had been "forgotten for 100 years." He envisioned a greenway from the Sellwood Bridge in southeast Portland to Ross Island to the north. Developing the west bank of the river south of downtown was part of his overall concept of an engaging waterfront.

The Portland Development Commission wanted to develop 8.7 acres in the south waterfront area by building housing, retail space, and a marina. The agency had narrowed the proposals to two—one from Norcrest and the other from Cornerstone Development Company, an experienced, well-financed Seattle company that was 80 percent owned by the Weyerhaeuser Corporation. Four equally weighted criteria would be considered: (1) the developer's record and finances, (2) the purchase price and timetable, (3) the economics of the proposed development, and (4) the quality of architecture and urban design. Norcrest enlisted architect Bing Sheldon and his firm SERA to come up with a design. Waterfront Commons, as they called it, included 608 housing units, most of them condominiums, with a focus on middle-income, one- and two-person households. An additional 107 apartments would be built when market conditions improved and warranted the investment. The Cornerstone Development proposal included 510 condominiums, 25 percent with scenic views and most facing interior courtyards. Their plan added a luxury hotel and an outdoor strip of retail along the riverfront.

Waterfront Commons was intended as a companion to McCormick Pier. A similar greenway would give the waterfront "a harmonious design," the *Oregonian* reported, and the review panel described SERA's design as a "very ordered kind of 'Emerald City.'" Because 80 percent of units were designed to have a view of the river and Mount Hood, Norcrest could maximize profit by charging $50 more per square foot. All of the midrise units would have balconies or gridded solariums to take advantage of the view. Retail shops and restaurants would face the marina and be adjacent to a public parking area. Landscape architect Charles Moore, whose firm had designed the Wonderwall for the 1984 Louisiana World Exposition in New Orleans, was chosen to design a one-acre public garden modeled on the Tivoli Gardens in Copenhagen.

A key point of the Naito design was that the waterfront was meant for everyone, and Moore's approach was in harmony with that goal. "The best architecture, an inclusive architecture," he said, "required listening to [users' preferences] but also their dreams and homesick fantasies." The garden would incorporate European design elements, with formal pathways and plantings to create an area that fostered diversity and social interaction. From the east side of the river, Norcrest proposed, the garden would be a "visual front yard" for Portland's downtown. Delicate lighting would give it a jewel-like appearance, and a pedestrian bridge would allow ready access from downtown.

Norcrest intended to rely on conventional floating-rate (variable) construction financing, industrial revenue bonds, multifamily

Bill in the 1980s

housing revenue bonds, and its own capital. The company's time-table was eight years from acceptance of the proposal to completion. But the committee judged that, although Norcrest had the superior design, Cornerstone's $1 billion in available financing, experience in developments of that size, and faster timetable merited the bid award. In response, Bill wrote an op-ed for the *Oregonian*, critiquing, among other things, the failure of Cornerstone's proposal to meet the design requirements. He questioned the long-term feasibility of building mostly one-bedroom $80,000 condos without a view of the river. He also doubted the viability of the retail strip, which would be several hundred feet from parking, saying that Norcrest would never put one of its own shops in such a location.

Bill was chagrinned at losing the bid but for no longer than a week, he claimed, following his own advice to "never look back." But losing the South Waterfront bid tested his philosophy in a way that no other business endeavor had—and it had cost the company $250,000 in the process. He was not spiteful or resentful, having learned as a Nisei that the best defense was a good offense—that is, the best way to disprove doubters is to be successful in spite of them. It was his version of *gonbaru*, toughing it out. "I feel I should take punishment as a samurai would, with a smile," he said. "There are these bastards trying to do us in and I go out there, go out there and fight these bastards like a samurai. . . . It actually gives me strength to accomplish what I do. And, to take on frustration much easier." Dwelling on losses, no matter the cause, served no purpose.

Bill rarely engaged in personal attacks. If he wanted to react negatively to something, he was more likely to do it in a nonconfrontational and joking way. When *Willamette Week,* a weekly newspaper in Portland, moved into the Shoreline Block on Second Avenue and Burnside, Bill presented them with a framed copy of a *Willamette Week* cover that asked, "Is Old Town Dying?" But losing the South Waterfront bid was different. Architect David Soderstrom remembered it as the only time that he saw Bill get angry—he described Bill as "absolutely furious." It was anger borne of hurt, not frustration over a lost business opportunity. By 1983, Bill felt like he had given so much to the community that he was owed the benefit of the doubt. PDC had been able to point to a lack of solid financing as an excuse, because First National would not extend Norcrest the line of credit it needed. The family had been with the bank since before the war and that rejection felt personal. After all, he had proved that he and the company were a sound investment when he delivered on McCormick Pier despite all the reasons it should have failed.

Many speculated about other reasons Norcrest lost the bid, but the real reason was probably the simplest one: Cornerstone represented outside investment at a time of bad economics in the city. Out-of-state money addressed an unspoken sense around Portland that the city might not be worth investing in. In a similar way, being awarded the South Waterfront bid would have addressed Bill's sense that he wasn't good enough to be American, a nagging sensation that never truly left him and fueled his rapacious need for success. Despite his hurt, and likely because of it, Bill wasted little time moving on. He completed his most audacious projects in the following years, perhaps because taking on big financial risks was a rebuke of the rejected South Waterfront bid. It may have been a way of saying, "Never doubt my abilities again."

The South Waterfront project did lead him into one of his strongest political relationships, with Mayor J. E. "Bud" Clark, who served two terms between 1985 and 1992. Clark was a political newcomer who ran his own business, Goose Hollow Inn, and had participated in neighborhood associations. He was also an unexpected winner in the 1984 mayoral contest against Frank Ivancie. Many property developers and businessmen were wary of Clark and his inexperience, as well as his colloquial way of speaking. When he showed up at Norcrest's offices to solicit campaign money and support, Bill warmed to him immediately, in no small part because Clark believed that Bill should have won the South Waterfront development bid. Clark was also smart and forward-thinking, and he had an off-the-cuff, affable personality. Importantly, he had attended Reed College for almost three years, where he had taken Humanities 110 and other required classes. That meant, to Bill, that he had "the influence of the most important courses." Being a Reedie was a shortcut to gaining Bill's trust.

Part of Clark's charm was his folksy manner, but even Bill was slightly taken aback when he and Bill Wyatt, the executive director of the Association for Portland Progress, arrived at Portland City Hall to find Clark in lederhosen. Any buyer's remorse was erased when, despite it being ten in the morning, Clark asked if they'd like a beer. He threw open the door of a small refrigerator, revealing end-to-end Budweiser cans. Bill partook, cementing the beginning of a deep friendship.

As a political novice, Clark struggled in a difficult first term with multiple scandals and an initial struggle with the mechanics of governing. Almost immediately, he was engaged in a power struggle with the Portland Bureau of Police. In 1985, Clark fired two white police officers for wearing T-shirts that read "Don't Choke 'Em, Smoke 'Em" after a Black man died from a choke hold in an encounter with Portland police. The response from the Portland Police Association was aggressive outrage directed at Clark (the officers were eventually reinstated). There were also internal governance issues at city hall, with staffers stepping on commissioners' toes. Most of those issues were attributed to inexperience, but they caused ongoing problems with commissioners, their staff, and with some of the community organizations they were working with. Some local activists worried that Clark was moving away from them and toward the business sector, and the business sector worried that he was more concerned with crafting his public image than creating substantive planning for the city.

Criticism floated around from all sides but never from Bill. Chuck Duffy, who worked in the mayor's office, recalled in 1996 after Bill's death that "sometimes, just talking to him made us feel better because he always kept moving to the next problem, the next issue, the next plan." Bill could see that the mayor had "a heart" and good character, which meant more than any temporary setbacks. It was much like how he saw Portland. And Clark was mayor because of a deep, sincere, guiding love of Portland. His missteps could be forgiven and, importantly, overcome. Wyatt believed Clark was Bill's favorite mayor, not because of his policy stances or accomplishments but because he was there for the right reasons. For his part, Clark was deeply appreciative of Bill. "It is tremendously reassuring to me," the mayor wrote him in 1988, "to know that you are always ready with encouragement, support and, I hope, criticism, when it is needed." In a way, Bill acted as a go-between, translating Clark's policies into easily appreciated terms for the downtown business community while influencing Clark's opinions on policies that directly affected businesses. Bill's capacity for compassion and understanding, coupled with a willingness to invest time, paid dividends for everyone. In the end, Bill called Clark Mr. Mayor, and Clark called him Mr. Vision. Together, they would see Bill achieve his greatest and most lasting real estate success.

The area around Guild's Lake, in northwest Portland, was part pastureland, part swampy marshland, but it would become home to Bill's most daring development. It was where Chinese farmers grew vegetables in the late 1800s, and in 1905, it was where businessmen and other Portland boosters staged the Lewis & Clark Centennial Exposition, the world's fair that put Portland on the world map. The fair was wildly successful, with 1,588,000 paid admissions walking through the elaborate gates from June 1 to October 15. When the fair closed, the land was sold for future development, and the ornate Spanish Renaissance–themed buildings were deconstructed. Landscape architect John Charles Olmsted, who designed the fair, had hoped the land would be turned into a park, but instead, Guild's Lake was filled in and converted to industrial land. One building that remained was the Forestry building, a three-story log building—what some called the largest log cabin in the world—located on what would become Vaughn Street.

In 1920, Montgomery Ward, the successful mail-order business, decided to build a distribution center and warehouse on Vaughn Street, not far from the Forestry building. The company's engineer, W. H. McCaully, designed the nine-story, almost 600,000 square feet, steel-reinforced building to be functional. Trains entered and deposited goods through a large opening in the center of the structure, creating a U-shape, and packages were dropped from the upper floors into a spillway and sorted at the bottom, where workers coasted around on roller skates. It was a design suited to the retailer's needs without ornamentation. The surrounding area was home to a Hooverville during the Depression and Guild Lake Courts, a housing project for workers, during World War II.

By the early 1980s, the Montgomery Ward building sat vacant on eighteen acres. To the south, Northwest Twenty-Third Avenue and Nob Hill were developing into a retail and restaurant district, with Vaughn Street largely dividing it from the industry to the north. Mobil Oil owned the Montgomery Ward building in 1984, and two offers to buy it were outstanding: one proposed to tear it down and construct smaller warehouses, and the other wanted it to grow tomatoes hydroponically. For several weeks, Bill talked with broker Paul Breuer about the possibility of buying the building. Finally, on a Thursday in September, he looked at Breuer through the stacks of paper on his desk and said, "I've made up my mind—we're gonna buy it." He had already purchased tickets for the two of them and his son Bob to fly to Chicago, where Mobil Oil's real estate headquarters were located. And off they went to negotiate. From Portland, Sam would approve the final deal—a thirty-day option to purchase the building and surrounding property.

But Sam had not wanted to take the risk on such a large project. He was too risk-averse and too parsimonious; minimal renovations in Old Town buildings suited him more. Sometimes Bill got Sam's approval for ventures like Montgomery Park by conceding other issues related to the mercantile and retail divisions, in which Sam had a greater personal interest. The concessions could be larger orders for the wholesale business or opening another retail store, like new locations for Import Plaza or Made In Oregon. But Bill and Sam shared the accolades the company received for its real estate developments, because Sam went along with them, if reluctantly. And without Sam, there would have been no capital upon which to branch out into real estate development. It was, after all, his and their father's return to Portland after the war that had revived the business. So, the brothers found ways to move forward, making sure each got enough of what he wanted while keeping the business successful, and projects like Montgomery Park went ahead.

Part of Bill's justification for buying the Montgomery Park building was that a ramp to nearby Interstate 405 would soon be completed, which would give freeway traffic easy access to the property. The question was whether there was enough demand for office and retail space to sustain a million-square-foot building, especially with a depressed economy. And even with the freeway connection, the building could be too far from downtown to draw tenants. There was also the question of which road the planners would use to direct traffic to the building. Access from Vaughn Street would create a straight shot from the ramps on and off Interstate 405, but access from Nicolai Street would require drivers to take more streets to get to the building. John Southgate of the Portland Planning Bureau thought the Naitos "were finally making a mistake. I didn't see how they could feasibly make money from a building isolated out of the heart of the city."

The option was contingent on Norcrest's ability to get Portland City Council to approve $28 million in industrial development revenue bonds. Otherwise, Norcrest could afford to buy the building but do nothing with it. Montgomery Park required an enormous, complicated renovation, whose success the company would depend on because of the size of financial commitment it required. Without the bonds, it would have been impossible. With only thirty days to meet the terms of the agreement with Mobil Oil, Norcrest had to move fast to secure the bonds and get approvals from PDC and city council. Obtaining the financing took a leap of faith by the City of Portland, a leap it had been unwilling to do with the Naitos' bid on the South Waterfront development. Bill offered the nebulous idea of turning the building into a trade center, which he claimed at the time was based on a "gut feeling."

When he appeared before the PDC in October 1984, he admitted that most of the details had not been worked out and that he couldn't make any real promises. "I've never run one of these," he said, referring to a trade market. Despite the "still sketchy" proposal, the plan was approved. Bill signed the purchase agreements on Hide's birthday. The building cost $6.5 million to buy, and it would take another $28 million to renovate and remodel it, $8 million of that from Norcrest's capital and $12 million in a conventional mortgage in addition to the revenue bonds. To alleviate some of the risk, the company sought and received a national and local historic landmark designation for the building, which ensured tax credits of 25 percent of construction costs.

The decision by the Portland Historic Landmarks Commission to identify the Montgomery Park building as a historic building was not without controversy. The *Oregonian* described the building as having no apparent architectural or historical significance and editorialized against the designation. During the hearing, when Bill called the former warehouse a "crystal palace," a reference to its glass exterior, his description drew chuckles from the commission, a tacit agreement that the building had limited visual value. The lone dissenting voice to the eventual vote in favor was architectural historian William Hawkins, who pointed out that "it's just big" and asked whether that was enough to warrant designation.

The Naitos' had two counterarguments that won designation: the building was on a historically important site, which made it worthy of protection, and Montgomery Ward was a precursor to major department stores and an important employer in the area. Furthermore, the building had been the site of a significant labor event. In December 1944, seven Montgomery Ward warehouses, including Portland's, had been taken over by the US Army after the company refused to follow World War II labor directives. Employees were told they were working for the United States and that any employees of draft age who contested would be sent directly into military service. Norcrest received landmark designation for the building, with no conditions. With the funding sorted, the largest renovation of a historic property in Oregon at the time began. Montgomery Park would be Bill's most lasting success and proof of Sam Naito's claim that to succeed in business "the most important thing is using a lot of common sense and imagination."

Bill, with Portland
mayor Bud Clark and
Vancouver mayor Bryce
Seidl, showing a model
of Montgomery Park

The building was 300 feet by 300 feet, larger than a Portland city block, and SERA had nine architects working on the project. When fully remodeled, it would have 750,000 square feet of leasable space. Tom Cole, the project manager, had to figure out how to combine showrooms, exhibit halls, and office spaces in a former warehouse with no apparent adaptive use and a large gap down the middle. To fill that gap, Bill proposed a barrel vault, a semicircular arch traditionally found in cathedrals and railway stations. But a barrel vault would not have allowed for any windows, leaving the top of the gap to function like a closed ceiling. Bing Sheldon countered with the idea of an atrium, a feature they had used so successfully in the Galleria. The potential for nine stories of natural light filling the interior was enticing, and it would make the building unique in the Portland area. Bill agreed.

In a building more than six decades old, another challenge was to meet current seismic codes. KPPF engineers performed a nine-month structural analysis to prove that extensive and costly shear walls were unnecessary to meet regulatory requirements. Government grants helped ameliorate energy upgrade costs, and a $528,000 grant from the Bonneville Power Administration paid for a nontraditional energy system. All forty thousand panes on the building's exterior had to be reglazed, and BPA consultants worked with SERA and P&C Construction to create a unique heating and cooling system. Using a heat pump system designed by McCormick Mechanical, excess heat and cold was distributed by water loops that connected the building's interior and exterior: heat created in the building during the day was removed to a 50,000-gallon insulated water tank and then used in the morning to heat the building. Through this feat of ingenuity, energy costs were expected to be half of conventional heating and cooling.

The scale of the building's energy and fire safety systems resulted in an integrated communication network with direct-digital controls created by Broadway Electrical—a first for the Portland area. In addition, nontraditional lamps that used less energy by burning cooler were installed, as well as a lighting control system that automatically turned lights off at six o'clock on weeknights. Tenants could manually turn lights back on, which allowed Norcrest to charge for extra electricity use.

For years, the ten-foot-tall letters on the roof that spelled out "Montgomery Ward" had been lit at night, visible far to the east across the Willamette River. Bill negotiated a deal with Montgomery Ward that allowed him to rename the building Montgomery Park, an inexpensive solution that required replacing only two of the sign's letters. The advertising benefit of the sign was incalculable. Bill also had a seventy-foot-tall tower constructed of old railroad tresses installed with a weathervane and a clock face on the corner of Twenty-Seventh Avenue and Nicolai Street—"a sort of Eiffel Tower, but smaller," he called it. He made sure existing maple trees and rose bushes were preserved, and he planted sixty red oaks and six hundred rhododendrons to mitigate the swath of concrete parking lot in front of the building. A Japanese sand garden with a water fountain was created near the main entrance, which, itself, had a water feature.

The parking, more than a thousand spaces, was one of the property's greatest assets, and each tenant had a guaranteed amount included with the lease. Fan lights lined the front of the building, a vestige of the 1984 New Orleans world's fair, designed by architect Charles Moore and purchased at auction by Norcrest. The fans became the symbol of Montgomery Park on stationary and business cards and in advertising. Flagpoles bought at the same auction displayed US and Oregon flags. By getting the financial support of the city and incorporating Moore's artwork—the architect who Bill had intended to design the park for the South Waterfront development—Bill had achieved some of his failed Waterfront Commons plan. It was his emphatic way of putting any doubts to bed.

Inside Montgomery Park, four twenty-five-year-old *Ficus* trees from Florida brought greenery into the lobby, flanking the escalators and stairs to the second floor. The space between the escalators led to large banquet halls. What appeared as marble and granite on the floor was actually painted concrete, providing a retail appearance at a wholesale price. On the second floor were a restaurant and a convenience store. A second set of escalators, bought at auction at a significant savings, connected the second floor to a free-standing third-floor walkway. In between was a plaza where tenants could eat lunch while listening to daily piano performances. In the evening, the area could be transformed into an event space under the stars. From the back of the atrium, four high-speed glass elevators scaled the height of the building. Sheldon was surprised that Bill had approved the custom elevator cabs, each with a $30,000 upcharge, but by the time prospective tenants had ascended in those gorgeous elevators and looked out on the atrium, Bill explained, they wouldn't care what the actual office looked like. He was following the old broker adage that the lobby sells the space.

With so much vacant space, Bill had to create the illusion that it was full. He declared Montgomery Park a temporary convention facility and wholesale trade market for Portland and rebranded the top floors the Montgomery Park Design Center. Bill had "the thought in the middle of the night," he said, but he had actually visited other wholesale marts and conducted an informal survey of potential tenants. He also had connections from the Galleria, where a significant number of the city's wholesale clothing manufacturers and reps had space after its opening in 1976.

In 1977, when Seattle Trade Center's apparel mart had opened, the industry began to decline in Portland. Between 1980 and 1986, Oregon lost twelve thousand clothing and textile-manufacturing jobs. But the Made in USA movement was now gaining momentum, and having an apparel trade center to rival Seattle's would bring business back to the city at a good time. The Design Center, which was closed to the public, allowed architects and designers to view furniture, carpets, fabrics, and other interior design elements. Three floors were remodeled as permanent showrooms, three floors as wholesale space, and three floors as office space. The vice president of leasing for Montgomery Park, Glen Robins, announced Norcrest's intention to rejuvenate the apparel business, and the company made inroads. Montgomery Park's rental prices were sometimes half of the cost elsewhere, and it attracted wholesale trade organizations from Seattle, Los Angeles, and other West Coast cities.

But there was also an image problem to overcome. "Almost everyone in this city has spent some time in the waiting room of the old catalog company," Bob Naito explained shortly after the building opened. "And everyone knew how run down it was." Then there was the distance from downtown, which remained an impediment. People had to be willing to come to the building to see the changes. Bill, his sons Bob and Ken, and Glen Robins worked long hours to schedule trade shows and to attract local tenants and national apparel companies to fill the top floors and get people coming through the doors.

The financial peril caused by the purchase and renovation of Montgomery Park cannot be overstated. Norcrest took on $40 million in debt between 1984 and 1988, with all of the Old Town properties used as collateral. To default on one payment would have meant losing almost all of Norcrest's real estate portfolio. Bill sold the Estate Hotel, the Foster Hotel, and the Shoreline Block to make mortgage payments—the only time he ever sold buildings. Between 1988 and 1990, the company was in the deep red for the first time in its history, and by 1993 cash flow for the company had fallen by 50 percent.

When bank regulators reviewed the company's loan with First Interstate, they found it was nonperforming on zero accrual, meaning the bank was no longer earning interest on the loan because of non-payment for ninety days or more. The bank was preparing to write it down, which would have reduced Montgomery Park's book value and labeled it an impaired asset. In a move that saved them both, Bob Ames at First Interstate moved some of the bank staff to offices in Montgomery Park. The space was leased at a mere nine dollars a foot, which was just enough additional income to allow Norcrest to make the payments. Ames then leased the vacated bank building space for more than nine dollars a square foot, making a net gain for the bank. This arrangement saved Norcrest from default and bought them the time they needed to make the building a success.

It is easy to look at the accomplishments of the Naitos' historic renovations and assume their company was just one of many that took on such projects. But many investors, attracted by the idea of preserving buildings and the tax incentives that came with it, failed, partly because they didn't fully understand the finances of it and often put more money into renovations than they could recover through rents later. The Naitos' renovations were successful partly because of Bill and Sam's rapacious desire to save money. Bill ran every rehab and redevelopment project from his hip pocket, with many decisions requiring his personal approval. The rehabilitation of the Phillips Hotel—which Norcrest renamed the Captain Couch Square in 1978 in honor of John H. Couch, the original owner of much of the property in northwest Portland—is a good example.

Located on First Avenue and Couch Street, the Phillips had been built as a workingman's hotel in 1906. Norcrest began renovating the building in 1977, but seismic codes required expensive bracing. There was never a costly seismic upgrade that Bill believed was justified, and he became an immovable object when confronted with them. His first introduction to Governor John Kitzhaber was friendly until the subject of seismic code legislation came up. "Seismic is shit" was his curt response before walking away. And when David Soderstrom, whose architectural firm was on the river side of a Naito building, asked Bill what the firm should do if the Big One hit, he advised dryly, "Well, Dave, you go out on your balcony and jump." The company got around the seismic requirement for the Phillips Hotel by building an inexpensive plywood roof that held the building together from

Captain Couch Square

above rather than relying on expensive bracing below, saving tens of thousands of dollars. Bill called it the Norcrest method of buying wholesale and renting retail.

Preserving a historic building was also bureaucratically challenging. If architectural plans filed with the Bureau of Buildings didn't meet code, then they were returned for revision. Those decisions could be appealed, but multiple appeals were usually required before a building permit was issued, taking up a good deal of time and resources. And there was always the issue of tenants to fill the buildings. In Portland, there was competition from high-rises like the Pacwest Center and the US Bancorp Tower, which were going after the same small and mid-size tenants. As the *Wall Street Journal* put it in 1977, "Renovating old buildings isn't a business for those seeking a quick move to easy street."

Bill and Sam had the benefit of being successful in a business where they had become savvy about budgeting, forecasting, and money management. Neither could have imagined running a real estate empire when they were young and working in their father's gift store, but their ambitions had grown far greater than his. What did Hide, an immigrant houseboy, think as he watched his sons grow

Hide and Bill, 1950s

a multi-million-dollar empire? He was adamantly opposed to both borrowing and loaning and certainly would have disapproved of the loans the company took out to buy property. Hide had been fifty-eight years old when Bill returned to Portland to join the business, and his active participation in decision-making dwindled rapidly as his sons took over the company. His conservatism had served him well before the war, but in the postwar era there was a disconnect between his philosophy of business and economic reality.

In 1980, Hide wrote to both of his sons about the pleasure he felt as he had watched their successes, and he forgave their outstanding loans from decades earlier to make their success "more complete." But he maintained a desk in the company offices through his seventies and always seemed to know what was going on. At the age of ninety-four, he even managed to give his sons "hell for buying a lot of 'dead' [retail] stock," Bill joked. And as ever, he was quiet and steady, aware of greater forces but not changed by them. Hide died on August 9, 1989, having achieved everything he had hoped for his family, despite the setbacks of World War II and the struggle against racism in his adopted country. His was the quintessential immigrant success story—a hardworking man who came to a foreign land with next to nothing and died with a legacy business for his children. Norcrest China Company was renamed H. Naito Corporation in his honor in 1992.

CHAPTER 18

When the company purchased Albers Mill in 1985, Sam confessed, "You couldn't find a worse-looking building." Located on the north side of the Broadway Bridge, the seventy-year-old, six-story brick building had been left vacant for two years. Since then, the riverbank had eroded, and the pilings had deteriorated. The building was slowly falling into the Willamette River. The smell of fermenting grain—and the thousands of river rats feasting on it—flowed over and through one end of the McCormick Pier apartments, and wheat dust floated into the swimming pool, creating a chlorinated oatmeal. Tenants were offered reduced rent for the units around the pool to compensate them for the inconvenience, but there were enough complaints that Bill decided to spend $225,000 to buy the mill.

Aside from the nuisance value, there was important history connected to the building. Henry Albers, a German American, had been unjustly arrested for sedition during World War I and had died a sad shell of himself, despite being exonerated. Bill understood what that must have been like and had empathy for Albers's struggle to overcome the effects of bigotry and war hysteria. While debating whether to clean out Albers Mill to make it usable as a warehouse for Norcrest or lease it to a local grain firm, Bill read that Hilton Hotels had turned a grain elevator in Ohio into a hotel. He began thinking about what the mill on the Willamette could become. A hotel could never succeed so far from the downtown core, but he saw something else in the decaying mess—an office complex. Montgomery Park had taught him that anything was possible.

SERA Architects and P&C Construction completed the renovation of the 124,000-square-foot mill in 1987 for $12 million. Over half of that cost, $6.7 million, came from federal grants secured by Senator Mark Hatfield to create the Wheat Marketing Center, a joint project of the Oregon Department of Agriculture and Oregon State University. The Department of Agriculture had asked Rick Gustafson to create the center. When he had been a first-term Oregon state legislator in 1975, Gustafson had met Bill and Sam at an awards ceremony where the brothers were recognized for their work to improve the environment. Since then, he and Bill had often teamed up on projects. Albers Mill became one of them.

The Oregon Wheat Commission had long advocated for a marketing center, which would include a public information area, a laboratory for product development and troubleshooting, meeting rooms and offices, and a conference center. At the time, almost a third of America's wheat was distributed through Portland, and trade missions visited the city from countries such as Japan, Taiwan, and South Korea. A Wheat Marketing Center, the commission believed, would be an ideal way to showcase the industry.

Bill submitted two proposals for the center, one for Montgomery Park and one for Albers Mill. Out of the six sites being considered, Gustafson thought the Albers proposal was "brilliant" and offered the best long-term return on investment for the center. Part of the success of the proposal was Bill's willingness to do what was necessary to create a successful partnership. There are always winners and losers in the public sector, he believed, but both sides have to win in business before a deal is possible. But the complications were considerable, including a requirement by the Wheat Marketing Center group, which was going to cover 80 percent of the cost, that it had the right to approve every lease. That item was a deal breaker, Bob Naito said, but Bill overruled him. "Actually," Bill explained, "I want you to, so that if it goes bankrupt, I'll have someone to blame." The Albers Mill project, according to Hank Sakamoto of the Wheat Marketing Commission, was a demonstration of Bill's "indomitable spirit" and his determination to get a deal done.

In the end, Norcrest contributed the building and the land, valued at $1.2 million, to a fifty-fifty partnership with the Oregon Wheat Commission, which provided $4.8 million in cash as equity for the renovation. Norcrest would secure a loan for the money needed over that amount, which would be repaid through the proceeds from leasing other parts of the building. The Wheat Marketing Commission

Albers Mill, circa 1985

contributed another $3.6 million to the partnership in order to receive a yearly distribution of 8 percent ($336,000). It was a complex but fair arrangement.

The renovation was complex as well. Dale Campbell, the P&C Construction project manager, called it a "logistical nightmare." Norcrest had to secure a submerged land lease as well as water rights, since the Willamette River flowed under half of the building and fluctuated three feet with the tide. Pile caps—large concrete slabs placed on top of pilings to provide stability to structures above—had to be replaced, which meant divers had to check for underwater wires, powerlines, and pipes. The pile caps required riprap supports, but there was only a two- to three-week window to put them in because no work could be done when salmon were migrating up the Willamette. One day, when Campbell was trying to figure out how the piers could be replaced while keeping the building in place, the rotten wood gave way under his feet. If he hadn't caught himself, he would have fallen thirty feet to a rocky beach below. Over 40,000 tons of rock was eventually brought in to stabilize the land.

There were also animal control problems. A lynx had been living in the mill, feasting on nutria, which are rodents the size of small beavers. When the lynx was caught and removed, the nutria population skyrocketed. One day, shortly after Norcrest's proposal was submitted, the company's real estate manager, Doug Campbell, led Bill, Senator Hatfield, and his assistant Gerry Frank on a tour of the property in hopes of gaining the senator's support. On a set of rickety stairs, Campbell's flashlight found a large nutria above them, which jumped on one of the men before escaping. When the group reached the top of the stairs, they found a scene of carnage—a great horned owl and a peregrine falcon had gotten inside a pigeon trap and gorged themselves. In an attempt to deal with the nutria problem, P&C put cats in the buildings, who failed to dent the population and disappeared in short order. It was daunting turning Albers into a functioning building, but luckily the wildlife did not deter Senator Hatfield's support.

There were also regulatory issues. The height of the building was a potential problem. At six floors that reached seventy-eight feet, the mill qualified as a high rise and was subject to strict regulations. Bill met with city officials weekly until he finally obtained an exemption. Then the city sought to have sprinklers placed under the decking, at a cost of $60,000. Officials were unmoved by Bill's argument that sprinklers wouldn't actually help if there was a fire, considering that part of the decking was over water. But Bill had sufficient faith in his persuasive powers that he told P&C to lay down the decking but not attach it. He eventually got his way with the city, and the decking was nailed into place.

The public greenway along McCormick Pier was extended past Albers Mill, creating a 1.6-mile-long path from the River Queen Restaurant to the Morrison Bridge. To maintain the integrity of the original building but still expand its size, a 30,000-square-foot attached building was added over the water. The extension was distinctly modern, painted a shade of ecru to contrast with the red brick of the mill. In the end, Albers Mill had 119,000 square feet of rentable space, and its original company signs were restored. In addition, the Naitos hired local artist Hugh Boatright to restore paintings of Albers Mill's product labels—Albers Oats, Buckwheat Flour, and Flapjack Flour—on four large silos next to the Broadway Bridge. Boatright had been a POW during World War II, and when he met with Bill he told him he held "no grudges against the Japanese, who held me prisoner." Without missing a beat, Bill dryly responded: "The US held us prisoner, and I hold no grudges either." Boatright did research on the images to get the coloring and detail as historically accurate as possible. He loved the work, he said. "It's a nice feeling to actually put your hand on history."

Albers Mill's proximity to the Willamette resulted in innovations that saved both energy and money. Water from the river was pumped through a heat exchanger in the building, helping cool the building in the summer and warm it in the winter. The system was similar to the one installed at Montgomery Park, upgraded and redesigned because of the building's proximity to the river. The city wanted the Mill's existing silos filled with water, with a distribution system as a failsafe should the primary system fail, at a cost of $300,000; Bill's mind went straight to an alternative. What about a pipe running to the river, where Portland's fireboats could pump water into Albers Mill? It was inexpensive and efficient, and it made the fireboats indispensable at a time when they were threatened with defunding.

The project also resulted in other Naito money-saving tricks, like the "Gusnaitoson Fountain," named with a mashup of Rick Gustafson and Bill's last names. A concrete wall to the north of Albers Mill was going to cost $50,000 to remove, but Gustafson and Bill came up with the idea of running water from the river through a pipe over the wall to create a water feature. Inside the building was a large pedestal that, according to Bill, called for a sculpture. Unwilling to part with the cost of an original piece of art, Bill had a salvaged wheat scale placed in the space. Then, to deal with a defunct water tower on the roof, Bill called Gustafson with one of his classic questions: "It will take $15,000 to take it down or $150 to put lights on it and make it look like a holiday celebration—what should I do?"

The Wheat Marketing Center opened in 1987. To celebrate, Joan Biggs, who did most of Norcrest's public relations work, organized Agrifair, a farmers' market with produce, wine, and microbrews along with nurseries that sold plants highlighting Oregon's agricultural bounty. Local restaurants provided food, and there was an evening celebration for Cycle Oregon riders, who were part of an annual long-distance bicycling trip. Governor Neil Goldschmidt and Senator Hatfield attended the festivities. The private-public partnership was a model, the senator said, and proof that Bill and his cadre of professionals could "make silk purses out of sow's ears." Bill called Albers Mill the "crown jewel" of his empire and praised the crew who had made it possible. It was, he said, "really icky work but we all got together and did it!"

Albers Mill was possible because of the political relationships the Naito Brothers had built over the decades. They were never on the same boards or involved in the same civic endeavors, part of the balance to limit friction between them. Because of that, there were few issues in the city that a Naito brother did not touch. Sam was on the Oregon Department of Transportation Commission and a commissioner for the Port of Portland, where he focused on getting more international flights, expanding the airport, and creating additional parking. Bill served on Mayor Bud Clark's Portland Future Focus committee, the state's Advisory Committee on Historic Preservation, and the city's advisory committee to the Economic Improvement District. He brought optimism and laughter to meetings and could be counted on, architect Karl Sonnenberg wrote, to "inject humor into any meeting, get something decided and done, and put a positive spin on any situation." Because of this level of engagement, their calls were always returned and their projects considered.

Albers Mill was Norcrest's last big, risky renovation. By then, Bill and Sam had transformed Naito into a household name, and as Dick Mimnaugh, president of Portland Apparel Association, said in 1987, "I think one would have trouble finding people in Portland who have negative things to say about the Naitos." It was a large accomplishment for two men who had been considered enemies of the state during World War II. They had been in Portland before the war and after, when, as historian Jewel Lansing writes, "a national Urban League official called Portland 'the most prejudiced [city] in the west,' a place that discriminated 'just like any Southern town.'" Portland's brand of discrimination and its racism were institutional, understated, and comparatively nonviolent, making it more difficult to address because there was an illusion that race was not a problem in the city.

In most photos of business organizations and nonprofits taken in the 1970s and 1980s, Bill or Sam was often the only person of color. Penetrating the arenas of power—in business and government—was difficult. The Arlington Club opened in 1881 as an "refuge for white businessmen with big bank accounts." It did not allow a Jewish member until 1969 and didn't allow women to become members until 1991. Sam was its first member of color, in February 1979. Given their expulsion from the city during World War II, this was a tremendous and unexpected outcome for the Naitos. Their success was a testament to their tenacity and single-mindedness. Like their father, they believed that their business had to succeed regardless of the racism that stood in the way.

After so much success, Bill could put a positive spin on Executive Order 9066: "Sure there were adversities in those days. But I think adversities sharpen and toughen people. From adversities come greater self-confidence and self-discipline, and the ability to face crises. These kinds of people are the ones who come up with dreams." And Bill took his experiences and made himself available for advice and comfort to those trying to break through the city's racial barriers. In the early 1970s, Jeanette Spencer was part of the initial group of vendors at Saturday Market. "As a black woman trying to start my own business," she wrote in a condolence card after Bill's death, "I often felt alone; I particularly lacked mentors who could guide me into Portland's then almost exclusively white business world. Bill generously shared his wisdom with me." He and his brother hadn't just blazed the trail; they were there to guide others along it, too. When Sam Brooks, the owner of a temporary jobs agency, joined the Chamber of Commerce as its first African American board member, Bill was the first to introduce himself, and thereafter Brooks saved a seat at the meetings for Bill, who was always late. Just as Bill's stamp of approval on city policy would ensure support from the business community, so would his endorsement of people. The doors he opened were an important part of his legacy.

CHAPTER 19

From helping found organizations like the Oregon Nikkei Endowment and the Association for Portland Progress to cooking charity dinners and nagging the city council about "ugly" stop signs, Bill was constantly giving his time to nonprofit organization and causes. By the late 1980s, he admitted that he got "more bang out of the public area" than he did from work, and he used his influence wherever he could. Referring to himself as a "local busybody," Bill worked to make Portland a strong, livable city outside of his direct business interests, resembling economist Adam Smith's optimistic ideal of the capitalist whose self-interest reverberates to society's good. Bing Sheldon thought he was "probably the only developer" he knew who consistently saw "a public purpose in whatever he [did]." In his own way, Bill acted as Portland's conscience. As an admirer put it after his death, he was "a champion of all those things that make a city human, make it alive."

The city was his "love affair," *Downtowner* editor Maggi White said, a place where his strong emotional attachment meant doing everything possible to make it better outside of business. "He plants trees to benefit another generation," Roman statesman Cicero wrote, a quote that Bill kept under the glass on top of his desk, and an ideal he followed through two of his great loves: trees and reading—pivotal parts of his childhood. While his father had worked tirelessly on the family business, Hide had almost always made time to tend his Japanese garden. His skill as a gardener was known around the neighborhood, and his talent with bonsai was recognized in 1965 at the first meeting of the Activities Council of the Japanese Garden Society in Portland, whose members included Governor Mark Hatfield and his wife Antoinette. Bill inherited this love of nature and its cultivation. "It gives me great pleasure to watch things grow," Bill explained. "I'm in love with small miracles."

He felt early on that city streets should have trees to "humanize harsh buildings." But the idea of sidewalks lined with trees was not universally accepted in early 1960s Portland. Architect Lewis Crutcher, a member of Portland's Art Advisory Committee, had brought up trees in the city in September 1957, arguing that they provided both beauty and shade. When the Metropolitan Improvement Committee planted trees in concrete tubs around downtown a couple of years later, the *Oregonian* reported that "derided at first, only a short year later the greenery has won over its critics." In 1963, in response to city council's decision to remove a sixty-three-year-old elm on Flanders Street, Crutcher and others formed Tree Lovers of Portland. "You'll cut down that tree over my dead body!" Crutcher warned. Luckily, both his and the elm's lives were spared.

The city did not have a tree program in 1963, so it was the Naitos who took the initiative and planted sweetgum trees in the sidewalks and parking lots of the Globe Hotel and Fleischner-Mayer for their new Import Plaza store and headquarters. The city gave them permission to cut up the concrete, and they planted the sweetgums without city assistance. Those long-living sweetgums, deciduous trees that have colorful foliage in fall, are now over sixty feet tall. By 1976, the city and the Skidmore Fountain Village Association had joined together to plant and maintain trees throughout Old Town. That same year, Bill was named chair of Portland's Park and Street Advisory Committee, which would become the Urban Forestry Commission. In his twenty years on the commission, he oversaw the planting of over thirty thousand trees and attended countless tree-planting ceremonies. He also attended "a zillion 7 a.m. meetings with angry people," according to David Judd, executive assistant to Parks Commissioner Mike Lindberg. Many of the committee's decisions were controversial and tempers could become hot, often because a business wanted to cut down trees to make way for a building and neighbors sought to prevent it. Judd felt that many who came before the commission did not get the result they wanted but felt they received a fair hearing, with Bill finding "the middle ground between developers and surrounding people."

At one point in the 1980s, though, some staffers suggested to City Commissioner Mike Lindberg that it was time for Bill to leave the commission. He was a dominant personality in whom some ideas went to die, and new blood was needed, they argued. They talked Lindberg into telling Bill that it was time to step down. The two of them had a close friendship developed over years. Bill had chaired all of the commissioner's political campaigns between 1980 and 1996. When Mayor Goldschmidt had left city council in 1979 to join President Carter's administration, Lindberg had been appointed to take his seat. Almost immediately, he faced a reelection campaign, but he had no public name recognition and no campaign structure. Then Bill showed up. He had watched Lindberg's career as director of the city's Office of Planning and Development, had spoken to several people, and was willing to chair the campaign and take charge of fundraising.

Bill's method was effective but unconventional. He asked people he saw on the street—a tenant, a business associate, a stranger—for a donation, saying that whatever money they had on them was great. When he went around collecting rent, he asked his tenants to consider donating to the campaign. If it was a retail shop and the owner didn't have a check, he would say, "Just open your till." Bill then showed up at Lindberg's office and emptied his pockets, spilling out crumpled bills and coins, unsure who had given what. The donor was often "some guy I ran into on the street." Lindberg thought of their relationship as a "partnership" and considered Bill's loyalty unprecedented in politics. Because of their closeness, Lindberg felt that he could persuade Bill to step down as the forestry chair, but he had barely broached the subject before he found himself leaving their meeting with an enthusiastic "I'm so glad you're going to stay on, Bill!"

After Bill died in 1996, Urban Forestry's manager, Brian McNerney, referred to Bill as "the backbone of Portland's Urban Forest." In his capacity as chair, Bill fiercely advocated for every tree in the city, always asking in the first instance, "What is good for the trees?" When Portland's Bureau of Maintenance unintentionally damaged six elms, an angry Bill called a special meeting to address the bureau's conduct and policies. "It's a shame—a dirty shame," he lamented, "to have to remove something grown there for 75 years." He blamed the city's "insistence on perfectly flat sidewalks" and pointed to Beacon Street in Boston to demonstrate that uneven sidewalks can work.

He wanted Portland to be the best—Portland "should always go first class," he once suggested—and in this instance it meant having

the best urban tree canopy in America. He worked closely with Bill
Roberts of PDC to plant trees along downtown streets and advocated
for requiring that trees be planted in the center of new parking lots
and also for compensating property owners when they saved trees.
During the improvement of Eighty-Second Avenue, a major thoroughfare on Portland's east side, in 1988–1989, he argued that trees
were vital to the project. Businesses, especially car dealerships, were
opposed, fearing that trees would block the view of their signs and
businesses. But Bill prevailed, and 177 trees were planted. Those same
business owners were some that celebrated the trees the most.

For Bill, trees were like historic buildings—old, often under-
appreciated, keepers of history, and in need of a tireless advocate.
Despite his intense parsimony and belief in minimal government, Bill
proposed and campaigned hard for a tree maintenance levy in 1984,
hoping to raise $1.2 million each year to "preserve and maintain the
beauty of neighborhoods and the city as a whole." Trees were also
like children, he argued, who needed to be cared for to keep them
healthy and growing. In 1992, he supported Ballot Measure 1, which
provided up to $250 million in bonds for the state to buy and maintain
parks and recreational facilities. Three years later, he threw his support behind Ballot Measure 26-6, Metro's Open Spaces Initiative. The
measure permitted the regional land use commission to issue $135.6
million in general bonds to preserve local land for parks and trails;
maintain water quality in rivers and streams; protect salmon, trout,
and steelhead; and provide areas for walking and picnicking. In Bill's
estimation, buying the land before it was purchased by developers
would "save zillions" for Metro, an unusual stand for a developer
but evidence of his approach to urban development and environmental conservation. Voters had to "bite the bullet," he said at the time,
and do what was in the best interest of the city. "Just imagine what
Portland would look like without Washington Park, Laurelhurst, the
north-south park blocks and the waterfront," he warned. When the
measure passed, Metro acquired over five hundred acres of land to
protect and conserve.

One of Bill's unfulfilled dreams was to have the North Park
Blocks connected to the South Park Blocks. His idea stretched back to
the turn of the twentieth century, when landscape architect Frederick

Law Olmsted said that the goal of urban parks was to "draw users away from the city," using "the wilderness experience . . . to impose itself on all the senses, capturing one's attention." Parks were the "lungs" of the city, he said, providing relief from urban noise and congestion. John Charles Olmsted, Frederick Olmsted's son, tried to put that philosophy into action when he created a master plan for Portland in 1904, which would have created parks throughout the metropolitan area on both sides of the Willamette River. But as many discovered over the years, while there was support for the idea there wasn't the political will to pay for it.

Half a century earlier, real estate investor Daniel Lownsdale, along with four others, had agreed to give the city a narrow stretch of twenty-four blocks to be developed as a unified park that would also serve as a firebreak between Lownsdale's property and the forested hills above. Litigation between his heirs and the city resulted in several of the midtown blocks between Salmon and Starks Streets being developed. Landowner Benjamin Stark refused to follow through on the donation with his plots. The result was the separation the South Park Blocks from the North Park Blocks by development and Burnside Avenue. To the south, the parklike blocks were lined by what became known as the city's cultural district, with Portland State University, the Portland Art Museum, the Oregon Historical Society, and Schnitzer Concert Hall. The blocks to the north suffered from their proximity to Skid Road. In the mid-1980s, Bill suggested putting restaurants and an aquarium on either side of the blocks to increase their use. "You have to be willing to think of anything" to attract people to the park, he said. It never came to be, but that didn't stop him from pushing for other ideas and causes.

His professed hobby was "to rebuild the city." He lived by a belief that citizens of a city were like trees who gave a place vitality and wisdom. "People with pride in where they live," he said in 1995, "that's what makes a city work." That's why he invested in nonprofits large and small. In 1991, the Galleria celebrated its fifteenth anniversary with a $1.2 million remodel and held a party—Viva! Galleria. The proceeds from the event went to fourteen of the nonprofits that had offices in the building, including Coalition Against U.S. Military Intervention in the Middle East, League of Women Voters, Oregon

NARAL, Right to Privacy, Water Watch, and Physicians for Social Responsibility. The Galleria also gave space to Our Children's Store, which benefited seventy children's charities, ranging from Albertina Kerr and Doernbecher Children's Hospital to Oregon Food Bank and Boys and Girls Aid Society of Oregon.

Bill donated his time and energy to more than thirty nonprofit boards and task forces, as well as countless projects and fundraisers. His practice was to sleep whenever he could, and he was notorious for falling asleep in meetings and at events, engaging in the Japanese practice of *inemuri*, the art of earning participation credit for being present despite having one's eyes closed. In 1988, he explained why he spent so much time working for causes he cared about: "What else is there? My kids are grown. I have a loving wife. I don't golf, I don't have hobbies. I have time and energy. Besides, there is a Japanese proverb about leaving the world a little bit better for having been here."

One of the nonprofits closest to his heart was his work on the transition of the Multnomah County Library system from decades of private ownership to county control. Bill had long given libraries credit for his success—they are "sacred areas," as he put it—and Multnomah Central Library, just a few blocks from Hide's gift shop, was his "second home" when he was a boy. Because Hide and Fukiye spoke and read only Japanese at home, Bill relied on libraries and librarians to help him learn English. He became an avid reader and thought of libraries as his second mother, places of sanctuary where he could learn without interruption or fear of criticism. It was the library that had saved his family in Salt Lake City during the war by giving him information about chicken husbandry.

In October of 1989, when frustration with the private association that had run the county libraries since 1907 had finally come to a head, over 70 percent of county residents had library cards at the county's fifteen libraries. Many citizens were invested in the idea of a more inclusive and open management system. The initial thought was an independent trust, which would safeguard the libraries against political whims while also making it more responsive to the public. Don Barney, a consultant and lifelong supporter of libraries, and Bill's friend Bill Failing were appointed by Multnomah County Commission chair Gladys McCoy to select trustees for the new trust's board.

Bill chairing the first library board meeting, September 1990; copyright the *Oregonian*

Bill Naito was their first choice and only choice as president. He accepted and was prepared to take responsibility for a $6 million endowment. Libraries were vital to democracy as First Amendment institutions, Bill believed, and they needed to be protected from the sometimes negative impulses of politicians and cultural trends. Libraries needed to be acknowledged as the independent cornerstone institutions they were.

But by January, there had been movement toward giving the libraries over to the county instead, turning what would have been the trust board into an advisory board. Bill argued unsuccessfully against the change. The county assumed full control by the end of 1990, but Bill did not let the idea of the libraries' independence die away. As the library's director, Ginnie Cooper, remembered, "He made the political decision makers and the business leaders in our community pay attention." Fifty percent of the budget relied on levies every three years, which created uncertainty for the library system. Bill tried but failed to get a utility tax passed, because the utilities, as he had predicted, "scream[ed] like stuck pigs" at the idea. So, he insisted on and oversaw an additional bond measure campaign in 1993. With the support of businesses in the county, it passed by a large margin. One of the projects it was intended to fund was the renovation of the Central Library.

The Central Library building, an English Renaissance–style structure built in 1913 and designed by architect A. E. Doyle, encompassed an entire block between Yamhill and Taylor Streets and Tenth and Eleventh Avenues. Of all the historic renovations that Bill worked on, this was the one he had the greatest emotional and intellectual connection with. "We've got the finest park system," he said. "We also need . . . a library that represents quality. We have people who believe in our community, believe in the United States; I think that's important." For him, a great library was connected with being American; one could not exist without the other. Democracy relied on educated citizens, and education relied on free access to information.

The Central Library closed for two years for the renovation, which included critical structural, seismic, and electrical upgrades. George McMath, A. E. Doyle's grandson, was one of the architects. A terrazzo was built for the ground-floor lobby, reading rooms were expanded, bookcases were bolted to concrete in case of earthquake, more computer facilities were created, and a coffee bar was installed. Bill scrutinized every aspect of the Central Library work, with much of his focus on the usability of the building, including air conditioning, comfortable chairs, and easy access to books instead of having them hidden away in the stacks. But he also emphasized, in his words, the "frosting"—the elements that gave Central Library class and elegance, such as putting mirrors in the elevators. He also made sure carpets in nonpublic areas were serviceable, not ornamental—an easy way to save money. Paul Bragdon, a member of the trust board, called it Bill's "love of the mundane." Bill's fellow board members honored his contribution by naming the main lobby after him after his passing. Ginnie Cooper considered him "the library's personal champion." Trees and books, parks and libraries, people and causes—these were Bill's passions, because they were the backbone of the city but also easily overlooked. Political expediency and more pressing matters often left them as low priorities to people in power, but Bill spent a lifetime shining a spotlight on them.

Back row (from left to right): Natalie, Will, Kirsten, Bill, Micki, and Erica. Front row (from left to right): Jack, Alex, and Wes

In his personal life, Bill was enjoying the next generation of Naitos, one that he envisioned would inherit the family business someday. Between 1978 and 1979, three of his four children married, and their children were born within a couple years of each other, beginning in 1980. The combination of his age and the birth of his grandchildren caused the first slowdown in his work schedule. Even when he and Micki bought property on the Oregon Coast in the Salishan Resort's gated residential community in the early 1970s, Bill continued to work as much as possible, even with the home's exceptionalism. The Gleneden Beach property sat above the beach, with a sloping hill covered with plants and trees leading to it. The house they commissioned was designed by Saul Zaik, a graduate of the University of Oregon's architecture program and designed in the Northwest Regional style. Zaik took those modernist impulses and adapted them to the landscape and climate. Constructed on stilts, the house sat on the hillside, with large bay windows creating a seamless transition between the ocean and house on the west and the house and the trees on the east.

Spending weekends at the beach house, which meant not working on Saturday, proved easier for Bill with his grandchildren than with his children. But at the beach, it wasn't all sandcastles and ice cream treats at the Salishan Marketplace. A path near the house ran along Salishan's golf course, with the Siletz Bay on the other side. Bill wasn't a golfer, but he knew there were plenty of them in Salishan. When the tide was low, he rolled up his pants and walked with his grandchildren through the tidal muck, instructing them on how to find errant golf balls with their toes. Bill would then hose them off and sell them to the golfers. He was teaching his grandchildren never to forgo a chance to make a business, even when on vacation. Opportunity was everywhere he looked—to learn, to teach, to make money, to seek change, and to leave things better off than how he found them.

CHAPTER 20

Bill once told landscape architect Robert Murase that the Japanese American Historical Plaza, created in Waterfront Park in 1990, was "the most important thing" he had "ever done in his life." He had only occasionally referred to his experiences during World War II in public before, but it was clear to most who worked with him that what had happened to him and other Japanese Americans during those years was never far from his mind. When the Board of Realtors named Bill and Sam First Citizens of Portland in 1982, he remarked, "I came back through the city they threw me out of. Then they made me first citizen. That's not bad." A framed copy of Executive Order 9066 hung next to his desk in the White Stag, a reminder of a wrong that had been done and that he had overcome. If someone mentioned it, he would tell them about that time in his life. It was how Bill kept forced removal and the American concentration camps in the minds of those he met. The Naitos had avoided imprisonment, but Bill had internalized many of the emotions of those who had been. His therapist in Chicago noted that during sessions he "merges his accomplishments with the postwar success of Japanese-Americans as a group." Sharing the accolades came with sharing the trauma for him.

But those experiences during World War II were largely unknown outside of the community. One of the first events to draw the public's attention to the imprisonment of Japanese Americans during World War II was the Day of Remembrance in Seattle on November 25, 1978, organized by the Evacuation Redress Committee. Not many Issei had spoken about their time between Pearl Harbor, expulsion from their home, and imprisonment in the decades since the war, and only a few had sought redress for the harm they had suffered. Some still carried a sense of shame for having been accused of disloyalty, something that Bill had felt keenly. But there was also a deeper unresolved issue: there was really no way to rationalize what happened to them and to give it meaning. At its core, forced removal and imprisonment meant that they had not been wanted, and it had left an intellectual and emotional void for many Issei. James Oda, who was imprisoned in Manzanar before joining the US Army, wrote that in the camps they were "non-mummified living dead." Returning from the camps had not resurrected them. But unlike their parents, many of whom had endured the wrongs in silence, Bill and many second-generation (Nisei) and third-generation (Sansei) Japanese Americans could not pretend that it hadn't happened. They needed an official acknowledgment from the United States government of the wrong that had been done.

Part of this was due to the unintended results of EO 9066, from expulsion to the camps, which had upended traditional family structure. Japanese American children watched as their parents were emasculated and their authority rendered hollow by the government. Nisei children grew up with a sense of independence, often playing unsupervised outside because their "home" was too crowded. In the camps, Issei were forbidden to act as leaders of community groups, the US government fearing that they would foment disloyalty. Generational differences manifested in heated debates and sometimes physical violence. Issei had a stronger connection to Japan than their US-born children did, and most Nisei had never been to Japan at all. In their former lives, those differences weren't outwardly disruptive, but in the pressure cooker of the prison camps they caused division, resentment, and anger. And EO 9066 itself made Nisei less obedient to authority. It was hard to justify obedience to a government that had destroyed their lives, despite its claim to be a beacon of democracy and so different from the authoritarian regimes they were fighting overseas. The hypocrisy was loud and unavoidable.

As one prisoner described it, "We developed a very negative attitude toward authority. We spent countless hours to defy and beat the system. Our minds started to function like any POW or convicted criminal." Some said that the camps, because of the scarcity of nearly everything from clothing to food to access to a bathroom, fostered an attitude of self-preservation that led to selfishness. There was little room for respect for authority or traditional community hierarchy. And, as decades passed, the hate and fear that had gotten them imprisoned in the first place didn't disappear. Even Bill's persistent optimism couldn't deny certain realities: in the greatest country in the world, racism and bigotry against people of Japanese ancestry had never gone away. When Karl Klooster, a columnist and cartoonist for *This Week* magazine, praised the Naitos' efforts in Old Town in 1985, he received an anonymous call, bitterly criticizing people with Japanese heritage. As late as 1989, Bill received hate mail suggesting that being Japanese American was nothing to be proud of and that the US military should have clubbed Emperor Hirohito "to death like baby seals." On the fiftieth anniversary of Pearl Harbor, there were US veterans who did not distinguish between the Japanese who had launched the attack and the Japanese Americans who were punished because of it.

For Bill, the need for an official acknowledgment from the United States government was necessary to prove his belief that the United States was, in fact, the greatest country on earth. After a world war in which the United States came out arguably its greatest victor, he was a part of an intoxicating sense of invincibility and infallibility. His parents had chosen America as their adopted home for a reason, and he grew up loving it. Once, as Made In Oregon general manager Linda Strand, a white woman, was about to go into a meeting with Japanese importers, Bill reminded her, "Now, Linda, remember—don't let them forget who won the war." In other words, be confident. Americans shouldn't back down to anyone. That the United States was a place where dreams did come true was a conviction held by many, including those who had been evacuated from their homes and imprisoned in the camps. Bill had an absolute faith in the United States Constitution, and the country had to live up to its promise by righting this wrong.

In 1948, the federal government had attempted reparations through the Evacuation Claims Act, but the forcibly removed and prisoners who had been incarcerated bore a heavy evidentiary burden to prove their claims for lost property. The Justice Department contested each claim, an admission that they wanted to limit payouts, and only a third of those eligible filed for compensation. The actual financial loss to the victims of EO 9066 was estimated at from

$281 to $845 million (between $4 and $11 billion in 2023 dollars), but only $37 million of the $148 million claimed under the act was distributed. More importantly, the act admitted no wrongdoing or civil rights violations by the government, and accepting compensation meant foreswearing future claims against the government. The act was intended as a definitive end to further investigation into internment, and redress years later sought to rectify that attempt to turn a blind eye.

Beginning in 1970, several advocacy groups comprising Nisei and Sansei began to talk about seeking reparations and a public apology from the US government. The civil rights and Black Power movements had fueled the idea, empowering many to be more vocal about their experiences as Asian Americans in the United States. The Japanese American Citizens League voted to pursue redress in 1970, 1972, and 1974, but nothing much came of it. There was a split between those who wanted judicial and congressional redress and those who wanted to do nothing, afraid of a racist backlash and believing it would fail. Finally, in 1979, there was enough support to begin lobbying Congress.

When the Commission on Wartime Relocation and Internment of Citizens was formed a year later, Japanese Americans represented less than 1 percent of America's population; half of them lived in Hawai'i. The history of Executive Order 9066 and the forced removal and imprisonment of Japanese Americans was not widely known west of the Rockies, and it was not part of the history taught in schools, even in cities like Portland where expulsion took place. In order to get a redress bill passed, Congress had to be educated about not only the facts of imprisonment but also the importance of acknowledging that it was wrong.

Former prisoners recounted their experiences over and over—in person, in phone calls, and in writing. They had silently born the indignities of the past, but now they bravely exposed them to strangers. After three years, the commission released a 467-page report, *Personal Justice Denied*, which recommended a joint resolution, signed by the president, that apologized for forced removal and imprisonment, established a foundation for research and education, and paid reparations of $20,000 to each survivor. Unlike the Claims

Act of 1948, the money was not for financial loss but for the loss of constitutional rights.

Opposition in Congress lasted for five years, with financial redress as the largest issue. Some members worried about setting a precedent that would lead to reparations for African Americans and Native Americans. Others thought it was repugnant to attribute a monetary amount to suffering or to require money to make the apology meaningful. Bill thought that, instead of personal checks, the $1.2 billion should fund twenty professorships of civil liberties across the United States. Civil rights were continuously under threat, he argued, and they needed to be protected through public knowledge and awareness. Those who had survived the loss of their civil rights during World War II should be given ways to defend them for younger generations and future citizens, since they could speak firsthand about the consequences of Executive Order 9066.

In the end, a coalition of liberal Democrats and conservative Republicans who were committed to the Bill of Rights agreed that reparations were necessary, and Congress passed the Civil Liberties Act of 1988 by a vote of 257 to 156. All of the hard work and pain of reliving the memories of imprisonment bore fruit, and Congress issued a public apology and reparations to each living survivor. "For these fundamental violations of the basic civil liberties and constitutional right of these individuals of Japanese ancestry," the act read, "the Congress apologizes on behalf of the nation." President Ronald Reagan affirmed that constitutional rights had been trampled: "The sad chapter in our history, when Japanese Americans living on the West Coast were interned during World War II, teaches us an invaluable lesson: that our Constitution is based on a belief in the innate, God-given worth of every individual, and that this worth cannot be denied without diminishing and endangering us all."

Norman Mineta, a congressman from California who had been imprisoned at Heart Mountain as a youth, spoke proudly about the bill: "Today we are no longer ashamed or ignorant of our history." He was also the keynote speaker at Portland's Redress Celebration Dinner, which Bill helped support by hosting over five hundred people at Montgomery Park for an event sponsored by the Portland chapter of JACL and other Japanese American organizations. The gathering honored local activists and organizers who had helped with the redress movement, but for most of the Issei who had lost their businesses, homes, farms, and investments, reparations had come too late. By 1989, two hundred survivors of the camps were dying every month. Hide, who was ninety-six, died just months before he would have received his $20,000 check.

To Bill, however, the passage of the Civil Rights Act was evidence of American excellence. As he told the *Oregonian* on the fiftieth anniversary of Pearl Harbor, "What the evacuation meant was we were guilty when we really weren't. It was tearful. We were just as loyal as our neighbors—a bum deal. But remember, this is a great country where the admission of an error can be made!" Still, even with the public apology, and maybe because of it, Bill did not feel complete, partly because it seemed that only the Japanese American community knew about it, and Congress was arguing over funding the bill. In order to pay reparations to survivors over seventy years old, Congress would have had to appropriate $320 million. Instead, it appropriated $20 million, which JACL's national president called "a joke." Congress never did set aside the full amount.

But the money would not have made Bill whole. In 1979, he gave a lecture at the Commons Club, a Reed College breakfast series in which community leaders were invited to give personal talks about their life experiences. He told the early morning gathering how affected and hurt he had been by war hysteria. The pain was tangible in his words. Dorothy Hirsch, the president of Reed's alumni association, later regretted that the audience had not been larger to hear him. At Bill's memorial in 1996, Reed College President Paul Bragdon remembered that talk as "one of the more memorable experiences" of his own life. Even though Bill had achieved so much by not holding grudges, Bragdon said, he "never wanted to let go of those emotions." He wanted to use his experiences and emotional reaction to them to achieve greater good for the community by always asking, "Are we where we want to be and are we headed in a good direction?"

By the late 1980s, Bill planned to do something in Portland—in his hometown—that would be personal and lasting, something that would be a reminder of past mistakes so they would not be repeated. "If we don't have history," he said, "we are like sheep," and the long

legislative battle for reparations had brought to the surface feelings
Bill had stomached throughout his life. He had experienced a "trauma
in the first degree," and he needed something more. Robert Murase,
a landscape architect in Seattle, had the same impulse. When he was
four years old, he had been imprisoned as a Sansei with his family
at Topaz in Utah. He served in the military for two years and was
horrified by the Vietnam War, so he went to Japan, where he devoted
himself to its arts and culture. He came to appreciate and master the
use of stone and rock in Japanese landscape architecture, whose "gardens provide a keen sense of *wabi*, the absence of any ostentatious
element, and a sense of humility and melancholy." In San Francisco in
1965, as the campaign for reparations was just starting, he had tried to
create a memorial to the Japanese American experience during World
War II, but there had been little support. After he and his family
moved to Portland in 1979, he approached the JACL with an idea for
a memorial. At about the same time, his sons went to work for Bill at
Norcrest, young students of the Norcrest School of Economics.

Murase met Bill in 1987. The two bonded over the idea of a com-
memorative garden, and Bill became a man possessed, unwavering in
his determination to see their vision fulfilled. Murase had heard about
Bill's parsimonious nature, but Bill said to forget about money when
it came to the Japanese American Historical Plaza. He would pay for
everything and get reimbursed, if possible, later. The original proposal
had three guiding ideas: Opening Out, making known the history of
Japanese people in Oregon; Awareness, making the violation of their
civil rights known; and Enlightenment, creating an understanding
that national principles of freedom and fairness transcend race. The
plaza took a long two years to complete. Mark Sherman—a Norcrest
employee, a recent Reed College graduate, and Bill's righthand man
on the project—described getting city approval as an "obstacle course
of people that really resisted." Hank Sakamoto, who had worked
with Bill on Albers Mill and now the Plaza, described it as a "typical"
challenge for Bill, but one that "others with less vision and less courage might not have started."

In 1988, when the city told Bill they wanted to expand Waterfront Park north of Burnside, directly across from Nihonmachi, he
and Murase knew that the memorial had to be created next to the

history it was honoring. The city proposed a variety of less prominent locations for the plaza, partly because of the resistance to the subject matter: Judy Murase, Robert's wife, believed that the prospect of having Asian faces at the front door to the city was driving some of the opposition. The heads of Portland's major bureaus met with Bill to tell him that the memorial was simply not possible, noting the bureaucratic hurdles that would have to be cleared and how unlikely it was that was going to happen.

At the time, the City of Portland had no standards regarding memorials on city property, and there was another memorial being considered on the waterfront for slain Portland Police officers, as well as a children's play area. At the request of the Landmarks and Design Committees, a citizen committee was created to establish criteria for city memorials, which had the unspoken benefit of delaying a decision about the plaza. No one in the city wanted to be the one to tell Bill that the memorial couldn't be located in Waterfront Park, despite most believing that would be the outcome. But Bill was undeterred. "His whole heart and soul was in it," Oregon Nikkei Endowment member Nobi Masuoka remembered.

The city continued to push back against the plaza's subject matter. It was, they warned, a park seemingly dedicated to an American mistake. Bill emphasized that the focus would be on the Bill of Rights, which ought to apply to all Americans, regardless of ethnicity. "What is more important than the Bill of Rights?" he once asked a reporter. "Nothing." In addition, he believed that the story of American concentration camps was not exclusive but one that every American had to heed. The purpose of the memorial, Murase explained, was to show that "there's an interrelationship to all cultural groups." The plaza would focus on Japanese Americans, but what happened to them could happen to anyone who was on the wrong side of the majority. Bill also emphasized that the plaza was not meant to be a cemetery but a place where people could gather for multiple reasons.

In the end, it was Bill's personal relationships with decision-makers that tipped the result in his favor. All of the public and private projects Bill had done over the decades helped him make the plaza a reality. He was a "master planner," with a mental checklist of everything necessary to complete the project, from bureaucratic approvals to media exposure. "He saw how things had to be done," Judy Murase remembered, "and wasn't going to let anything get in the way." Mike Lindberg was parks commissioner, and Bill had planted the idea with him early. It had been a sunny day, and Bill asked if Lindberg could see the waterfront. Yes, he could. "Wouldn't it be nice to have cherry blossoms there?" Yes, it would. "Well, I've got someone in Japan who will donate them" to be planted on Waterfront Park, but that donation would be contingent on building the memorial. When the Japanese American Historical Plaza was finally approved in 1989, Bill reminded city council that "in this very room, the City Council passed an ordinance [in January 1942] canceling all business licenses held by Japanese residents." Now there would be a park honoring those who had suffered from that policy. The commissioners' approval came with a requirement that the community raise half million dollars to fund an endowment that would pay part of the construction costs and future maintenance fees.

Oregon Nikkei Endowment (ONE), a nonprofit, was created by Portland's Japanese American community, with Henry Sakamoto as president, Joseph Mine Wahl as vice president, Judy Murase as secretary, Dr. Matt Masuoka as treasurer, and Scott Sakamoto as public relations chair. Together with board members Jean Matsumoto, Robert Murase, Hisako Saito, Lury Sato, Miyuki "Miki" Yasui, and Dr. James Tsujimura, the board moved the idea of a memorial toward reality. Judy Murase had "never seen such a smooth, positive group." A key individual was Mark Sherman, whom Bill "loaned" to ONE from Norcrest almost full time. The group met three to four times a month in Murase's study and ate dinner together in Chinatown, usually at Hung Far Low, a restaurant that had opened in Old Town in 1928. Bill tried to host each dinner, but at the end of every meeting a board member would claim responsibility for the evening's check. After a few drinks, Bill would regale the group with stories of his childhood when Hide had taken him to the same restaurant.

When the revocable permit was officially granted for the plaza on June 29, 1990, Norcrest financially guaranteed performance of Oregon Nikkei Endowment to maintain the plaza under the permit's terms. Bill was head of fundraising, something he had done for political campaigns and nonprofit organizations for decades. When he told the board how much money they needed to raise—half a million dollars—everyone "fell on the floor" in shock, remembered Sakamoto. But Bill was nonchalant. "Don't worry," he said. "It'll be no problem—everyone here just write a check for $5,000." The project brought the Japanese American community together as nothing had since before the war. Imprisonment eradicated Nihonmachi and other neighborhoods, and those who had returned to Portland had scattered across the city. Through the fundraising campaign for the plaza, organizations and people found solidarity in donating.

Bill paid for a model to make the memorial more tangible to potential donors. He left no stone turned, no personal contact untouched, and reached out to Chamber of Commerce board of directors, Business Youth Exchange donor lists, Oregon State Bar members, Portland State University Foundation Corporate Associates Program donors, and Reed College alumni. Even US Senator Bob Packwood provided a list of potential donors. It was as if all of Bill's connections over decades had been building to this. A breakthrough came when the Collins Foundation and the Meyer Trust committed donations. It was no coincidence that former Norcrest School of Economics student Ken Thrasher was Fred Meyer's CFO at the time. Portland's sister city, Sapporo, also made a donation, as did the Portland Development Commission. People rarely turned down a request from Bill, knowing that if they came through for him, he would come through for them.

Robert Murase, meanwhile, had to focus on adapting his vision for the plaza to practical necessities, like allowing for smooth turns for bikes at the south end of the plaza, lowering an amphitheater area to prevent conflict with a potential trolley, and accommodating underground utility lines. The Portland Police demanded that there be no tall structures that could act as hiding places for the drug-dealing common in Old Town at the time. When the design plan was initially rejected, Bill made the entire board attend the follow-up meeting; he understood that it would be much harder to reject the project to their faces. The revised plan received approval.

The challenge in designing the plaza was to make the unknown both known and relatable. While most memorials are based on common knowledge, the Nikkei were still discovering their own history.

In 1985, there had been substantial friction over the creation of a Japanese American National Museum and its impact on regional groups. The push for redress had brought to light how much history there was to preserve but also how much had to be processed. Many Sansei had only a partial understanding of what their parents and grandparents had gone through during World War II, and some Nisei had been so young at the time that they couldn't remember the experience. A National Japanese American Historical Society newsletter in 1988 reported that "many Nisei had often felt that the Issei story had been scrubbed so clean, most often by Sansei, that it had become sterile." How to tell a story to the wider public when the narrative within the community was still muddled?

Murase's final design of the plaza reconciled these issues into a space meant to serve many functions: an acknowledgment of the history of Japanese immigrants and America's mistake in imprisoning them and Japanese Americans in World War II, a place of healing, a gathering space, and a pleasant place to walk. He used a traditional Japanese/Chinese aesthetic of four gateways into the plaza with animal spirts. The northern entrance—the tortoise gateway—was a large stone "set in the low earthen mound that evokes hope for a peaceful long future." The western entrance off Burnside—the tiger gateway—was flanked by bronze columns sculpted by Jim Gion, a Portland artist who had studied in Japan. Faces of the Japanese American experience, from farmers and family to soldiers and internees, were etched into the bronze.

On the east side, with the dragon gateway fronting the river, ninety cherry trees were planted along a small hill, a donation from the Japanese Grain Importers Association. A large granite stone engraved with the names of all ten prison camps was placed in the center, with a stone walkway curving around it. Against the hill of trees was the Blue Dragon wall, lined with large boulders with bronze plaques. Murase requested that the stones be set by Masatoshi Izumi, an apprentice of Isamu Naguchi, a sculptor and designer who died in 1988. Born in 1904 to a white mother and Japanese father, Naguchi had been transformed by bigotry following Pearl Harbor. He started Nisei Writers and Artists Mobilization for Democracy and asked to be placed in a camp, where he hoped to use his art to improve conditions (he left after seven months when his efforts failed). Masatoshi Izumi spent twenty-five years as Naguchi's top assistant and apprentice.

Bill gave Izumi an apartment at McCormick Pier for the time it took him to complete his work on the plaza. Izumi could not speak English but was able to facilitate placement of the stones without difficulty. With the Murases translating, he described the function of the stones: "This particular project relates to history, and that's very good, especially to using natural stones. It's a very outstanding project, and we have a sense of history, of natural stone and its age." Stones at the southern entrance—the phoenix gateway—were large and singular to represent the single men of the first wave of Issei. Then the stones slowly joined together to make a unified wall, representing the community that came to be over time. Short verses were taken from the work of Hisako Saito, Shizue Iwatsuki, and Lawson Inada. Saito, a founding member of ONE, had been imprisoned in Minidoka as a twenty-nine-year-old. Iwatsuki had carved out a commendable life in Hood River before being imprisoned at Tule Lake and Minidoka. Inada, who had been imprisoned as a four-year-old with his family in Jerome, Arkansas, edited the poems to fit on twelve stones. A professor of English at Southern Oregon State College and Poet Laureate of Oregon, Inada said that the closest he had been to Japan was Import Plaza, but the project was of profound importance to him. Initially, he had considered including more text, but that might have detracted from the other aesthetic parts of the plaza and its overall experience. That concern caused him to swing in the opposite direction, considering pictographs to almost completely eliminate the impact of words on a visitor's experience. Eventually, he decided on a happy medium between the two: a series of haiku on the rocks.

Haiku left the main portion of the plaza "artistically sound, clean, 'shibui,'" which balances simplicity with complexity. The haiku interacted with each other, like a community, with voices echoing around each other. Taken together, they told the story of Japanese immigrants in Oregon, coming to America, adapting to a new country, war and imprisonment, and returning home and starting anew. "With new hope / We build new lives. / Why complain when it rains? / This is what it means to be free." A gap in the wall represented the jarring

Stone in the Japanese American Historical Plaza

effect of incarceration. Inada wanted to avoid a "tombstone effect" by keeping the writing free of politics, preachiness, and angry emotion or meaning. With regard to the camps, he tried to create irony and keep the message positive, which, he said, "is what we did in real life anyway." The Bill of Rights was emblazoned in bronze on a stone, along with President Reagan's public apology. The bronze was intended to darken over time and the rocks to gather moss. Murase wanted the plaza to have *wabi*, the Japanese aesthetic that highlights imperfection, impermanence, and spiritual longing.

At the opening ceremony on August 3, 1990, the Japanese American Historical Plaza was not yet finished, and there was bare dirt instead of grass. Almost a thousand people attended, many of whom were survivors. Bill had picked that weekend because the Greater Portland Reunion of Japanese-Americans was to take place. Joan Biggs, a public relations consultant who had done other work for Bill, remembered how "crystal clear" the day was, with "the bluest sky" as a backdrop. It was also hot, and, at one point Bill crossed the street to the Globe Hotel Import Plaza store, grabbed as many Japanese sun umbrellas as he could, and gave them out to elderly attendees.

Twenty years later, Biggs could still remember the "deep emotion" of the opening celebration. A long row of American flags lined the memorial, and men who had served in the 442nd Regimental Combat Unit and 100th Battalion provided the color guard. The Pledge of Allegiance was recited, and Secretary of State Barbara Roberts read a proclamation by Governor Neil Goldschmidt making August 3, 1990, Japanese American Citizens Day. Nola Sagai Bogle sang "America the Beautiful," emphasizing that the plaza was meant to benefit all Americans. It was Bill's gift to US democracy.

Oregon Supreme Court Justice Michael Gillette delivered a speech dressed in his judicial robes at Bill's request. It was important, Bill felt, to have a visible symbol of justice at the ceremony. "What is the reason for creating a memorial?" the justice asked. "It seems to me that the answer to that is clear. Because without a memorial, without a physical gesture of remembrance, we can, we may, we will, forget." Consul-General Akira Watanabe paraphrased a Japanese haiku poet: "Do not seek to follow / In the footsteps of Men of Old / Seek instead what they sought." At the end of the ceremony, Bill helped release a hundred white friendship pigeons into the air, symbolizing peace and renewal. They circled twice around the crowd and then flew away into the clear blue sky. The Portland Fire Department fireboat shot out red, white, and blue water, capping off the ceremony in patriotic fashion.

Harriet Sherburne of the city's Design Committee later said that the "audience involvement" at the dedication "drew us all together as a community of caring citizens." Oregon US Senator Bob Packwood noted that the plaza was "at once a solemn reminder of dark times and a celebration of honor and prosperity." One of its most important supporters through the process, Commissioner Mike Lindberg had not realized the emotional impact the plaza would have until he saw it in person. It was everything Bill had hoped to create, but he didn't stop there. He also requested that a sign with the plaza's name be placed on Interstate 5. It was small gesture but deeply meaningful, signifying its importance beyond the Japanese American community. After the plaza opened, Mark Sherman curated a book commemorating the plaza, *Touching the Stones*, and Bill turned to Joe Erceg, the tenant who had been with Norcrest the longest, to create the design. He gave a copy to everyone he could, including President Bill Clinton and Vice President Al Gore, who were in Portland for a Pacific Rim economic summit.

For Bill, the plaza and its companion book were far more significant than an apology and reparations could ever be. When he took fellow Reedie Norman Lezin through the plaza, "he glowed with pleasure over every rock, every poem," despite the chilly rain, recalled Lezin in a condolence letter. It was a vindication. "More personally satisfying to me," Bill said in 1993, "is that the Plaza has helped to remove the mark of Enemy from the Japanese American community here. What we built is a symbol of the many contributions Japanese Americans have made in Portland, not purely for our own private gain, but for the betterment of the broader community we live in." A critical element of the plaza's power was the tours conducted by ONE volunteers, including Bill. Fifth-grade teacher Marianne Sweeney took her class on one of Bill's tours of the plaza. In her thank-you card to him, she wrote that "the cherry trees in full bloom [stood] still to hear you unlock the message of the 'talking stones.'" She recounted how moving it was for the students and parents to listen while he spoke "so eloquently about their rights as Americans."

Bill's White Stag offices were just across the street from the plaza, and he often called City Commissioner Lindberg to complain about graffiti on the stones or to ask for the sprinklers to be turned on if homeless people were loitering there. But he also called just to draw the commissioner's attention to how beautiful it was: "Look out your window, Mike. Isn't it a beautiful day and a wonderful city?" He watched over the plaza like it was his own.

Bill and the rest of the Oregon Nikkei Endowment board agreed that the next step was to create a museum as a companion to the plaza. He had been a supporter of the Japanese American National Museum in California, and an unfulfilled part of the reparations bill had been for research and public education. So, in fall of 1989, he started in earnest to pursue the idea of a permanent Japanese Cultural and Historical Center in Portland, along with a traveling exhibit. The estimate for a museum in Portland was between $5 and $6 million dollars, but in 1990 President Bill Clinton appropriated a *total* of $5 million for research and education, leaving Bill and other Japanese Americans to organize and fundraise for museums on their own.

Bill leading a tour of the Japanese American Historical Plaza, early 1990s

By 1996 Bill was making plans to renovate the Bickel Block on Front Avenue and Couch Street for the newly conceived Oregon Nikkei Legacy Center. His death that year delayed the process, but his brother Sam eventually donated space for the center in the Rich Hotel. The last generation of Issei in Oregon was dying, and efforts were made to archive oral histories, photos, and documents. "We wanted to save the cultural basis of the community because it could disappear on us in no time," Sam said at the opening ceremony in 1997. In 2004, the museum moved to the Merchant Hotel, a fitting location to house Nihonmachi's story: before Executive Order 9066, it had been the home of Japanese offices, a grocery store, and offices of *Japanese Oregon Weekly*.[1] Inside the museum, a permanent exhibit told the history of the Japanese American immigrant experience, from arrival through imprisonment and return. It was the final piece of a project that was Bill's legacy to the city and its Japanese American community.

---

1   In 2021, the museum rebranded itself as the Japanese American Museum of Oregon and moved to 411 NW Flanders Street.

It also honored his father by commemorating Issei who had achieved so much and would no longer be at risk of being forgotten.

In 1941, Minoru Yasui, a Portland lawyer born in Hood River, had intentionally broken the military curfew on Japanese and Japanese Americans to challenge its constitutionality. He lost his case when the US Supreme Court upheld the law. After emerging from solitary confinement in prison and then months in Minidoka concentration camp, he was admitted to the Colorado state bar and in 1952 helped pass the Immigration and Nationality Act, which allowed Japanese immigrants to become citizens. In 1983, when Yasui received Oregon ACLU's MacNaughton Award in honor of his life works, he quoted Alfred Lord Tennyson's "Ulysses." Bill kept a clipping of the quote on his desk. When Tennyson wrote "to strive, to seek, to find, and not to yield," he was describing a man who had been through battles and seen much of the world, a "grey spirit yearning in desire to follow knowledge like a sinking star, beyond the utmost bound of human thought." It had taken Bill "50 years to get off that letter 'E' [for enemy] all over my Japanese face," he said in 1993. But it was also evidence that he should never give up and never stop striving, no matter the odds and no matter his age.

CHAPTER 21

Bill's love of greenspaces and the city of Portland extended to his final project, a classical Chinese garden. He was brought in to the project by Donald Jenkins, curator of Asian art at the Portland Art Museum, but he already knew about it because of city council member Mike Lindberg. A Chinese garden had been Lindberg's idea from several years before. It was an exciting concept, and Bill embraced it with passion. Portland needed a companion to the Japanese Garden in Washington Park, he thought, and a Chinese garden in Old Town could become a focal point for the area. A public Chinese garden fit with his vision of Old Town as a multicultural neighborhood, one that honored the part it had played for many people in Portland, from Germans and Scandinavians to Irish, Greeks, and Sephardic and Russian Jews. So, between 1991 and 1996, Bill served as a director of the Classical Chinese Garden Society.

Bill had always supported Chinese culture and history in Old Town, hoping in the 1970s that it would become like Grant Avenue in San Francisco. He had cheered city council's adoption of the Chinatown Development Committee's redevelopment plan, which included bilingual signs, ornamental streetlights, and the China gate in the neighborhood. In 1989, he celebrated the designation of New Chinatown/Japantown on the National Register of Historic Districts. He believed that a classical Chinese garden would be yet another attraction for Old Town and would look "just wonderful on a postcard." It would also counter Old Town's reputation as an open drug market, caused by the influx of heroin into the neighborhood in the early 1990s.

Bill used the prospective garden as an incentive for the Oregon Department of Transportation to move its headquarters into the NW Natural building on Third and Everett. He used the Chinese garden as evidence of who ODOT's neighbors would be, going to lunch with many of the agency's employees and showing them renderings of the garden as part of his pitch. It was a bit of chicken and egg: the garden was an enticement for ODOT to move to the neighborhood, and the presence of ODOT warranted investment in the garden. The approach worked, and it turned out to also be a critical part of finding a location for what would become known as the Lan Su Chinese Garden.

For that to happen, Bill used his political connections, and together with city council member Mike Lindberg, who was still head of the Portland Parks Bureau, they got Mayor Vera Katz fully on board with the project. Bill had great respect for the politicians he had worked with over the years, but he had never wanted to enter politics himself. Mayor Bud Clark and others had urged him to run for mayor throughout the 1980s and 1990s, and businessman Emery Zidell had offered him a $10,000 donation as incentive to run, but he resisted all calls to seek elected office. Politicians lived in a what-have-you-done-for-me-lately universe, he thought, where voters demanded instant results. It was a struggle to get people to trust in long-term solutions when problems loomed large in the here and now. Working for someone else, including voters and campaign donors, would have hampered his ability to try new things and would have eaten up his time with bureaucracy. Bill was also opposed to doing a "lousy job" that would require him to attend early-morning meetings and late-night banquets, he explained in 1991. As he told entrepreneur Sam Brooks, sometimes it was better to be the kingmaker than the king.

A classical Chinese garden had been a dream of Mike Lindberg's since 1985, when he visited China. He brought the idea before city council in 1989, when he presented an elaborate study of a garden, cultural center, and museum. But it was Vera Katz who would become the driving force behind Lan Su. The first woman speaker of the Oregon House of Representatives, Katz had wanted to become a lawyer but was discouraged because of her gender. So she volunteered for political campaigns and was eventually elected to a seat in the Oregon legislature. She and Bill likely crossed paths during her first term in the early 1970s because of her interest in public housing and health care.

In July 1975, a horrific fire swept through the Norcrest building that housed Erickson's Saloon and the Pomona Hotel, killing thirteen people. The city's updated 1972 fire code had not been enforced, and multiple buildings in Old Town had violations similar to the one that led to the Pomona tragedy. In response, Mayor Goldschmidt convened a citizens committee to balance the need for owners to meet fire safety requirements with the hundreds of people who would be left homeless by closing noncompliant buildings. He appointed Katz as chair. Part of the committee's focus was to encourage hotel owners to renovate their buildings rather than tear them down. As part of her work on the committee, Katz organized a tour of Old Town in 1975 for US representative Les AuCoin, who sat on the Housing and Community Development subcommittee. The tour included Sam and Bill.

When Katz ran for mayor in 1992, she was up against Earl Blumenauer, a member of the city council. Bill backed Blumenauer in the race, saying he was the better candidate for mayor and that Katz was better suited for superintendent of Portland Public Schools (PPS). Katz had been chair of the Joint Ways and Means Subcommittee on Education in the legislature and had been a formidable leader, and Bill thought she would be a natural fit for PPS. But Bill also had a personal history with Blumenauer. When Blumenauer was a student at Lewis & Clark College, he had worked with Bill's eldest son, Bob, then a sophomore in high school, on a campaign to lower the voting age. That was the beginning of Bill's support for Blumenauer's long career in law-making, which he supported by donating space and even an occasional and "painful" small cash contribution. But Katz won the contest. Bill thought Blumenauer came off as "too serious," and he suggested that he wear a bowtie to soften his appearance. Blumenauer thought it was a bit rich coming from Bill: "thinking about someone like Bill giving *me* fashion advice," he recalled in 2009. Blumenauer gave it a try, wearing bowties on and off in the coming months, and in 1996 he won election to the US House of Representatives.[1]

Bill embraced Katz as mayor, and she embraced the Lan Su project. In 1988, Mayor Bud Clark had formalized a sister-city relationship with Suzhou, which had offered to send gardeners to Portland

---

1 When Blumenauer arrived at the Capitol, Senator Mark Hatfield pulled him aside and said, "You wear those bowties, right? Wear them every day." He has, and he has won reelection ever since.

to install a true classical Chinese garden in exchange for Portland's help in developing Suzhou's wastewater system. Clark visited Suzhou the following year, a few weeks after city council gave its blessing to a privately funded garden. In 1990, the Classical Chinese Garden Society submitted a model of the prospective garden, estimated to cost six to seven million dollars. Both Vancouver, BC, and Seattle had plans for their own classical Chinese gardens, and there was a growing appreciation for creating classical gardens to honor Chinese heritage and culture. In 1991—the same year Donald Jenkins got Bill involved—the society began to host events to drum up community support and raise money.

Mayor Katz executed the agreement with Suzhou to partner with the city to create the garden and put a trade center in the Galleria. At the signing event with the mayor of Suzhou and Katz, Sean P. Nelson of the *Asian Reporter* watched as Bill entered and gave Katz a big kiss on the lips. Katz joyfully exclaimed, "Oh, I must have done something right to get a kiss out of you!" But despite that initial joy, the project struggled to make substantial gains, in part because there was no location and no money. Bill knew that acquiring the land was probably easier than raising cash, and he believed that the building and parking lot owned by the natural gas utility, NW Natural, offered the best opportunity. He suggested a meeting between Katz and Bob Ridgeley, head of NW Natural.

Andrew Haruyama, from the city's Office of International Relations, was impressed with Bill's ability to facilitate the negotiations between NW Natural and the city. In truth, Bill's negotiation consisted of constantly calling—nagging, more accurately—Ridgeley about the property until he finally wore him down. In March 1995, Portland City Council voted unanimously to option NW Natural's 176-space parking lot on Third and Everett for ninety-nine years for one dollar. In exchange, the city had to replace the parking spaces and the Garden Society had to come up with private money to pay for the garden. Bill was named the chair of fundraising for the project in 1995 and began campaigning to raise the projected six to seven million dollars necessary to fund construction. Mayor Katz created a steering committee, directing Commissioners Charlie Hales and Mike Lindberg to help raise money. Bruce Allen of the PDC and Haruyama completed

Bill in the White Stag offices, framed Executive Order 9066 visible on the column behind him

the group. Raising the money was always going to be difficult, but there were other knotty issues. A consensus on the project had to be reached in Old Town among its many interest groups, activists, and cultural communities. The *Oregonian* characterized the road ahead as "a virtual minefield on its three-year journey to fruition."

Just as the Classic Chinese Garden Society had settled on the NW Natural parking lot location, Mental Health Services West threw a wrench in the plans. The company had purchased the Royal Palm Hotel building across the street, where it wanted to open a shelter for homeless people with mental conditions. Organizers could not think of a less attractive neighbor for the Chinese garden. The plan also raised concerns among members of the Chinese community, who felt that they had been ignored during the approval process for the shelter. "It seems like another example of the Chinese community being treated like second class," noted Bruce Wong of the Chinese Consolidated Benevolent Association and president of the Classical Chinese Garden Society. The CCBA appealed the city's decision to award a permit to Mental Health Services. The animosity over the situation caused the coalition that had come together in support of the garden to fall apart. After the CCBA removed its support for the garden, both sister-city associations withdrew from the steering committee. They couldn't continue their involvement without local Chinese support and, furthermore, the city hadn't properly acknowledged Chinese cultural practice when it approved the shelter. It became a considerable distraction. Andrew Haruyama, the point person for the project in the mayor's office, was frustrated and dispirited, and he relied on Bill, who coached him through the process and reminded him not to get bogged down in petty grievances. Look at the big picture, Bill advised, and the details will sort themselves out.

Bill fell ill in late April 1996 and was hospitalized shortly after the news hit that the Chinese garden was in trouble. When Mayor Katz called to ask him if there was anything she could do for him, his answer was, "Build the garden." When Bill passed away soon after, Mayor Katz declared that the garden would be built, with or without the involvement of the sister-city associations. The project was already too far along, in her estimation, and while she hoped the sister cities would return to the project, she would not allow the shelter to stop the garden. There was a balance that could be achieved in the neighborhood, she believed, between social services and a beautiful, intimate garden.

Then there was the financing issue. Only $100,000 had been raised of the roughly $12 million that was now needed to complete the project, and there was no plan for going forward. Like many projects where Bill was in charge of fundraising, there hadn't been much structure put in place, and the effort relied on him for his energy and connections. To kick the campaign back into gear after Bill died, a Classical Garden Project Executive Committee replaced the steering committee, Bobbe Blacher was hired as director of development, and a trust led by Bob Naito was formed to raise the money. In 1999, after raising $8.8 million in private funds and obtaining $2.9 million in tax increment financing from PDC, work began on Lan Su Garden, the Garden of Awakening Orchid. The sixteen-ton rock garden was created in China and shipped to Portland in pieces, holding fast to traditional Chinese philosophy while being transported across the

Pacific Ocean. Lan Su's chief designer, Kuang Zhen Yan, described the philosophy behind Suzhou's style: "What's important is not how it looks. What's important is how it makes you feel when you're in it." It was an idea that was at the core of Bill's approach to relationships and life.

No one can know how early Bill realized that his sickness was serious. The diagnosis of aggressive cancer was made on April 30, 1996, but he had been sick with what was thought to be pneumonia eight weeks earlier. Bing Sheldon noticed subtle changes that suggested he wasn't well, and Bill missed a Reed College board meeting, which he had never done. Those close to him noticed that his behavior was becoming erratic. But he kept his suffering to himself. He called his son Bob back into the business and hired a commercial property manager to review the company's properties and to hire a property manager specifically for Montgomery Park.

Still, Bill seemed unperturbed by his impending death. On his desk, he kept a copy of the poem "Thanatopsis," by William Cullen Bryant, which describes death not as an end to be lamented but as a beginning to be welcomed.

So live, that when thy summons comes to join
The innumerable caravan, which moves
To that mysterious realm, where each shall take
His chamber in the silent halls of death,
Thou go not, like the quarry-slave at night,
Scourged to his dungeon, but, sustained and soothed
By an unfaltering trust, approach thy grave,
Like one who wraps the drapery of his couch
About him, and lies down to pleasant dreams.

Two weeks before his death, he showed up for a Portland Parks Bureau tour, where he spoke of his hopes and plans for the future. He managed through his obvious discomfort and encouraged the crowd to support the Urban Forestry Commission. Perhaps most telling, he appeared before a Skyline Elementary School class to speak about Japanese Americans and his experience as a second-generation immigrant. He was hospitalized shortly after.

Bill died on May 8, 1996. The news broke during city council's afternoon session, where members were stunned and saddened. The next day, his grandchildren lit Rudolph's nose on the White Stag sign. A public viewing and a burial service were held at Willamette View Cemetery, with full military honors in tribute to his service during World War II. A hundred people with umbrellas gathered around the small building where the family sat with his coffin, standing in a torrential downpour to pay respects to a man who had been important to them.

A public memorial was held at the Japanese American Historical Plaza. Bill had requested that four faiths be represented, since he was not sure whom he might meet in the afterlife. Rabbi Joshua Stampfer of Congregation Neveh Shalom, Reverend Julie S. Hanada-Lee of Oregon Buddhist Temple, Reverend George Uyemura of Epworth Church, and Reverend Richard Berg, CSC of Downtown Chapel of St. Vincent de Paul, gave their blessings. "America the Beautiful" and "Amazing Grace" were sung, and the speakers included Reed College president Paul Bragdon, Mayor Bud Clark, fellow Reedie Bill Clawson, Norcrest School of Economics alum Sho Dozono, Lan Su Garden promoter Donald Jenkins, architect Bing Sheldon, nephew Tim Sonley, son Bob, brother-in-law Per Sjogren, and Sam. Per Sjogren read a poem Bill had selected by Johann Wolfgang von Goethe, both in the original German and in English:

> Your fortunate eyes
> What all you have seen,
> May it be as it will.
> It was lovely to me.

Everyone received a Japanese green maple seedling to plant.

Bill always advocated for renaming places and things in honor of others, and there was a rush to find something to name after him. "The goal of naming a landmark," he wrote in an op-ed attempting to get something named after Governor Tom McCall, "should be more than simply to pay tribute to a great man Oregonians knew and loved. Rather, the goal should be to memorialize Tom McCall and that for which he stood so future generations will know the importance that

this generation placed on Oregon's natural heritage and on preservation of the state's livability." Renaming Front Avenue, which ran
through Old Town along the Willamette River, was suggested multiple times, "to let his name be the beginning of the area that he had
done so much for," as one letter to the editor suggested.

Meanwhile, in the summer of 1996, many private organizations
renamed awards after him: Portland Chamber of Commerce William
S. Naito Outstanding Service Award; Historic Preservation League
of Oregon William Naito Award for Community Preservation; Livable Oregon Bill Naito Main Street Citizen Award; and Commercial
Association of Brokers Bill Naito Award. The Urban Forestry Commission created the Bill Naito Community Trees Award. The first
floor of Multnomah County's Central Library became the Bill Naito
Lobby, and the Portland Police Museum put up a memorial in honor
of its longtime supporter. The National Trust for Historic Preservation
dedicated its fiftieth conference to Bill, calling him "an individual who
truly made a difference in preservation, in short, a preservation hero."
Norcrest employees created a memorial fund at the library, and Noella
Aufmuth, a Norcrest baby, ran in a race to raise money for cancer
research in his memory. The following year, the Oregon Symphony
dedicated a performance of Beethoven's Third Symphony to Bill.

In the end, Front Avenue was renamed Bill Naito Parkway to
honor his commitment to the Old Town neighborhood. Portland
City Council violated its own law by waiving the requirement that a
five-year wait period pass after a person's death before honoring them
with a renaming tribute. The Portland Chamber of Commerce did not
oppose the decision. "We could've waited," Mayor Katz explained,
"but when Bill visits with us, he says you gotta do it and you gotta
do it now. . . . In the spirit of Bill Naito, we're going to do it and do it
right now." The parkway was unveiled at Front Avenue and Yamhill
forty-six days after Bill died. It was fitting having his name on the
north-south axis of downtown, a stretch of road he had nursed from
the divisive Harbor Drive to an open public park. A livable Portland
was his gift to the city that had once been unlivable for him.

In 1951, Bill would have said that he was going to become a professor, probably at the University of Chicago with his mentor Milton
Friedman. Many Japanese Americans who suffered the injustices of

Executive Order 9066 found the Midwest far more welcoming than the West Coast, and Bill would have expected that he and Micki could have carved out a successful life there, away from his family in Portland. But only a year later, he found himself living back with his parents on Burnside and finding his way into the family business. Did he have any regrets? In 1988, when he received an honorary doctorate from Linfield College, he said he didn't: "There is no funner career than being an entrepreneur. There is tremendous enjoyment in building your own business. I wouldn't trade the life I had."

EPILOGUE

Norcrest's buildings created a tangible legacy in the city, as did all Bill's civic works, but Bill's family business didn't have the same longevity. It's unlikely that he foresaw that his family business of historic renovations would bring a certain infamy as well. After his death, there was almost instantaneous infighting over control of the business. It is partly his fault, and because of his own arrogance, that there was not a better succession plan in place. The existing plan at the time of his death—that the surviving brother would inherit one extra controlling share upon death of the other—was based on an unrealistically optimistic view of the family dynamics, even by Bill's standards.

In the late 1980s, Bill compared the family business to the "Japanese truck gardening farms that were so prevalent during the '20s and '30s." This was tongue-in-cheek but also true: most members of the family were employees of Norcrest at some point. It was a running joke that no one knew where the family ended and the business began. And Bill *was* the business—its talismanic leader who appeared impervious to everything and kept almost total control of it. It is impossible to hypothesize a Norcrest without Sam, but Bill was its engine, and that's why it struggled to continue in the same forceful, dynamic vein in his absence. The balance that he had achieved with his older brother did not transfer beyond the two of them, and the result was two lawsuits between the family members. The settlement from the second trial resulted in Sam keeping the mercantile and retail divisions, and the real estate properties spinning off into a new business for the remaining family members.

It was not what Bill would have wanted, but it didn't diminish the legacy of livability that he left the city through his projects and also the people. Patrick LaCrosse, of the Portland Development

Commission, described Bill's impact: "His opening line for years was that this is a great city and a great day, and we've got a great future. If you were around him long enough, you'd believe it."

NOTES ON SOURCES

Personal Family Library

A significant part of my research relied on my personal library of Norcrest and Naito family letters, notes, newspaper clippings, and photos. This includes scrapbooks, kept by Norcrest employees and the family, containing newspaper articles and correspondence throughout the years. In addition, I have Norcrest's marketing materials for its buildings and the research into the histories of the buildings and their historic designations. Twelve employees also gave the company their written recollections of Norcrest when the company sold the White Stag building in 2015, which I have.

I have corporate documentation, such as board minutes and bylaws, from Norcrest's many years. In addition, I have many files related to the two lawsuits that resulted after Bill's death. I also received a sizable number of letters, notes, and business paraphernalia that had been on Bill's desk at the time of his death, as well as other papers and photos that had been collected by his wife, Micki. This includes the family's slides, which she went through with me to describe where they were taken and what was happening at the time. She also gave me all of the get-well and condolence cards that Bill and she received at the time of his illness and death, which numbered in the hundreds.

Interviews

I held group interviews throughout 2017 with the following people:

First Interstate/Wells Fargo banker Robert Ames
P&C Construction owner and manager Dale Campbell
Former Norcrest employee Sho Dozono
Vintage Trolley founding board member Bill Failing
Urban planner Rick Gustafson
City of Portland forester David Judd
Former Norcrest employee Keane Satchwell

Portland city commissioner Mike Lindberg
Architect Jack Miller
Bill's daughter and former Galleria manager Anne Naito-Campbell
Portland Planning Bureau senior staff member Rodney O'Hiser
Consultant Ruth Scott
Architect Roger Shiels
Former Made In Oregon manager Linda Strand
Former Norcrest employee Ken Thrasher
Port of Portland executive director Bill Wyatt

Individual interviews were held with the following people:
Former Oregon governor and Portland mayor Neil Goldschmidt in
2017
Norcrest employee Richard Lenhart in 2009
Bill's widow Micki Naito throughout 2009 to 2017
Linda Strand in 2017

The Oregon Nikkei Endowment (now Japanese American Museum of
Oregon) conducted many interviews and oral histories which I relied on.
Businessowner George Azumano in 2009
Public relations specialist Joan Biggs in 2004
US representative Earl Blumenauer in 2009
Reed College president Paul Bragdon in 2009
Real estate broker Paul Breuer in 2009
Entrepreneur Sam Brooks in 2009
Dale Campbell in 2009
Norcrest real estate manager Doug Campbell in 2009
Portland mayor Bud Clark
Reed College alum Bill Clauson in 2009
Sho Dozono in 2009
Graphic designer Joe Erceg
Bill Failing in 2009
Author Gerry Frank in 2009
Rick Gustafson in 2009
Phil Kalberer in 2009
NW Natural CEO Gregg Kantor
Businessowner David Kobos in 2009
Portland Mayor's Office of International Affairs Andrew
Haruyama in 2009

Professor of architecture Suenn Ho in 2009

Mike Lindberg in 2009

Oregon Nikkei Endowment founding board member Nobi
    Masuoka in 2009

Oregon Nikkei Endowment founding board member Judy Murase
    in 2004

Older brother Samuel T. Naito in 2003

Historian Chet Orloff in 2009

Oregon Nikkei Endowment founding board member Henry
    Sakamoto in 2009

Architect George "Bing" Sheldon in 2009

Former Norcrest employee Mark Sherman in 2004

Roger Shiels in 2009

Architect David Soderstrom in 2009

Linda Strand in 2009

Real estate broker Donn Sullivan in 2009

Former Norcrest employee Ken Thrasher in 2009

Portland Development Commission chair Bruce Warner in 2009

Norcrest employee Jean Weitzel in 2009

Public relations specialist Karen Whitman in 2009

Bill Wyatt in 2009

Oregon Nikkei Endowment founding board member Miyuki Yasui
    in 2004

Chapter 1

In writing about Portland's turn-of-the-century history, I relied on books
by Carl Abbott, *Greater Portland: Urban Life and Landscape in the
Pacific Northwest*, *Portland in Three Centuries*, and *Portland: Planning,
Politics, and Growth in a Twentieth-Century City*; as well as Jewel Lansing's *Portland: People, Politics, and Power*. Contemporaneous articles
from the *Oregonian* in 1918, 1919, and 1937 also provided context.

For information on the Meiji Restoration and turn-of-the-century
Japan, I used Edward Steidensticker's *Low City, High City* and S. C.
M. Paine's *The Japanese Empire*. Several *Oregon Historical Quarterly* articles provided background on the Issei experience in Oregon,
including "A History of Oregon's Issei, 1880–1952," "The Nikkei in
Oregon, 1834–1940," and "Myron Louie Lee: Portland's Louie Chung
(1876–1926)."

Chapter 2

Much of Bill's recounting of his childhood can be found in two articles by Charlotte Babcock, MD, his psychotherapist: "Personal and Cultural Factors in Treating a Nisei Man" in *Clinical Studies in Culture Conflict* in 1958, and "Psychoanalysis and Follow-Up: The Personal and Cultural Meaning of the Experience of a Nisei in Treatment," in *Psychotherapy and Training in Clinical Social Work* in 1980. Other remembrances came from articles in the *Oregonian* in 1989 and 1993; the *Downtowner* in 1988; the *Business Journal* in 1996; and *Metro: The City Magazine* in 1985, as well as an interview of Sam Naito by the Japanese American Museum of Oregon.

Historical context was found in contemporaneous articles in the *Oregonian* and the *Oregon Journal* in 1920, 1923, 1926, and 1939, as well as Abbott's *Portland: Planning, Politics, and Growth in a Twentieth-Century City*. Ruth A. Sasaki's *The Loom* provided a fictional account of the experience of being Nisei in America during the same time as Bill.

Chapter 3

In addition to contemporaneous articles from the *Oregonian* from 1935 and 1942, I also relied on newspaper articles from the *Utah Nippo* from 1942 through 1944, the *Utah Chronicle* in 1942, the *Neighbor* in 1983, and *Metro: The City Magazine* in 1985. *Missing Stories: An Oral History of Ethnic and Minority Groups in Utah,* by Leslie G. Kalen and Eileen Hallet Stone, provided great insight, as did *An Editor for Oregon: Charles A. Sprague and the Politics of Change* by Floyd McKay.

Bill's personal accounts drew from interviews with the Oregon Holocaust Resource Center in 1994, *Northwest Reports* in 1992, Oregon Public Broadcasting's *Oregon Portraits: Bill Naito* in 1990, the psycho-analysis articles referenced above for chapter 2, and his own personal writings in 1993 and 1994. I also relied on *Righting a Wrong* by Leslie T. Hatamiya, *Only What We Could Carry* edited by Lawson Inada, and the *Oregon Historical Quarterly* articles referenced for chapter 2.

Chapter 4

This chapter relied on personal correspondence and remembrances of Bill's fellow service members after his death in 1996, as well as his own in *Oregon Portraits*. James Oda's *Heroic Struggles of Japanese Americans* and Stone Ishimaru's *Military Intelligence Service Language School US Army* also provided context.

Chapter 5

This chapter relied on articles from the *New Yorker* in 1944; *Saturday Evening Post* in 1952; the *Downtowner* in 1990; the *Oregonian* in 1981, 1983, 1988, 1990–1991, and 1996; *Oregon Magazine* in 1995; and *Metro: The City Magazine* in 1985. Remembrances came from Bill's speech, "A Personal Experience of Human Rights" in 1993, and in condolence correspondence in 1996 from Steven Koblick, Art Leigh, Fred Rosenblum, David Wu, as well as Paul Bragdon's speech at Bill's memorial service.

Insight also came from interviews with Bill's close friends and colleagues, including Joan Biggs, Neil Goldschmidt, Mike Lindberg, Chet Orloff, and Bill Wyatt. John Okada's *No-No Boy* also provided important understanding of the Nisei experience in postwar America.

Chapter 6

Multiple personal interviews with Micki Naito, as well as extensive correspondence between her and her brother Lorne between 1940 and 1947, formed the backbone of most of the chapter, as well as an interview by the Japanese American Museum of Oregon of Bill's close friend Bill Clauson. Bill's interview with *Metro: The City Magazine* in 1985 and an *Oregonian* article of the same time were also relied on.

Chapter 7

Personal interviews with Richard Lenhart, Bill Wyatt, and Nobi Masuoka helped to inform this chapter, as well as articles from the *Hood River News* in 1945; the *Oregonian* in 1945, 1971, and 1990; *Oregon Journal* in 1956; the *Downtowner* in 1978; *Business Success News* in 1980; and the *Asian Reporter* in 1999. Greg Robinson's *A Tragedy of Democracy: Japanese Confinement in North America* helped with understanding the aftermath of exclusion and imprisonment.

Chapter 8

For this chapter, I relied heavily on articles from a wide range of publications: the *Oregonian* in 1959–1960, 1963, 1974, 1990, and 1994; *Oregon Journal* in 1963, 1968, and 1975; *Lake Oswego Review* in 1982; *Historic Preservation Magazine* in 1981; the *Downtowner* in 1987; the *Oregon-Columbia Constructor* in 1987; *Daily Journal of Commerce* in 1987; and the *Neighbor* in 1983. An interview with Dale Campbell of P&C Construction also helped inform Norcrest's relationship with the company.

Chapter 9

The story of Old Town's revival relied on reporting from numerous publications: the *Oregonian* in 1973–1975, 1978–1979, 1987, 1989, and 1991; *Oregon Journal* in 1974–1975, 1977, and 1981; *Willamette Week* in 1977; the *Downtowner* in 1989; *Northwest Neighbor* in 1994; *Old Portland Today* in 1975; *Historic Preservation Magazine* in 1981; and *Urbest* in 1990, as well Kathleen Ryan's *Burnside: A Community*. Context was provided, in part, by an interview with Chet Orloff, *Oregon Portraits*, and correspondence from advertising executive Jack Matlack.

Chapter 10

The stories in this chapter came from articles in the *Oregonian* in 1975 and 1978–1981; *Oregon Journal* in 1981; the *Asian Reporter* in 1995; *Willamette Week* in 1977; *Reed Magazine* in 1978; and *American Preservation* in 1977. Also informative were cards and letters of condolence after Bill's death in 1996, including those from Liden Ward Dardevich, Mel Katz and M. Russo, and Steve Burdick. Roger Shiels and Robert Ames were quoted from their interviews, and Richard Moe and Ruth Rhyne from their correspondence.

Chapter 11

Personal interviews were critical to this chapter, including with Neil Goldschmidt, Bill Wyatt, and David Soderstrom, as well as Paul Bragdon's remarks at Bill's memorial service and at a City Club of Portland talk a month later. Broker Don Barney also spoke at the City Club talk. Also helpful were articles in the *Business Journal* in 1986 and 1996; *Lake Oswego Review* in 1986; and the *Oregonian* in 1989 and 1996.

Chapter 12

For the story of Portland's revival, I used articles in the *Oregonian* in 1960, 1961, 1965, 1968, 1972; *Oregon Journal* in 1965, 1969, 1971–1972, and 1979; *Old Portland Today* in 1975; and *New York Times Magazine* in 1958 (quoted in Ray Ginger's *Modern American Cities* in 1969). Carol Abbott's *Portland: Planning, Politics, and Growth in a Twentieth-Century City* and *Greater Portland: Urban Life and Landscape in the Pacific Northwest*, as well as Steven Reed Johnson's "The Myth and Reality of Portland's Engaged Citizenry and Process-Oriented Governance," in Connie P. Ozawa's *The Portland Edge*, provided important context.

Interviews with Neil Goldschmidt, Rodney O'Hiser, and Mike Lindberg were also provided key information to this chapter.

Chapter 13

This chapter used information in articles from the *Daily Shipping News* in 1991; the *Oregonian* in 1986, 1991, and 1994; *Oregon Journal* in 1966; and *Business Journal* in 1994. I also relied on interviews with Earl Blumenauer, Rick Gustafson, Portland mayor and city commissioner Charlie Hales (by KINK FM radio station in 1996), and Karen Whitman.

Chapter 14

I relied on articles in the *Oregonian* in 1973, 1976–1977, 1985, and 1987; *Oregon Journal* in 1946, 1960, 1975–1976, and 1978; the *Downtowner* in 1983; *Democrat-Herald* in 1978; *Reed Magazine* in 1978; *Portland Metropolitan Guide* in 1997, and *Metro: The City Magazine* in 1985. Quotes came from a letter from Judith Head at the announcement of Bill's illness and George "Bing" Sheldon's remarks at Bill's memorial service, as well as personal correspondence from the time and after Bill's death. Personal interviews were noted in the text, including with Neil Goldschmidt, Dale Campbell, and Ruth Scott. Other information was taken from the City of Portland's *Leadership and Vision: The Story of the 1972 Downtown Plan* video, *Oregon Portraits*, and *Northwest Reports: The Enemy Next Door* television program from 1992.

Chapter 15

I used articles from the *Oregonian* in 1959, 1976–1978, 1983, 1985–1986, and 1990; *Oregon Journal* in 1973, 1976, 1982, 1983; the *Neighbor* in 1983; and *Willamette Week* in 1994. Personal interviews with the Japanese American Museum of Oregon and the author are attributed in the text, including Jack Miller, Karen Whitman, David Judd, Rodney O'Hiser, Roger Shiels, and Sam Brooks. Robert Baldwin was interviewed by Ernie Bonner in 1994. Richard Brandman and Lana Nelson provided quotes, as well as correspondence from Rick Williams in 1995 and *Oregon Portraits*. Context was provided by Carl Abbott's "Centers and Edges: Reshaping Downtown Portland" in the *Portland Edge*.

Chapter 16

This chapter relied on articles from the *Oregonian* in 1979 and 1980; *Oregon Journal* in 1973 and 1976; *Daily Journal of Commerce* in 1980 and 1987; the *Neighbor* in 1983; the *Downtowner* in 1987; *Sylvia Porter's Personal Finance* in 1985; and *Old Portland Today* in 1975; as well as Carl Abbott's *Portland in Three Centuries*. Personal interviews quoted in the text were with Neil Goldschmidt, Rodney O'Hiser, Bing Sheldon, Donn Sullivan, and Earl Blumenauer.

Chapter 17

I relied on articles from the *Oregonian* in 1978, 1983–1985, 1987–1988, and 1992; *NW Neighbor* in 1996; *Building Operating Management Magazine* in 1986; *Daily Journal of Commerce* in 1982; *Oregon Journal* in 1978; *Willamette Week* in 1987; *Portland Business Today* in 1985; *DNR/ Magic* in 1989; *Wall Street Journal* in 1977; and the *Downtowner* in 1983 and 1988. Quotes from personal interviews with the author and Japanese American Museum of Oregon are noted in the text, specifically from Paul Breuer, Robert Ames, and David Soderstrom. Additional quotes came from correspondence from Bud Clark, testimony from the 1999 trial *Naito v. Naito*, *Oregon Portraits*, and Charlotte Babcock's two articles cited in the chapter 2 notes. An analysis of the work of Charles Moore can be found in *Charles Moore: Buildings and Projects 1949–1986* by Robert A. M. Stern, with Raymond Gastil.

Chapter 18

A personal interview with Rick Gustafson in 2017 provided critical insight into this chapter, as well as articles from the *Oregonian* in 1984 and 1989; *Daily Journal of Commerce* in 1989; and *DNR/Magic* in 1989. *Portland in Three Centuries* by Carl Abbott and *Portland: People, Politics, and Power, 1851–2001* by Jewel Lansing were also important. Quotations came from interviews with Dale Campbell, Hank Sakamoto at a City Club talk in 1996, *Oregon Portraits*, and personal correspondence from Karl Sonnenberg in 1996. Jeanette Spencer's quote came from her letter of condolence.

Chapter 19

I relied on articles from the *Oregonian* in 1960, 1968, 1984–1985, 1988–1989, 1991, and 1994–1996; *Gateways* in 1996; *Northwest Magazine* in 1985; *This Week* in 1988; *New York Times Magazine* in 1966; *Cincinnati Enquirer* in 1995; *Business Journal* in 1994; and the *Downtowner* in 1989, as well as Chet Orloff's article, "If Zealously Promoted by All: The Push and Pull of Portland Parks History," in the *Portland Edge* and *Oregon*

Portraits. Personal interviews with David Judd, Mike Lindberg, and Bill by the Oregon Holocaust Resource Center in 1994 provided important context, in addition to letters of condolence from Brian McNerney and Ginnie Cooper and an OPB interview with J. Clayton Hering shortly after Bill's death.

Chapter 20

For insight into the effects of Executive Order 9066 and the redress movement, I relied on several books, including James Oda's *Heroic Struggles of Japanese Americans,* Wendy Ng's *Japanese American Internment during World War II: A History and Reference Guide,* and John W. Powell's *Education for Maturity*. Bill wrote "A Personal Experience of Human Rights" in 1993 to describe his own feelings about the effects of Executive Order 9066.

I used articles in the *Oregonian* in 1953, 1988, 1990, 1996, and 1997; *This Week* in 1985; *New York Times* in 1989; the *Asian Reporter* in 1996; *Daily Journal of Commerce* in 1991; *NJAHS Focus* in 1988; *Oregon Humanities* in 1991; and the *Downtowner* in 1993, as well as *Oregon Portraits*.

I relied on interviews by the Japanese American Museum of Oregon of people who were involved in the creation of the Japanese American Historical Plaza, including Mark Sherman, Judy Murase, Miyuki Yasui, and Hank Sakamoto. I also used personal correspondence at the time from Lawson Inada to Bill and others throughout 1990 as he curated the poems on the stones.

Touching the Stones contains the remarks of Justice Michael Gillette and Consul-General Akira Watanabe from the opening ceremony, as well as details about the Plaza. Comments from those in attendance at the opening ceremony came from personal correspondence from Harriet Sherburne, US senator Bob Packwood, and Norman Lezin. Other comments came from interviews with Linda Strand and Mike Lindberg, correspondence from Dorothy Hirsch and from H. Krueger, Paul Bragdon's remarks at Bill's memorial, and Hank Sakamoto's at the City Club's talk in 1996.

Chapter 21

I used articles from the *Oregonian* in 1983, 1991, 1992, and 1994–1997; *Daily Journal of Commerce* in 1995; and the *Asian Reporter* in 1996, along with personal correspondence, interview with Earl Blumenauer, and remarks by Paul Bragdon at Bill's memorial.

INDEX

Page numbers in *italics* indicate illustrations